PROTECTING WHITENESS

PROTECTING WHITENESS

WHITELASH AND THE REJECTION
OF RACIAL EQUALITY

*Edited by Cameron D. Lippard, J. Scott Carter,
and David G. Embrick*

Foreword by Eduardo Bonilla-Silva

UNIVERSITY OF WASHINGTON PRESS

Seattle

Copyright © 2020 by the University of Washington Press

Composed in Warnock Pro, typeface designed by Robert Slimbach

24 23 22 21 20   5 4 3 2 1

Printed and bound in the United States of America

All rights reserved. No part of this publication may be reproduced or transmitted in any form or by any means, electronic or mechanical, including photocopy, recording, or any information storage or retrieval system, without permission in writing from the publisher.

UNIVERSITY OF WASHINGTON PRESS
uwapress.uw.edu

LIBRARY OF CONGRESS CATALOGING-IN-PUBLICATION DATA
Names: Lippard, Cameron D., editor. | Scott Carter, J., editor. |
    Embrick, David G., editor. | Bonilla-Silva, Eduardo, writer of foreword.
Title: Protecting whiteness : whitelash and the rejection of racial equality /
    edited by Cameron D. Lippard, J. Scott Carter, and David G. Embrick ;
    foreword by Eduardo Bonilla-Silva.
Description: Seattle : University of Washington Press, 2020. |
    Includes bibliographical references and index.
Identifiers: LCCN 2020015380 (print) | LCCN 2020015381 (ebook) |
    ISBN 9780295747989 (hardcover) | ISBN 9780295747996 (paperback) |
    ISBN 9780295748009 (ebook)
Subjects: LCSH: Racism—United States—Philosophy. | Racism—
    United States—History. | Race discrimination—United States. |
    United States—Race relations.
Classification: LCC E184.A1 P775 2020 (print) | LCC E184.A1 (ebook) |
    DDC 305.800973—dc23
LC record available at https://lccn.loc.gov/2020015380
LC ebook record available at https://lccn.loc.gov/2020015381

The paper used in this publication is acid free and meets the minimum requirements of American National Standard for Information Sciences—Permanence of Paper for Printed Library Materials, ANSI Z39.48–1984.∞

To our children: We hope that your America will be a place that accepts all and treats everyone with dignity, respect, and admiration.

CONTENTS

Foreword by Eduardo Bonilla-Silva xi

Introduction. The Resurgence of Whitelash: White Supremacy, Resistance, and the Racialized Social System in Trumptopia
DAVID G. EMBRICK, J. SCOTT CARTER, AND CAMERON D. LIPPARD 3

PART I. THE IDEOLOGICAL REINFORCEMENT OF WHITE SUPREMACY

1. Post–Color Blindness? Trump and the Rise of the New White Nationalism
ASHLEY "WOODY" DOANE 27

2. The Unblackening: "White" License and the "Nice Racism" Trope
JOHNNY E. WILLIAMS 43

3. Political Correctness: A Genuine Concern for Discussion or Slippery Language Rooted in Racial Animosity
J. SCOTT CARTER AND J. MICAH ROOS 57

4. Diversity Regimes: How University Diversity Initiatives Shape White Race Consciousness
JAMES M. THOMAS 71

PART II. THE REENTRENCHMENT OF WHITE SUPERIORITY IN AMERICAN INSTITUTIONS

5. Institutional Racism Revisited: How Institutions Perpetuate and Promote Racism through Color Blindness
   CHARLES A. GALLAGHER   89

6. Prison in the Street: What Market-Based Bipartisan Reform Means for Racial Stratification
   KASEY HENRICKS AND BETHANY NELSON   103

7. Settler Culture and White Property: From the Bundy Ranch Standoff to the West Virginia Coalfields
   REBECCA R. SCOTT   117

8. Local Immigration Enforcement: Shaping and Maintaining Policies through White Saviors and Economic Motivations
   FELICIA ARRIAGA   132

9. Recruiting White "Victims": White Supremacist Flyers on College Campuses
   DAVID DIETRICH   151

10. The Whitening of South Asian Women
    BHOOMI K. THAKORE   165

11. Colorful Art, White Spaces: How an Art Museum Maintains White Spaces
    SIMÓN E. WEFFER, DAVID G. EMBRICK, AND SILVIA DOMÍNGUEZ   179

PART III. WHITE EMOTIONS, EXPRESSIONS, AND MOVEMENTS

12. White Noise: How White Nationalist Content Creators Reproduce Narratives of White Power and Victimhood on YouTube
    C. DOUG CHARLES   197

13. Blue Lives Matter: Police Protection or Countermovement
    MARETTA MCDONALD   210

14. Echoing Derrick A. Bell: Black Women's Resistance to White Supremacy in the Age of Trump
    MARLESE DURR   224

15. Solidarity and Struggle: White Antiracist Activism in the Time of Trump
MARY K. RYAN AND DAVID L. BRUNSMA 240

Conclusions. Where Do We Go from Here? Structural and Social Implications of Whitelash
J. SCOTT CARTER, DAVID G. EMBRICK, AND CAMERON D. LIPPARD 255

List of Contributors 267

Index 271

FOREWORD

EDUARDO BONILLA-SILVA

In 2015–2016, far too many social scientists waited to issue analytical pronouncements about the potential impact of a Trump victory. Some argued that they did not have "systematic data" on the matter at hand and others that it was not their place to comment on politics. Much like Max Weber, they hid behind "objectivity" to say or do anything while the wind of authoritarianism was clearly blowing with hurricane force in the nation. They remained working in their beautiful offices solving social puzzles while the world around them burned down.

Three years after Trump's election, the devastating impact of what I have called "authoritarian populism" (Bonilla-Silva 2019a) is still being felt. *Protecting Whiteness* is what social science needs at this time: a bold, multipronged, and theoretically sophisticated effort to examine the growth of open white male hostility in America. This collection gathers under one roof some of the best critical minds in sociology and tasks them with explaining what the editors label "the rebirth of White resistance." Their contributions are parceled out in sections dealing with ideology, mobilization of white resistance, spatial racism, movements and countermovements, and a powerful conclusion addressing the all-important matter of what is to be done.

As the editors do a masterful job at summarizing what each author brings to the table in their introductory chapter, I use this opportunity to ponder aloud about some of the themes and ideas in the book. The first thing I want to raise is eminently political. The rise of authoritarianism reveals both the *race* and the *class* contradictions of America. If race is the modality through which class is lived in America, we need to untangle how the race-class nexus operates. If, as the authors of this volume clearly show, Whites frame their mostly class-based pain as a racialized phenomenon, how do we undo this perception? What kind of new politics and interventions do we need to fracture this reading? I am on record stating that blaming poor Whites as "the racists" is ultimately a losing game that will alienate them further from the possibility of joining a progressive economic populist movement. But I am not a fool and recognize that White workers feel deeply that their pain is indeed race-based (Bonilla-Silva 2019b). Thus, we cannot just proceed with a class-is-all appeal hoping that it will miraculously unite the "workers of the world." What is needed is historical (how was the race-class nexus forged in America?) and theoretical analyses, bolstered by serious practical political efforts to engage the White working class. Abandoning members of that class as "deplorables" or assuming that they are racially incorrigible in the quest for criminal justice and economic reform will not do.

My second observation is about the nature of the racial polity and the ideologies at play. Despite Trump's clear authoritarianism, strongly endorsed by a significant segment of his supporters, race domination does not depend on the behavior, practices, and views of *Trumpistas*. Whether in jobs, schools, or the streets of America, normative racial domination still operates along "new racism" lines (Bonilla-Silva 2001). People of color's socioeconomic standing is maintained not by the racial flame throwers of overt white supremacy that we saw in Charlottesville but by the sweet racial enchantment of regular White folks voting for Trump and calling for "the wall" to constructed. Their actions and views are hegemonic and happen in everyday spaces, thus having more of a consequence on racial outcomes in America than demonstrations against Confederate statue removals. However, we surely cannot just ignore the import of overt racism via populist rhetoric that has once again darkened the doorway of the US government and many other countries around the world. Ideological fields are always mixed up and articulate old and new discursive forms.

A real concern I have, and one I cannot prove empirically yet, is that the increase in old-fashioned racism has pushed color-blind racism to the right! I believe that the real danger of authoritarianism in America is the inoculation of color blindness as a healthy way of addressing racial matters, of liberal racism becoming the antidote to racism. Color-blind practitioners can now say, "Well, we did not recruit that black applicant because she was an inferior candidate, period." Just three years ago, they would have to ponder statements like those. What do I mean by "inferior candidate"? What are the standards we use for judging candidates' record? Are the differences in record or credentials sufficient evidence to judge the merits of applicants?

And, for those with purely instrumentalist concerns, "Will I be seen as a racist if I do not support at least one candidate of color in this process?" Today I think liberal Whites are unburdened by these questions as they seem to think that the real racists are the *Trumpistas*; hence, they have absolved themselves from racial sins.

The political implications of this shift are potentially monumental. Color-blind racism has been so far a contradictory dominant ideology. It always had to contend with the fact that color matters, that Whiteness exists, that White spaces and organizations are real. But if these realities no longer bring the least remorse or shame, then the doors that were slightly opened a while back by the social movement for racial redemption can be shut again. Thus, the effects of the whitelash may extend much farther than we think.

But I am optimistic about the future. In the midst of this storm, a storm reminiscent of the Reagan years, social movements have emerged to counter *Trumpismo*. The people have mobilized, some in concert with the Democratic Party, others independent of the party, and yet others within but critical of the party (e.g., representatives Alexandria Ocasio-Cortez, Ilhan Omar, and Rashida Tlaib). This is all potentially good news. Although the corporate forces that control America are working quite hard at corralling the party (i.e., bringing it back to the "center"), the space for possibilities has been created. We now discuss publicly, without much reluctance, many ideas and concepts such as Medicare for all, socialism, institutional racism, criminal justice reform, and the working class.

However, I also must, as comedian Larry David would recommend, "curb my enthusiasm." Having the space for thinking and doing things does not necessarily translate to new thinking and practices emerging. For this to happen, we need concerted efforts. We need politicking (yes, this is not a bad word) about the kind of movement we want and aspire to build. This is why I have been talking, lecturing, writing, and advocating for a new "rainbow coalition" that takes class, race, and gender equally seriously. For the workers of America to unite as a political force, we need a program and a relentless praxis that tells everyone they are part of the past, present, and future of the nation. Economic populism can work, but only if it is viewed by the people as the conduit to rework the social compact. Bernie Sanders's approach failed in the 2016 presidential election precisely because he could not work well on race and gender. The opening is there for radical possibilities to emerge, but nothing will transpire unless we all commit to make it happen.

This book, I suspect, will become an opening salvo in the campaign to fight the contemporary whitelash. It may also help analysts and activists alike reorient their politics to fit the new moment. I look forward to the conversations and engagements this book should engender and praise the editors and contributors for a job well done.

REFERENCES

Bonilla-Silva, Eduardo. 2001. *White Supremacy and Racism in the Post–Civil Rights Era*. Boulder, CO: Lynne Rienner.
———. 2019a. "'Racists,' 'Class Anxieties,' Hegemonic Racism, and Democracy in Trump's America." *Social Currents* 6(1): 14–31.
———. 2019b. "Feeling Race: Theorizing the Racial Economy of Emotions." *American Sociological Review* 84(1): 1–25.

PROTECTING WHITENESS

INTRODUCTION

The Resurgence of Whitelash: White Supremacy, Resistance, and the Racialized Social System in Trumptopia

DAVID G. EMBRICK, J. SCOTT CARTER,
AND CAMERON D. LIPPARD

O**N NOVEMBER 6, 2016**, some Americans wept while others rejoiced as Donald Trump became the forty-fifth president of the United States of America. His election represented more than just the election of another charismatic public personality, American millionaire playboy, or television star who never seemed to hold back on his racist and sexist comments. For many, Trump represented a renewed call to arms for a conservative war against twenty-first-century liberalism, the growing threat of Hillary Clinton's "feminist" agenda, and, particularly, Obama's America. Those who voted for Trump wanted to "make America great again" by building a wall to keep out "murderers and rapists" and setting up global economic deals that put "America first" and punished economic adversaries such as China, Canada, and Mexico for taking American jobs and earning higher profits. Trump supporters also wanted to stop discussion of diversity, same-sex equality, encouraging "socialist" programs of universal health care, and balancing economic prosperity across all social classes. As documented by the sociologist Arlie Hochschild in her research monograph *Strangers in Their Own Land* (2016), Trump's election helped justify the complaints of mostly white and often blue-collar men who were crying foul against a supposedly meritocratic society that had decided that they were "deplorable."

This disgruntlement gained a face with the election of Donald Trump. Rather than being rebuked by the Republican party and by citizens, Trump increasingly gained support for his directness and so-called lack of political correctness, especially on issues of race. He publicly lamented against undocumented immigrants, violence in inner cities, and Muslims entering the United States, without regard for public reactions. In the summer of 2019, he tweeted that four newly elected minority congresswomen should "go back" to "the crime infested places from which they came" despite three of the four being born in the United States (Rogers and Fandos 2019). As suggested by CNN commentator Van Jones, "This was a whitelash against a changing country, it was a whitelash against a black president in part. And that's the part where the pain comes" (qtd. in Grinapol 2016).

The lack of racial empathy expressed by the president is reflected in current public sentiment, particularly among whites. National polls reveal that a large chunk of white Americans believe that racism against blacks is a thing of the past but are concerned that whites are now the new targets of racism (Gallagher 2008; Gallup 2019). Also, a majority of whites now say they are satisfied with how blacks are treated (51%) and that blacks are treated fairly at work (67%), in neighborhood shops (76%), in restaurants, bars, theaters, or other places of entertainment (76%), in interactions with police (52%), and in getting health care from doctors (77%). Hence, it is not surprising that many white Americans now see policies opposing affirmative action or increasing border security as practical and legitimate answers to increasing their job security, economic prosperity, and even safety from foreign terrorism. As the sociologist Herbert Blumer has argued (1958), despite few personal experiences and overwhelming amounts of research to suggest otherwise, whites perceive that their economic, political, and social group position in America is threatened by ever-growing nonwhite populations.

Considering that many feel we are in a postrace society, it is common for white Americans (and some nonwhites) to minimize race or racism when confronted with examples of discrimination or mistreatment felt by nonwhites (Bobo, Kluegel, and Smith 1997; Bonilla-Silva 2001, 2003; Feagin 2010). Rather than agreeing that race continues to matter, many white Americans often rely on cultural stereotypes (e.g., laziness, violence) to explain away disadvantages faced by nonwhites. These deflective rhetorical strategies that deny the persistence of racism have come up repeatedly when discussing police brutality (e.g., Black Lives Matter vs. All Lives Matter or Blue Lives Matter; see Embrick 2015a, 2015b, 2016), Mexican immigration (Carter and Lippard 2015; Chavez 2013; Golash-Boza 2012; Lippard 2011), inequality in higher education (Carter and Lippard 2020; Carter, Lippard, and Baird 2019), and the failure of public schools due to continued racial segregation (Kozol 2005; Logan and Burdick-Will 2017). As such, many white Americans refuse to consider how race still shapes the lives of nonwhites despite countless examples and research to the contrary.

Such a lack of insight expressed by whites has been linked to the problem of "whiteness"—the idea that many whites do not see the privileges provided to them by virtue of the association with the white "race" while concomitantly ignoring the oppression that must occur against marginalized groups for whites to secure these benefits. Some scholars have attempted to situate whites in the larger societal context of white supremacy (Fredrickson 1982) or racialized social systems (Bonilla-Silva 1997, 2001, 2003). For example, the 2003 book *Whiteout: The Continuing Significance of Racism*, edited by Ashley "Woody" Doane and Eduardo Bonilla-Silva, represents one of the early attempts by sociologists to show how white racial attitudes have led to attempts to challenge debates concerning race in the United States as a matter of social inequality and a charge for social movements. Lest we be accused of glaring holes in unpacking the connections between whiteness and white supremacy, we acknowledge the central importance of precursors to this scholarship: those who recognized how identifying oneself as white also meant consciously or unconsciously committing to upholding white supremacy as normative. Indeed, James Baldwin (1980: 43) once noted that "to be white was to be forced to digest a delusion called white supremacy." In contrast, then, to be nonwhite was to be forced to *endure* the oppressions of living, nay existing, in a white supremacist society. Others such as Malcolm X, Frantz Fanon, Sojourner Truth, and Martin Luther King Jr., for instance, have noted the deep connections between whiteness and white supremacy, connections that ultimately meant more for nonwhites than just being ignored, dismissed, or counted as inferior. As Truth (1851) would contend, it would mean that to be a woman was to be white. In other words, in a white supremacist society, nonwhite women were not "real" women. Whiteness in a white supremacist society refers to more than just privileges afforded to one group or another; whiteness is about power, acceptance, and belonging, as well as a constant rewriting of history that centers whites while dismissing or discounting nonwhites. The black sociologist W. E. B. Du Bois (1903) remarked on this in his concept of the double consciousness of African Americans—the constant internal struggles faced by nonwhites who viewed themselves through the lens of a white racist society that held them in contempt (see also Fanon 1952; Cooper 1892).

But how might we best understand whiteness and white attitudes in the Trump era, as well as their outward manifestations? And how does "whitelash" manifest itself beyond intraindividual attitudes, reactions, and ultimately actions? That is to say, we are interested in how white Americans hold on to power, wealth, and privilege in the face of growing diversity and calls for racial equality in the twenty-first century. This volume is *not* a rediscovery of white folks' understanding of privilege in America. Rather, this volume demonstrates how whites use ideologies and institutions to reinforce, defend, and continue the privilege of whiteness, and thus white supremacy, in America. More importantly, it is white America's backlash (aka "whitelash") against racial equality that echoes in their cheers to make America great again . . . for them.

REFRAMING BACKLASH AS "WHITELASH"

In 1991, Pulitzer Prize winner Susan Faludi published an award-winning book titled *Backlash: The Undeclared War against American Women*. In this book, Faludi argued three main points. First, a backlash—a social and societal reaction against a perceived trend, partially driven by the media—erupted against women's rights in the 1970s. Second, evolving from that backlash were contestations that the women's liberation movement was to blame for most of the problems having to do with women's rights in the 1980s. The "blaming the victim" strategy would prove to be long-lived and, indeed, frequently used by individuals and institutions in the twenty-first century to counter gender equality issues in the workplace, such as gender wage inequality and sexual harassment. Third, backlashes were not new; rather, they should be seen as a historical trend with peaks that correlated with societal gains that leveled the playing field with regard to women's rights.

What we find most interesting is that the ideas Faludi presented on backlash against women's rights parallel many of the theoretical and empirical sociological studies on racism and ethnic oppression in the United States. Like other race scholars, we view white backlash, or whitelash, in different forms erupting at many points in US history, challenging the calls for the rights of nonwhites and the opposition to racial/ethnic oppression, whether those issues be economical, political, social, psychological, or even philosophical. For instance, the Reconstruction era history was rife with the backlash against the emancipation of black slaves (Browne 2007). This era witnessed the rise of Jim Crow laws, redlining, antimiscegenation laws, police brutality, and increased nonwhite incarceration rates not just in the American South but across much of the US. More violent and stark examples of whitelash include acts of white mob violence that attacked prosperous black communities in the early 1900s, which climaxed during the "Red Summer" of 1919, when ten major antiblack riots were carried out in concert across the

US (see Voogd 2008). Lynching African Americans and destroying private property to run blacks out of town also became common practices to deter and stifle African American prosperity after the Civil War.

Centuries later, there is reactionary "whitelash" toward correcting "mis-history" regarding slavery in the US—for example, reclassifying the Civil War as a war fought for states' rights rather than for the perpetuation of slavery and white supremacy.[1] Related to the whitelash against correcting US history, there have also been more recent moments of backlash toward the removal of monuments (e.g., Confederate statues) that celebrate or represent a nostalgic call back to days of overt legal racial oppression (Fortin 2017; O'Reilly 2017). We also see this backlash against progressive policies such as affirmative action (Carter and Lippard 2020; Carter, Lippard, and Baird 2019; Cokorinos 2003; Moore 2008), often with whites invoking the notion of reverse racism as a way to suggest that racism no longer exists. As described by many white Americans, affirmative action policies are problematic because they discriminate based on race and penalize hard-working white men. And we see this whitelash whenever immigration issues (see Montejano 1987) arise, in the creation of exclusionary state and federal laws to keep nonwhite immigrants out (see Carter and Lippard 2015; Lippard 2011), in media portrayals (see Chavez 2013), or in the private spaces of one's home (Picca and Feagin 2007). Finally, we also see whitelash at pivotal moments when there are perceived challenges to whiteness. The pushback against professional sports players kneeling (or not standing up) during the US national anthem during sporting events—a practice inspired by Colin Kaepernick[2]—is one recent example, but others include Gamergate[3] and statewide (e.g., Arizona) and national (see Green 2019) attacks on ethnic studies programs in secondary and higher education. Notwithstanding, whitelash is not only aggressive tactics to prop up white supremacy; it is also reactionary, in that whites attempt to stamp out any efforts made by marginalized groups or individuals to obtain racial equality and fair treatment. Although Colin Kaepernick was clear in his request for equal treatment and less police brutality for people of color by the police, President Trump and other prominent individuals eschewed such arguments and, in essence, banished Colin from full participation not only in the NFL but in society as well.

The sociologists Michael Omi and Howard Winant (2014 [1994]) argued that whites, through the use of various social institutions, have systematically and diligently challenged any racial or ethnic progress toward equality since the US Civil War. The shift to "New Racism" (Bonilla-Silva 1997, 2001, 2003)—whereby racism has become less visible, overt, or aggressively confrontational largely because of changes in the legal system—have given rise to unique but savvy ways to challenge calls and actions for racial equality. For example, since the civil rights movement of the 1960s, whites have increasingly minimized or ignored addressing racial inequalities over class inequalities, have favored laissez-faire explanations (Bobo, Kluegel, and Smith 1997; Bobo and Smith 1998) that blame minorities[4] for their social standing, or have couched resistance to equality in terms of neoliberal thought of supporting equality for all and not the truly disadvantaged. The last approach has increased particularly since the 1980s, pushing for policy reforms that particularly seem to have racialized outcomes (Saito 2009).

We adopt the term "whitelash," coined by CNN commentator Van Jones (see Grinapol 2016), to point out these moments of individual and systemic resistance by whites to hold on to their privilege and position in American society. In response to Trump's surprising win in the election, Jones's remarks reflected a general sentiment of some people—that Trump's victory was fueled, in some part, by a backlash against the perception of a changing country that would aim to promote more diversity and racial equality. Moreover, it was a backlash against the previous eight years with America's first black president. Whether or not that diversity would be critical of existing racial inequities would be largely irrelevant to the loud blustering of the Right (and some of the Left) that promoted fear of Muslims, inner-city violence, and immigration, for example, and continued to exploit and exaggerate stereotypes of folks of color. As Jones noted, the whitelash that fueled the election results showcased not just disagreement with multiculturalism but reactions to the very fact that the top elected US office was held by a black man for two terms.

In keeping with the general notions of backlash as reactions aiming to maintain the status quo in society and rebuking change—that is, reactions unfavorable to understanding or correcting existing racial, gender, and other inequalities—we define whitelash as individual, institutional, and structural countermeasures against the dismantling of white supremacy or actions, real or imagined, that seek to remedy existing racial inequities. Whitelash, we argue, is action and reaction that seek to maintain the white status quo; it is action and reaction against any progressive change that would call out racism, question white privilege, or suggest that racial equality is necessary to meet American ideals of fairness, in any of its forms. In a larger, sociological sense, whitelash is less about identity and more about fear of change, whether imagined or real. That is, whitelash has less to do with whites who are against issues such as immigration and more to do with maintaining white domination in all avenues of life and reinforcing the pillars that hold up white supremacy despite growing efforts to at least question it. To that end, whitelash reflects the action and reaction of individuals *and* institutions in the larger racialized social structures that have a possessive investment in whiteness (Lipsitz 1998, 2011).

In the following, we engage in the racial theories that inform how we understand racism and ethnic oppression in the US and how these theories serve to frame the overall picture of this book. We then outline how whitelash manifests itself at various societal levels, all of which serve to maintain the status quo of white supremacy in the US. Our theoretical map (see figure I.1) informs how we think about and synthesize the chapters in this book—each contributor highlighting one or more instances of how whitelash plays out in the context of the twenty-first-century, postracial rhetoric.

MAPPING WHITELASH

Our understanding of whitelash, which constitutes the collection of chapters in this book, is predicated on our understanding that white supremacy is part of the very fabric of American society and that racism reinforcing white supremacy is firmly embedded in its structural foundations. We draw from several racism scholars in thinking about whitelash, including Michael Omi and Howard Winant's concept of racial formations, Eduardo Bonilla-Silva's racialized social systems perspective, and Joe R. Feagin's systemic racism and white racial frame.

In his 1997 article published in *American Sociological Review*, Eduardo Bonilla-Silva posits racism as a global phenomenon in which racialized social systems are hierarchically ordered and in which people gain advantages and disadvantages depending on where they fit in the racial and social order (see also Bonilla-Silva 2001). Bonilla-Silva's intent was to address the lack of a structural theory of racism that would highlight the practices and mechanisms the dominant race put into place to secure and maintain their social standing at the top of the racial hierarchy. While the racialization of the world system is based on social, economic, political, and psychological relations of domination and subordination between groups at the top of the racial hierarchy and those below, Bonilla-Silva does note that historically, "the racialization of social systems did not imply the exclusion of other forms of oppression" and that "racialization occurred in social formations also structured by class and gender" (1997:470).

The sociologist Joe Feagin (2010) also highlights the structural, institutional, historical, and systemic racism that is unique to a country that was founded specifically to oppress blacks and provide advantages to whites. Feagin argues that the deep roots of racisms in US society have resulted in societal and institutional racist practices at all levels—economic, ideological, and political—that work to preserve white supremacy. White racial frame serves as the ideological arm of Feagin's systemic racism theory, a concept that provides a broader understanding of racism that includes visual images, emotions, and language, for example, as legitimizing and maintaining white supremacy.

By focusing on these critical examinations of American institutions and ideologies, we stay away from attempting to explain whiteness as simply white privilege. However, we do accept that whiteness is a prominent social force within American society and is working to stay in control and in charge. Moreover, as some scholars have suggested (i.e., Douglas et al. 2018; Moore 2008; Ray 2017, 2019; Saenz et al. 2007), American institutions have been and continue to be racialized structures that shape the varied outcomes we see today across racial groups in America concerning higher education, the job market, homeownership, and social mobility. As the sociologist Victor Ray (2017, 2019) has noted, organizations are racialized and thus imbued with racial meanings that help shape organizational hierarchies and interactions with the racial state as well as individual-level interactions.

Echoing some of Omi and Winant's thesis on racial formation and racial projects, we identify whitelash as collective action and reaction against change, real or perceived, that would challenge or dismantle white supremacy. The central message from Omi and Winant is that the state (and its institutions) plays a large role in the creation, shaping, and reproduction of racial categories and racial identities. Thus, race is fluid, dynamic, and highly dependent on the politics of white supremacy at different times in US history. Omi and Winant define racial formation as the process by which the aforementioned forces determine the racial order of society, the importance of racial categories, and the value-laden meanings attached to them. We agree and argue that whitelash occurs at different levels, including individual and institutional levels, not only to continue to secure white privilege but also to remind other groups of their "place" in American society. Racialized institutional policies and practices, as well as individual practices, that act to produce and reproduce the racial status quo all serve as examples of whitelash. These institutional mechanisms serve to maintain and solidify white supremacy in the US. Similarly, ever-changing racial ideologies that help folks make sense of the current racial and social order, and that often disregard or minimize racial fissures in society and reinforce white supremacy, are a type of white backlash too. We provide details below on the specifics of how we might think about whitelash at the structural, institutional, and individual levels (see figure I.1).

Structural

We follow the lead of scholars such as Bonilla-Silva and Feagin in understanding structural racism as the embedded practices within a given society that are designed to give unequal rewards to groups in society, and that are formalized as normative. More importantly, race and racism is historical and a part of the American DNA of understanding social mobility and group privilege or oppression. Beginning with the erasure of indigenous groups (Glenn 2015) and the enslavement of Africans to drive the American economy, racism has deep roots in the country's founding (Feagin 2010), and its tentacles extend politically, economically, socially, and ideologically. Omi and Winant (2014 [1994]) argued that race, and the notion that whites should be in charge of and benefit the most from any prosperity, was extensively included in government policies and institutional reactions at every turn. This foundational script was clear in the US Constitution, in which our democratic foundations and its system of governance kept out nonwhites (as well as women and indigenous folks) from participating in creating the free and capitalist society that would later be called the United States of America. In structural terms, whitelash also emanated from a number of racial ideologies that exist in the US, including racialized social systems (Bonilla-Silva 1997) that help whites (and some nonwhites) make sense of their place in the racial social order: color-blind racism (Bonilla-Silva 2003; Burke 2019), white racial frame (Feagin 2010), diversity ideology (Embrick 2008, 2011, 2018; see also Berrey 2015), racial apathy (Forman and Lewis 2006), or blaming the victim—what Karen E. Fields and Barbara J. Fields (2014) labeled as "racecraft." However, the point here is that race mattered and continues to matter because race and racism is part of the "soul" of America, particularly in its understanding of democracy, social mobility, equality, and oppression.

Institutional

Many of the contributions in this book focus on the institutional level, where racial mechanisms (see Hughey, Embrick, and Doane 2015) help maintain white supremacy through so-called normative and sometimes radical practices that maintain the racial status quo. Whitelash can occur as a result of real or perceived pressures that challenge existing institutional practices or seek to dismantle them. Similarly, whitelash can result in the creation of exclusive spaces that promote white supremacy. Organizational racial mechanisms include, but are not limited to, place, space, policies, programs, practices, methods, logic, and language (Ray 2019). Examples include the centering or recentering of whites by institutions that are important and central to understanding life in the US, including media that exacerbate the fears of a future US society in which nonwhites take over as the majority population. It also has been played out in the oversimplified notion of white loss, or whites being left behind if nonwhites have equal access to higher education and thus the chance to be socially mobile. Whitelash shows up in institutions when the American public ratchets up antiwelfare, anti–affirmative action, or anti-immigration rhetoric. Or it shows up in blindly following but also craftily using legal loopholes to support a president passing racist policies or federally protecting and supporting white national hate groups. The examples are many, and this volume offers several chapters demonstrating how white backlash happens throughout American institutions.

Individual

At the individual level, we draw on Eduardo Bonilla-Silva's advancement of racialized emotions (2019) as tied to collective movements that propel groups to react negatively to progressive changes or to perceptions of impending change. Moreover, these negative and collective reactions that we identify as whitelash are often driven by a sense of group position, particularly the notion that being white in America affords the group better access to citizenship, voting, property ownership, better jobs, and better wages (see Gallagher 2008). Herbert Blumer (1958) suggested that feelings of prejudice and the actions of discrimination by white Americans have largely been predicated on what they think they economically deserve as white American citizens. He argued that if whites felt that their group position (i.e., economic situation and social mobility) was in danger, then whites would lash out in prejudicial thoughts and discriminatory actions. When white Americans feel economically and politically threatened by various racial and ethnic groups, whitelash has often been deployed to restore the social, economic, and political order of white dominance. In addition, within the realm of racialized emotion, whites will feel attacked, degraded, and disrespected if other groups gain access to privilege, leading to negative and often violent emotional outbursts and reactions. This powerful mechanism has been the subject of the majority of the work in the social sciences to explain persistent racism and discrimination through racial resentment (Tuch and Hughes 2011), apathy (see Forman 2004), and fragility (DiAngelo

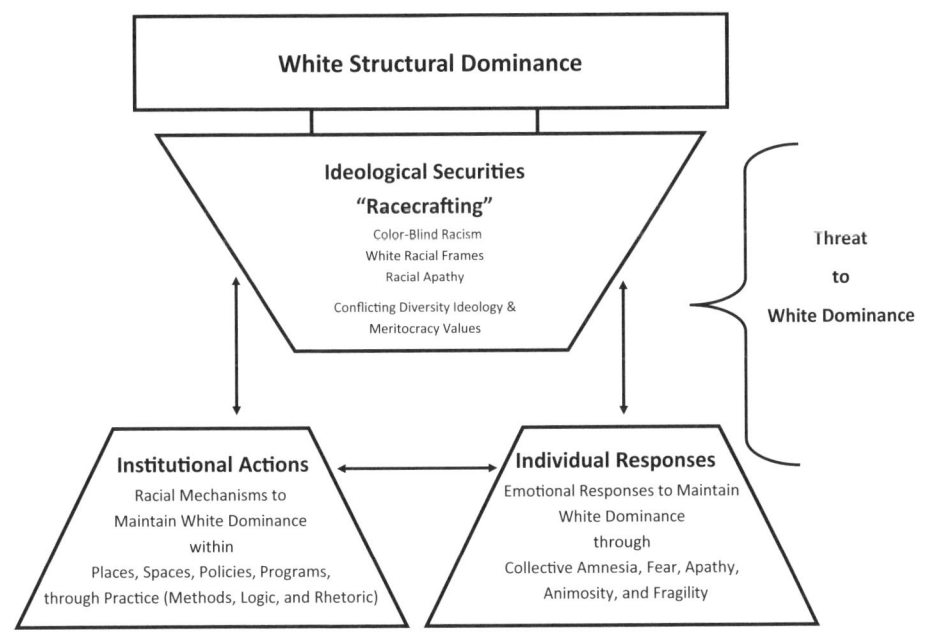

```
                White Structural Dominance

              Ideological Securities
                  "Racecrafting"
                 Color-Blind Racism
                 White Racial Frames            Threat
                   Racial Apathy
             Conflicting Diversity Ideology &     to
                 Meritocracy Values
                                            White Dominance

     Institutional Actions         Individual Responses
      Racial Mechanisms to      Emotional Responses to Maintain
     Maintain White Dominance          White Dominance
              within                      through
   Places, Spaces, Policies, Programs,  Collective Amnesia, Fear, Apathy,
  through Practice (Methods, Logic, and Rhetoric)  Animosity, and Fragility
```

FIGURE I.1. A theoretical map of white racism and "whitelash"

2018). The chapters in this book argue that ideological arguments are evolving over time, which calls for continued analysis. For example, findings by J. Scott Carter and J. Micah Roos, discussed in chapter 3, propose that the anti–politically correct (anti-PC) movement is really an ideological mechanism that President Trump and other conservative pundits use to cloak racial animosity. This finding flies in the face of the conservative position that an anti-PC position is important because pressure to be PC inhibits important debate on controversial issues. As such, conservatives contend that their ability to deal with issues is being blocked. However, findings from the Carter and Roos chapter do not support this. Rather, calls to end political correctness are steeped in racial animosity and are just another ideological mechanism to prop up white supremacy in a society growing more diverse over time.

To be clear, we see these levels (figure I.1) not as independent from one another but rather as integral to maintaining white structural dominance, each level working interdependently with the others to maintain the status quo. Thus, any deviance from white normativity is a threat to white dominance and subject to whitelash.

INTRODUCTION   13

NEW DIRECTIONS IN THE SOCIOLOGY OF RACISM AND ETHNIC OPPRESSIONS

Our aim in this book is to highlight scholarship that places white supremacy as the overarching concerns perpetuating racial inequalities in US society and fueling whitelash as a central response to attempts to change the racial social order. Our contributors examine the rise of "white consciousness" in resistance to social movements of inclusion, equality, and change. Further, our collection and vision continues Doane and Bonilla-Silva's (2003) interrogation of whiteness in several ways. First, we go beyond white attitudes and point out that there is indeed a "white agenda" in race politics and social relations. Although Omi and Winant's (2014 [1994]) seminal book, *Racial Formation in the United States*, has pointed out that this has been true for centuries in America, we take up this cause to expose specific ideologies and racialized institutional mechanisms that currently fuel racial animosity and reproduce racial inequality. Second, we note that there are variations of white resistance beyond the overt examples that we often visualize as clashes between individuals and groups at Ku Klux Klan rallies in places like Charlottesville, Virginia, in 2017. Rather, whitelash can occur in seemingly innocuous places. For example, it may be found in the media, where white normativity through institutionalized color-blindness hides agendas steeped in maintaining the US racialized social system. Whitelash may also be found on YouTube, a supposedly cosmopolitan site of web entertainment. In this volume, the work of C. Doug Charles demonstrates that "conservative" videos actually produce and reproduce ideologies of white supremacy through seemingly neutral rhetoric. Finally, we provide food for thought as to where we can go from here.

Protecting Whiteness presents three unique parts, focusing on the ideological reinforcement of white supremacy; the retrenchment of whiteness in American institutions; and white emotions, expressions, and movements.

The first part, "The Ideological Reinforcement of White Supremacy," examines intrapsychological whitelash in contemporary US society and how it affects racial dynamics, leading to the visible push and growth of right-wing groups and ultimately the rise of President Donald J. Trump. Collectively, these chapters highlight the notion of white ideology, which allows whites (and some nonwhites) to ignore the role of race in producing and reproducing inequality while pretending that whiteness is not a beneficial identity in the US. As Woody Doane states in chapter 1, color blindness—the proposition that race no longer predicts divergent racial outcomes in the US—has been highlighted by race scholars as one of the primary political mechanisms used to preserve white supremacy and racial inequality. In true color-blind fashion, individuals are able to minimize the role of race and racism even in the face of discernible racial malfeasance. However, as Doane describes, President Trump's ascension in modern politics has shaken the foundation of the color-blind theoretical frame.

In chapter 2, Johnny E. Williams similarly poses that the ideology characteristic of Jim Crow was quickly replaced by a more contemporary "nice racism" that acts to maintain the racial status quo in seemingly race-neutral ways. This new "nice racism" denounces individual acts of overt racism associated white supremacy while denying any involvement in seemingly neutral acts that reproduce such a system.

Carter and Roos use public opinion data in their chapter to connect rhetoric to negatively held racial attitudes. President Trump and other conservative pundits have led the charge on ending political correctness. While this charge did not start with President Trump (see the controversial work of Dinesh D'Souza and others), he has definitely pressed the controversy in contemporary debates over racial issues. The anti-PC stance is lauded by many as a way to allow debate over serious issues harming our society. Notwithstanding, Carter and Roos find that the call to end political correctness (even a general call with no emphasis on a particular issue) is less than genuine and is rooted in racial animosity.

Finally, in chapter 4, James M. Thomas points out that in the age of Trump, even seemingly positive institutional practices that move to diversify are co-opted and used to further reinforce the racist structure. In his study, universities enlist diversity initiatives led by seemingly race-conscious individuals to deal with inequality. However, these initiatives often structure white consciousness and minimize real problems of racism and discrimination. In so doing, real work that seeks to disassemble racist structures found in higher education institutions gives way to benign celebrations of differences (e.g., diversity initiatives).

Part II of this book, "The Reentrenchment of White Superiority in American Institutions," explores the role of American institutions as incubators for creating or fueling *whitelash*. These chapters highlight how ideas of superiority and color-blindness rally individuals to protect and preserve white supremacy in various public domains. In chapter 5, Charles A. Gallagher proposes that color-blind ideology, the dominant way of framing US race relations, is thoroughly embedded in all our nation's institutions. He suggests that "color blindness has gone from ideal to a normative" and is formally embedded in all major institutions such as churches, public schools, media, and even the Supreme Court. Gallagher highlights that such forces exist during turbulent times, providing the perfect environment for the resurgence of overt racism and the opportunity for someone spewing negative racial rhetoric, such as Trump, to win the US presidency.

In chapter 6, analyzing arguments advanced by the liberal ACLU and the conservative Right on Crime (RoC), Kasey Henricks and Bethany Nelson explain that a market-inspired racial project (such as government spending) may provide insight into why government officials, both Democrats and Republicans, are now supporting prison reform. In reflecting on prisons and their economic impact, Henricks and Nelson posit that both liberals and conservatives use color-blind frames and problematize "mass imprisonment."

In chapter 7, Rebecca Scott turns the reader's attention to settler colonialism and how it reproduces white supremacy. Most interestingly, Scott demonstrates that the settler colonialism ideology exists among both liberal and conservative activist groups—specifically, the Bundy ranchers and a group of Appalachians seeking to protect their mountains. She notes that the two groups become connected because they both represent the righteousness and morality of white America through settler culture.

In chapter 8, Felicia Arriaga outlines how local law enforcement became complicit in immigration control. She contends that while the partnership between local law enforcement and US Immigrations and Customs Enforcement (ICE) was apparent early on, subsequent collective amnesia of ICE's priorities and goals among local law enforcement have led to a reduction of sustained resistance against the implementation of anti-immigration policies. This amnesia, according to Arriaga, is produced and reproduced by the frames of white innocence, ignorance, and white savior mentality.

In chapter 9, David Dietrich argues that concern over white mobilization efforts should be taken seriously as white supremacy activism and hate crimes have grown. While rallies and speeches often gain a lion's share of the attention on college campuses, tactics such as flyers and pamphlets are overlooked but are more commonly used to promote white pride and attempt to mobilize students for the cause.

In chapter 10, Bhoomi Thakore demonstrates that the media also plays a powerful role in producing and reproducing a society that values "whiteness" over other traits. Thakore examines specifically how Southeast Asian women of color are represented in popular television media to understand the ways in which produced, created, and manufactured content reinforces this era's dominant ideologies of homogeneity and divisiveness. While representation is clearly increasing, there is a clear whitewashing of these Asian women, where certain characteristics (e.g., lighter skin color) are considered much more attractive than others.

Rounding out part II, Simón E. Weffer, David G. Embrick, and Silvia Domínguez illustrate how an institution devoted to the arts can be a place that facilitates "whiteness" and "elitism" and thus reinforces a racist social system that benefits whites at the expense of other, more marginalized groups. In so doing, erudite institutions, such as museums, prop up white supremacy and white normality while also stoking whites' fear with respect to their place in society, reinforcing the racial status quo in the most seemingly cosmopolitan places.

While the first two parts looked at how ideology, both individually and institutionally, can perpetuate the racial status quo, part III turns to white emotions, expressions, and movements. Authors discuss solutions for how might we be able to counter whitelash and dismantle white supremacy, and they provide insights into movements and countermovements that seek to fight back against racism, Trump, and attempts to minimize concerns of the marginalized groups.

In chapter 12, C. Doug Charles finds white victimization to be well represented in videos submitted to YouTube by individuals who also promote white supremacy. YouTube acts as an interesting setting to promote this ideology; because of the site's unique search algorithms, it is not always clear when viewers are tapping into white supremacy videos. Videos submitted by proponents of white supremacy commonly portrayed whites as besieged and beleaguered by a changing society that values diversity.

Maretta McDonald, in chapter 13, provides a discussion of a prominent countermovement. Titled Blue Lives Matter, this countermovement started in response to the Black Lives Matter social movement, which grew out of frustration with the "not guilty" verdict handed down in the Trayvon Martin murder case. Findings demonstrate that indeed Blue Lives Matter is used to counter a movement that seeks reform and to reify racial ideology within social structures, leading to the creation of laws that benefit one group over another.

In chapter 14, Marlese Durr turns to the role of women in the fight against Trump and racism today. Durr posited that many women rejected both populism's "Make America Great Again" and the neoliberal feminism of today. Durr noted that in response to the populism that led to Trump's election, women globally came to the "rescue" of women and fought for other marginalized groups as well, supporting issues such as immigration and health care reform, reproductive rights, the natural environment, LGBTQ rights, racial equality, religious freedom, and workers' rights. Thus, many women followed Derrick Bell's call and fought against President Trump's antiwoman and other marginalizing stances.

Lastly, in chapter 15, Mary Ryan and David Brunsma turn to activism by antiracists in direct response to the overt racism and bigotry of Donald Trump (as well as the current political climate surrounding his administration and in US politics more generally). This digital ethnography looked at twenty-three organizations' online information, including mission statements, activities, and discursive strategies and goals, to assess antiracist activism by whites. They conclude by offering some challenges facing antiracism in the Trump era. White allies must recognize their privilege, identify (at the direction of people of color) ways in which they reproduce white supremacy, and change those behaviors in ways that oppose racial hierarchies.

CONCLUSIONS

Given the discussion above, we propose that whitelash is a collective and historical process made up of actions and reactions of whites attempting to dismantle any challenge to the racial status quo or any calls made oppressed groups for equal rights and treatment. Furthermore, whitelash is backlash against diversity and diversity initiatives. From slavery to the rise of Donald Trump today, the fight to maintain power and control is perpetual. Accordingly, we see whitelash as a collective effort among whites to protest and prevent change, despite living in a shifting society that is growing more diverse by the day. Accordingly, we feel that the theoretical framework of whitelash will provide scholars with a conceptually and analytically agile tool to explain future actions and reactions among whites (and some nonwhites) who seek to maintain control and power in the face of growing protest over unequal treatment and fairness.

NOTES

1. For more on the movement to correctly educate on the history of US slavery, see the work being done by the Southern Poverty Law Center, https://www.splcenter.org/teaching-hard-history-american-slavery.
2. Colin Rand Kaepernick, acclaimed quarterback for the San Francisco 49ers for six seasons, received worldwide notoriety for sitting during the playing of the US national anthem at the 49ers' third preseason game as a means of protest against racism and white supremacy in the US. His (and others') protests received mixed reactions from the public that were further polarized

and intensified after President Donald Trump issued a series of statements condemning the action as unpatriotic.
3. Gamergate refers to an online harassment campaign and use of the hashtag #Gamergate beginning in 2014. The campaign centered on issues of sexism but included racism and homo/transphobia in video-game culture.
4. See the Moynihan Report (Moynihan 1965); see also Ryan 1976 for a classic take that refutes blame-the-victim arguments.

REFERENCES

Agerholm, Harriot. 2016. "What Is 'Whitelash,' and Why Are Experts Saying It Led to Donald Trump's Election?" *Independent*, November 9.

Anderson, Carol. 2017. *White Rage: The Unspoken Truth of Our Racial Divide.* New York: Bloomsbury USA.

Baldwin, James. 1980. "Dark Days." *Esquire.* October.

Becker, Amanda, and Richard Cowan. 2018. "Battle Looms in Congress over Money for Trump's Border Wall." *Reuters.* Retrieved March 1, 2019 (https://www.reuters.com/article/us-usa-congress-lameduck/battle-looms-in-congress-over-money-for-trumps-border-wall-idUSKCN1ND1GL).

Berrey, Ellen. 2015. *The Enigma of Diversity: The Language of Race and the Limits of Social Justice.* Chicago: University of Chicago Press.

Blumer, Herbert. 1958. "Race Prejudice as a Sense of Group Position." *Pacific Sociology Review* 1(1): 3–7.

Bobo, Lawrence, James R. Kluegel, and Ryan A. Smith. 1997. "Laissez-Faire Racism: The Crystallization of a Kindler, Gentler, Antiblack Ideology." Pp. 15–44 in *Racial Attitudes in the 1990s: Continuity and Change*, edited by Steven A. Tuch and Jack K. Martin. Westport, CT: Greenwood Publishing Group.

Bobo, Lawrence, and Ryan Smith. 1998. "From Jim Crow Racism to Laissez-Faire Racism: The Transformation of Racial Attitudes." Pp. 182–220 in *Beyond Pluralism: The Conception of Groups and Group Identities in America*, edited by Wendy F. Katkin, Ned Landsman, and Andrea Tyree. Urbana: University of Illinois Press.

Bonilla-Silva, Eduardo. 1997. "Rethinking Racism: Toward a Structural Interpretation." *American Sociological Review* 62(3): 465.

———. 2001. *White Supremacy and Racism in the Post–Civil Rights Era.* Boulder, CO: Lynne Rienner.

———. 2003. *Racism without Racists: Color-Blind Racism and the Persistence of Racial Inequality in America.* Lanham, MD: Rowman & Littlefield.

———. 2019. "Feeling Race: Theorizing the Racial Economy of Emotions." *American Sociological Review* 84(1): 1–25.

Browne, Jaron. 2007. "Rooted in Slavery: Prison Labor Exploitation." *Race, Poverty & the Environment* 14(1): 42–44.

Burke, Meghan. 2019. *Colorblind Racism.* Medford, MA: Polity Press.
Carissimo, Justin. 2016. "Van Jones Calls Trump's Surprise Victory a Whitelash against a Changing Country." *Independent,* November 9.
Carter, J. Scott, and Cameron Lippard. 2015. "Group Positioning, Threat and Immigration: The Role of Elite Actors and Interest Groups in Setting the 'Lines of Discussion.'" *Sociology of Race and Ethnicity* 1: 394–408.
———. 2020. *The Death of Affirmative Action? Racialized Framing and the Fight against Racial Preference in College Admissions.* Bristol, UK: Bristol University Press.
Carter, J. Scott, Cameron Lippard, and Andrew F. Baird. 2019. "Veiled Threat: Colorblind Racism, Group Threat and Affirmative Action." *Social Problems* 66(4): 503–18.
Chavez, Leo R. 2013. *The Latino Threat: Constructing Immigrants, Citizens, and the Nation.* Redwood City, CA: Stanford University Press.
Cokorinos, Lee. 2003. *The Assault on Diversity: An Organized Challenge to Racial and Gender Justice.* Lanham, MD: Rowman & Littlefield.
Cooper, Anna Julia. 1892. *A Voice from the South.* Xenia, OH: The Aldine Printing House.
DiAngelo, Robin. 2018. *White Fragility: Why It's So Hard for White People to Talk about Racism.* New York: Beacon Press.
Doane, Ashley "Woody," and Eduardo Bonilla-Silva. 2003. *Whiteout: The Continuing Significance of Racism.* New York: Routledge.
Douglas, Karen M., Gideon Sjoberg, Rogelio Sáenz, and David G. Embrick. 2018. "Bureaucratic Capitalism, Mass Incarceration and Race and Ethnicity in America." In *Racial and Ethnic Relations Handbook,* 2nd ed., edited by Pinar Batur and Joe R. Feagin. New York: Kluwer/Springer.
Du Bois, W. E. B. 1903. *The Souls of Black Folk.* Chicago: A. C. McClurg & Co.
Embrick, David G. 2008. "The Diversity Ideology: Keeping Major Transnational Corporations White and Male in an Era of Globalization." Pp. 37–42 in *Globalization and America: Race, Human Rights, and Inequality,* edited by Angela Hattery, David G. Embrick, and Earl Smith. Lanham, MD: Rowman & Littlefield.
———. 2011. "Diversity Ideology in the Business World: A New Oppression for a New Age." *Critical Sociology* 37(5): 541–56.
———. 2015a. "Two Nations, Revisited: The Lynching of Black and Brown Bodies, Police Brutality, and Racial Control in 'Post-Racial' Amerikkka." *Critical Sociology* 41(6): 835–43.
———. 2015b. "We Will Never Forget (Never Again): Massacre of the Charleston 9, Murders of Brown and Black Bodies, and 21st Century Amerikkka." *Issues in Race & Society: An Interdisciplinary Global Journal.*
———. 2016. "Minimizing the Roots of a Racialized Social System; Ignoring Gender: Lethal Policing and Why We Must Talk More, Not Less, about Race

and Gender." Response to "Lethal Policing: Making Sense of American Exceptionalism," by Paul J. Hirschfield (30:4). *Sociological Forum* 31(1): 233–36.

———. 2018. "Diversity: Good for Maintaining the Status Quo, Not So Much for Real Progressive Change." Pp. 1–9 in *Challenging the Status Quo: Diversity, Democracy, and Equality in the 21st Century*, edited by David G. Embrick, Sharon M. Collins, and Michele Dodson. London, UK: Brill Press/Haymarket Books.

Faludi, Susan. 1991. *Backlash: The Undeclared War against American Women.* New York: Crown Publishers.

Fanon, Franz. 1952. *Black Skin, White Masks.* New York: Grove Press.

Feagin, Joe R. 2010. *Systemic Racism: A Theory of Oppression.* New York: Routledge.

Feagin, Joe R., and Karyn M. McKinney. 2005. *The Many Costs of Racism.* Lanham, MD: Rowman & Littlefield.

Fields, Karen E., and Barbara J. Fields. 2014. *Racecraft: The Soul of Inequality in American Life.* New York: Verso.

Forman, Tyrone. 2004. "Color-Blind Racism and Racial Indifference: The Role of Racial Apathy in Facilitating Enduring Inequalities." Pp. 43–66 in *The Changing Terrain of Race and Ethnicity*, edited by Maria Krysan and Amanda E. Lewis. New York: Russell Sage Foundation.

Forman, Tyrone, and Amanda E. Lewis. 2006. "Racial Apathy and Hurricane Katrina: The Social Anatomy of Prejudice in the Post–Civil Rights Era." *Du Bois Review* 3(1): 175–202.

Fortin, Jacey. 2017. "The Statue at the Center of Charlottesville's Storm. *The New York Times*, August 13.

Fredrickson, George M. 1982. *White Supremacy: A Comparative Study in American and South African History.* Oxford, UK: Oxford University Press.

Gallagher, Charles A., ed. 2008. *Racism in Post-Race America: New Theories, New Directions.* Cary, NC: Oxford University Press.

Gallup. 2019. "Race Relations." https://news.gallup.com/poll/1687/race-relations.aspx.

Glenn, Evelyn Nakano. 2015. "Settler Colonialism as Structure: A Framework for Comparative Studies of U.S. Race and Gender Formation." *Sociology of Race and Ethnicity* 1(1): 54–74.

Green, Erica L. 2019. "U.S Orders Duke and U.N.C. to Recast Tone in Mideast Studies." *New York Times*, September 19.

Grinapol, Corinne. 2016. "Van Jones: 'This Was a Whitelash against a Changing Country': 'We've Talked about Everything But Race Tonight.'" *Adweek*, November 9. Retrieved February 1, 2019 (https://www.adweek.com/digital/van-jones-this-was-a-whitelash-against-a-changing-country/).

Hochschild, Arlie Russell. 2016. *Strangers in Their Own Land: Anger and Mourning on the American Right.* New York: The New Press.

Hughey, Matthew W., David G. Embrick, and Ashley "Woody" Doane. 2015. "Paving the Way for Future Race Research: Exploring the Racial Mechanisms within a Color-Blind, Racialized Social System." *American Behavioral Scientist* 59(11): 1347–57.

Kozol, Jonathan. 2005. *The Shame of the Nation: The Restoration of Apartheid Schooling in America*. New York: Crown Publishers.

Lippard, Cameron D. 2011. "Racist Nativism in the 21st Century." *Sociology Compass* 5:591–606.

Lipsitz, George. 1998. *The Possessive Investment in Whiteness: How White People Profit from Identity Politics*. Philadelphia: Temple University Press.

———. 2011. *How Racism Takes Place*. Philadelphia: Temple University Press.

Logan, John R., and Julia Burdick-Will. 2017. "School Segregation and Disparities in Urban, Suburban, and Rural Areas." *The Annals of the American Academy of Political and Social Science* 674(1): 199–216.

McCarthy, Justin. 2018. "Small Majority in U.S. Say the Country's Best Days Are Ahead." *Gallup*, July 3. Retrieved March 1, 2019 (https://news.gallup.com/poll/236447/small-majority-say-country-best-days-ahead.aspx).

Montejano, David. 1987. *Anglos and Mexicans in the Making of Texas, 1836–1986*. Austin: University of Texas Press.

Moore, Wendy L. 2008. *Reproducing Racism: White Space, Elite Law Schools, and Racial Inequality*. Lanham, MD: Rowman & Littlefield.

Moynihan, Daniel P. 1965. *The Negro Family: The Case for National Action*. Washington, DC: Office of Policy Planning and Research, U.S. Department of Labor.

Omi, Michael, and Howard Winant. 2014 [1994]. *Racial Formation in the United States*. New York: Routledge.

O'Reilly, Andrew. 2017. "Amid Charlottesville Backlash Some Are Asking If Stature Removal Push Has Gone Too Far." *Foxnews.com*, August 28. Retrieved February 1, 2019 (https://www.foxnews.com/us/amid-charlottesville-backlash-some-are-asking-if-statue-removal-push-has-gone-too-far).

Picca, Leslie Houts, and Joe R. Feagin. 2007. *Two-Faced Racism: Whites in the Frontstage and Backstage*. New York: Routledge.

Ray, Victor. 2017. "A Theory of Racialized Organizations." *SocArXIV*, April 15. Retrieved February 1, 2019 (http://osf.io/preprints/socarxiv/u75gr).

———. 2019. "A Theory of Racialized Organizations." *American Sociological Review* 84(1): 1–28.

Rogers, Katie, and Nicholas Fandos. 2019. "Trump Tells Congresswomen to 'Go Back' to the Countries They Came From." *New York Times*, July 14.

Ryan, William. 1976. *Blaming the Victim*. New York: Vintage.

Saenz, Rogelio, Karen M. Douglas, David G. Embrick, and Gideon Sjoberg. 2007. "Pathways to Downward Mobility: The Impact of Schools, Welfare, and Prisons on People of Color." Pp. 373–409 in *Racial and Ethnic Relations Handbook*, edited by Hernán Vera and Joe R. Feagin. New York: Kluwer/Springer.

Saito, Leeland T. 2009. *The Politics of Exclusion: The Failure of Race-Neutral Policies in Urban America.* Redwood City, CA: Stanford University Press.

Truth, Sojourner. 1851. "Ain't I a Woman?" *Civil Rights and Conflict in the United States: Selected Speeches.* Lit2Go Edition. Retrieved Jan. 14, 2020 (https://etc.usf.edu/lit2go/185/civil-rights-and-conflict-in-the-united-states-selected-speeches/3089/aint-i-a-woman/).

Tuch, Steven A., and Michael Hughes. 2011. "Whites' Racial Policy Attitudes in the Twenty-First Century: The Continuing Significance of Racial Resentment." *Annals of the American Academy of Political and Social Science* 634(1): 134–52.

Voogd, Jan. 2008. *Race Riots and Resistance: The Red Summer of 1919.* New York: Peter Lang.

Wingfield, Adia, and Joe R. Feagin. 2012. *Yes We Can? White Racial Framing and the Obama Presidency.* New York: Routledge.

Withers, Paul. 2018. "Christians Are the Most Persecuted Religion in the World—Reveals New Report." *Express*, June 22.

PART I

THE IDEOLOGICAL REINFORCEMENT OF WHITE SUPREMACY

CHAPTER 1

POST–COLOR BLINDNESS?

Trump and the Rise of the New White Nationalism

ASHLEY "WOODY" DOANE

On June 16, 2015, wealthy entrepreneur and television personality Donald J. Trump announced his candidacy for the Republican Party nomination for president of the United States. In his speech, Trump referred to immigrants from Mexico as criminals and rapists (Washington Post 2015). To some observers, this seemingly ended the Trump candidacy just as it was beginning, for Trump had willfully breached the prevailing racial etiquette that proscribed such overt displays of racism. But as we know, neither this nor many other racist remarks (Desjardins 2017) would derail Trump's eventual election to the position of president. For those who seek to understand racism in the United States in the twenty-first century, the success of the Trump campaign raises an important question: are the social forces that produced the Trump presidency a unique phenomenon, or do they portend a change in American racial ideology?

THE IMPORTANCE OF RACIAL IDEOLOGIES

Racist statements and actions do not occur in social isolation. They are not idiosyncratic examples of individual "hate." Indeed, racism exists in what Eduardo Bonilla-Silva (1997) has called a "racialized social system," a society where socially constructed racial categories have been deliberately employed to shape the distribution of wealth, power, and other social goods. And as I have argued elsewhere (Doane 2014a, 2017), racialized social systems are supported by *racial ideologies*, collections of beliefs and understandings about what race is and how social arrangements and practices should be racially structured. Alternatively, ideologies can be described as a mélange of elements that includes frames, narratives, symbols, stereotypes, discursive styles, and vocabulary (Bonilla-Silva 2018 [2003]). Ultimately, these beliefs and understandings become embedded in culture and, as such, serve as the "common sense" that shapes the worldview and everyday individual interactions of social actors.

For the purposes of this analysis, what is most important about racial ideologies is that they are inherently *political*. As Eduardo Bonilla-Silva has stated, racial ideologies are used to *"explain and justify"* (dominant race) or *challenge* (subordinate race or races) *the racial status quo"* (2018 [2003]:9, emphasis in the original). Consequently, there are *dominant ideologies*, which disproportionately shape political and social outcomes, and *oppositional ideologies*, which seek to restructure the racial logic of society. Politically, groups "weaponize" racial ideologies to attack or defend the existing racial order, for they provide the rationale for social policies and the organizing ideas for social movements (Doane 2007). In this political struggle, racial ideologies are used strategically to attract and mobilize supporters and to neutralize and discredit opponents.

The political nature of racial ideologies requires that they be dynamic and flexible in order to maintain their utility in intergroup struggle. This means that ideologies must continually be adapted to respond to opposing political claims and social movements, as well as social and economic changes in society (and, increasingly, in the world). For example, virtually everything that has happened in US history, from abolitionism to emancipation, territorial expansion and colonialism to industrialization, Reconstruction to the civil rights movement, has effected changes in racial politics, leading to the *evolution* of racial ideologies (Smedley 2007). And in the shorter term, racial events—occurrences whose emergence triggers a public discussion of issues of racism and racial inequality (Doane 2006, 2007)—such as "hate crimes," police shootings, the Katrina disaster, and the Obama campaign often require that proponents of a particular racial ideology adjust their rhetoric and possibly their worldview to incorporate these new events and to meet the challenges of their opponents (Doane 2014a). Consequently, it is essential that those who study racism and racial ideologies remain vigilant for changes.

"WHAT'S PAST IS PROLOGUE": THE EBB AND FLOW OF WHITE SUPREMACY AND WHITE RESISTANCE

The existence of white supremacy and white resistance in the United States in the twenty-first century can be understood only in the context of over four hundred years of European/white/American racism. Trump, the Tea Party, and other contemporary forms of white resistance are not new phenomena but the latest manifestation of an ongoing process. The United States is grounded in European colonial expansion and white supremacy and has been shaped by the ebb and flow of racial domination and resistance. The creation of "American" society was shaped by three core dynamics, all of which were directly linked to racism. First was the conquest and "ethnic cleansing" of the indigenous peoples of much of North America, which provided the physical and social space for the United States. The initial colonial beachhead on the East Coast was maintained through racialized warfare with Native Americans. Over three centuries, this conquest and colonization expanded across the North American continent and extended to Mexicans in the southwestern United States and native peoples in Alaska and Hawai'i. Second was the "triangular trade" and the enslavement of African Americans, which produced great wealth and served as a pillar of the nation's economic development. Enslavement and its aftermath—Civil War, Reconstruction, Jim Crow, and the civil rights movement—played a core role in the ongoing racialization of the United States and a racial discourse that focused on issues of "black and white." Finally, the US established a regime of racialized immigration, where immigrants who differed from the Anglo-American core culture were often viewed as suspect until proven white and differentially incorporated into (or in some cases excluded from) American society. Taken as a whole, these three dynamics not only shaped the creation and evolution of the United States but also were a major influence on its dominant culture, political organization, and social institutions.

Concurrent with the US colonial project and the physical establishment of white supremacy was the emergence of racial ideologies to legitimize these practices. From the beginning, conflicts over land and resources were swiftly followed by the "racialization of savagery"—the belief that conquest, dispossession, removal, and even genocide could be justified by casting Native Americans as inherently uncivilized and subhuman. Similarly, creation of institutionalized chattel slavery led to the emergence of an ideology of race—a worldview that increasingly melded politics and "science" to create a biological myth that supported enslavement on the basis of innate inferiority

(Smedley 2007). With the passage of time, this racial hierarchy was extended to other colonized peoples (Mexicans, Alaskans, Hawaiians, and Puerto Ricans) as well as immigrants who did not fit the "Anglo-Saxon" ideal for who is an "American." And on a broader scale, the idea of race was used to craft the idea of "whiteness"—an allegedly superior group of people who were destined to rule over inferior races. Over time, "white" became synonymous with "American" (Painter 2010), thus melding ideas of racial superiority into the national identity. This "whiteness/Americanness" in turn gave rise to the idea of American exceptionalism, as John Winthrop's "errand in the wilderness" evolved into the doctrine of Manifest Destiny—the idea that white/Anglo-Saxon Americans had a divine mission to spread civilization, democracy, and prosperity across the planet. These ideas continue today in the image of the US as the global superpower and the persistence of the ideology of American exceptionalism.

While dominant racial ideologies were used to legitimize the establishment and maintenance of the United States as a racialized social system, their use has not followed a consistent pattern. Historically, when white supremacy has been challenged, racist ideologies come to the fore and racial boundaries harden. This has been true since the early days of English colonization, when Virginia planters responded to the threat posed by the interracial alliance of poor whites and enslaved blacks during Bacon's Rebellion by institutionalizing enslavement and expanding participation in the Atlantic slave trade. In the eighteenth century, when Benjamin Franklin felt threatened by German immigration into Pennsylvania, he responded not only with ethnic slurs but also by questioning the immigrants' "whiteness." This pattern continued over the centuries, with increased immigration met with rising nativism (the Know Nothing Movement, the Chinese Exclusion Act, immigration restriction movements, and the imposition of quotas in the 1920s) and any semblance of advancement for African Americans (emancipation, Reconstruction) met with new forms of oppression such as the Black Codes and the creation of the Jim Crow racial order (Du Bois 1998 [1935]; Anderson 2016). And more recently, whites have responded to the gains of the civil rights movement and post-1965 changes in immigration and racial demographics with the racially driven Nixon-Reagan "wars" on crime, drugs, and welfare and the Trump attack on immigration. The point here is that *the white backlash or "resistance" of the Trump era is not new; it is simply the latest manifestation of a centuries-long defense of white supremacy.*

Throughout US history, these various episodes of white backlash or resistance have been supported by the dominant racial ideology, with its claims about the meaning of race, its blueprint for behavior, and its rationale for racial inequality and oppression. For much of this period, the dominant racial ideology was what can be called "classical racism" (Doane 2017), with core tenets of biologically distinct races, racially determined characteristics (e.g., intelligence), and the existence of a "natural" racial hierarchy (with whites, of course, occupying the top position). In the wake of the civil rights movement and other challenges to white supremacy, classical racism—or at least overt public displays of racism—became increasingly untenable. As many scholars of race have argued, it was replaced over the past half-century by color-blind racial ideology (Bonilla-Silva 2018 [2003]; Doane 2017).

COLOR-BLIND RACIAL IDEOLOGY AND THE TRUMP TRANSGRESSIONS

Color-blind racial ideology is grounded in the claim that the United States in the late twentieth and early twenty-first centuries is a "postracial" society in which race no longer matters and racism is no longer a significant obstacle to success for peoples of color. It addresses the problem of racial inequality's persistence through a number of discursive frames that "explain" phenomena such as economic inequality or residential and educational segregation as accidental or due to the actions (or inactions) of minorities themselves (Bonilla-Silva 2018 [2003]). And color-blind racial ideology is politically effective in that it conflates social aspirations (e.g., realizing Martin Luther King Jr.'s "dream") with the claim that this has largely been achieved. Over the past few decades, elements of color blindness have been employed by whites and their allies, individually and collectively, to deny or minimize racism and to defend white advantages. In the context of white resistance, color blindness has been used to attack affirmative action, school desegregation, and other race-cognizant programs used to address racial inequality. It is also used to portray racialized policies such as the "war on drugs," the "war on crime," and welfare "reform" as "race neutral" and, therefore, not racist.

Like all racial ideologies, color blindness is a fluid construction, continually adjusted to respond to changing circumstances or the discursive attacks of opponents—particularly antiracists using systemic racism consciousness ideology to assert that structural racism continues to be significant (Doane 2017). For example, color blindness has increasingly included claims of white "victimization" (e.g., "reverse discrimination") to the point where some surveys find that a plurality of whites see "racism" against whites as a more significant problem than racism against peoples of color (Norton and Sommers 2011). It is also able to incorporate the seeming contradiction of racist acts in a claimed "postracial" society by framing them as individual acts of hate or bigotry that do not reflect the larger society. This has the additional advantage of opening the door for arguments equating white racism with the "racism" of blacks and others—thereby effectively discounting four hundred years of history (Doane 2014a).

These are the rough parameters of the ideological/discursive arena into which Trump launched his campaign rhetoric in 2015 and 2016. As mentioned earlier, the surprise was that a series of racialized remarks did not end or irreparably harm his candidacy, for similar breaches of color-blind racial etiquette had severe consequences for others in the public eye (e.g., Michael Richards, Don Imus, Megyn Kelly, Roseanne Barr). Almost immediately, a "racial morality play"—a public trial of an offender—was set into motion, with harsh condemnation coming even from members of Trump's own party such as Paul Ryan, Lindsey Graham, and Mitt Romney. Yet Trump forged ahead, occasionally defending himself as the "least racist person" (Danner 2016) or using more racially coded language but making no significant change in his discursive approach to racial issues. And despite polls that showed 44 percent of respondents describing Trump as racist and a majority agreeing that he appealed to bigotry (Bump 2016), Trump succeeded in winning both the Republican nomination and, in November 2016, the presidency. Clearly, the "Trump card" overcame the existing color-blind racial etiquette.

A broader interpretation of what transpired is that the Trump campaign reflected the normalization of overt expressions of racism. Following the 2016 election, one supporter exulted that "Trump broke that P.C. barrier . . . made me feel comfortable again to speak out" and that "#WhiteShaming doesn't work anymore" (Kaleem 2016). White supremacist Richard Spencer asserted that Trump's election was "white Americans of all classes revolting against political correctness" (Kaleem 2016). In a publication titled "The Trump Effect" (Costello 2016), the Southern Poverty Law Center documented an increase in racial attacks and hate speech following Trump's election. And in a Connecticut high school basketball game, students from a predominantly white town used chants of "Trump" to taunt players on a predominantly black team (Blair 2017). These—and other—events lead to the conclusion that Trump's political discourse was part of a larger racial dynamic.

And the beat goes on. Since his election, Trump has continued his pattern of race-baiting. Following clashes in Charlottesville, Virginia, between white supremacists and antiracist demonstrators, Trump placed blame on "both sides," thereby equating white nationalist extremists with those opposed to racism (Desjardins 2017). He derided black football players who protested racist police violence as "sons of bitches" and called for their firing. In the winter of 2018, Trump referred to refugees from the Global South as immigrants from "shithole countries" (Dawsey 2018). And in the run-up to the November 2018 midterm elections, he repeatedly referred to the threat posed by a migrant "caravan" and supported a political advertisement featuring an immigrant "cop killer" who posed a threat to the United States (Herb, Sands, and Shortell 2018). And throughout the entire period, a plurality of Americans (49 percent) described Trump as racist (Cillizza 2018). All of these events represented a challenge to the hegemony of color-blind racial ideology.

THE NEW WHITE NATIONALISM: A CHALLENGING IDEOLOGY?

Drawing on the above discussion, I would like to suggest that we need to recognize the existence of the "new white nationalism" as a distinct racial ideology that has emerged to contest "color blindness" in the political and public sphere. To be clear at the outset, I am *not* making the assertion that the new white nationalism is replacing color-blind ideology as the dominant or hegemonic racial ideology. What I am claiming is that it has emerged as an alternative that needs to be taken into account in analyses of contemporary racism in the United States. Most scholars who study racism, myself included, have tended to focus on color blindness, while recognizing the persistence of white supremacist ideology (the offshoot of classical racism) and the existence of antiracist ideology (which recognizes the continuing significance of systemic racism and which I have elsewhere labeled as "systemic racism consciousness"—Doane 2017). Future analyses of racial discourse and ideology need to be able to account for the changing political and social terrain.

Before I proceed further, it is useful to consider the nature of ideologies. Because we so often focus on the content of ideologies (e.g., color blindness), we place less emphasis on their nature. Ideologies—and their use by individuals and groups—are complex. They are in a constant state of flux, buffeted by the ever-changing political and social context. They are inconsistent, as racial discourse may employ elements of multiple ideologies—e.g., using elements of both color blindness and more overt forms of racism—depending on the situation (Doane 2014a; 2017). Ideologies do not follow an unbroken path of progression from past to present. As Bonilla-Silva observes, "the hegemony of one form of racial ideology does not mean that at certain historical junctures a secondary form cannot be heightened" (2018 [2003]:223). And as Kasey Henricks (2018) has demonstrated, elements of color-blind racial ideology can be found in the debates surrounding the infamous "three-fifths" clause of the US Constitution. Similarly, W. E. B. Du Bois clearly describes President Andrew Johnson using the language of white victimization and "reverse discrimination" in his statement vetoing the Civil Rights Bill of 1866 (1998 [1935]:282–83). My point here is that racial ideologies are inherently messy—they are inconsistent and overlapping—and this reality poses a significant challenge for sociological analysis.

What, then, is the case for the "new white nationalism"? I have previously argued (Doane 2014a) that color-blind racial ideology is extremely flexible in its ability to incorporate events and ideas (e.g., the Black Lives Matter movement or the valorization of "diversity") that on the surface seemingly contradict the color-blind denial of racism. Jennifer Mueller (2017) extensively describes the creative strategies whites use to continue to defend color blindness despite evidence of persisting disparities in wealth and social advantages. And Bonilla-Silva (2018 [2003]) demonstrates the multiple ways in which Trump, despite his transgressions, also remained under the sway of color-blind ideology (e.g., continually maintaining that he is not a racist). Yet there is a point at which we stretch something so far that it loses all semblance of its original shape. If color blindness is everything, then it risks becoming nothing.

While space limitations require a condensed argument, I will begin by suggesting that the new white nationalism is not a simple return to past forms of overt racism (the Jim Crow era) but represents an emergent constellation of claims, understandings, and discursive strategies developed for changing social circumstances. Trump is not the cause of what is happening—which is why I believe that it is misleading to speak of "the Trump effect"—he is merely the most pronounced symptom. And as I asserted above, the "new white nationalism" is not, strictly speaking, new: it is the latest manifestation of cycles of white assertion and the defense of white supremacy that reach back to the origins of the United States. Even if we concentrate our analysis on the more recent past, I would argue that the phenomenon has clear roots that can be traced back to former Klan leader David Duke's 1990 Senate campaign in Louisiana and Patrick Buchanan's Republican presidential primary campaigns in 1992 and 1996 (and, going further, to the "Reagan Revolution" and the 1960s and 1970s "backlash" against the civil rights movement).

Content-wise, the "new white nationalism" can be broadly viewed as a mash-up of elements of color blindness and white supremacy that has been adapted to the present context. While a detailed analysis remains to be done, I would highlight the following areas:

Nationalism

American nationalism has been on the upswing since the September 11, 2001, terrorist attacks, the "War on Terror," and the two wars in the Middle East. If we view nationalism as going beyond patriotism to advocate for the interests of one's people and nation at the expense of others, then the claim can be made that American nationalism is currently at a high tide. With a campaign promise to "make America great again" and an inaugural address that asserted that "from this day forward, a new vision will govern . . . it's going to be only America first, America first" (BBC 2017), the Trump administration embarked on a series of steps designed to advance US interests, including initiating trade wars by imposing tariffs, withdrawing from international agreements (Paris agreement on climate change, Iran nuclear deal), and questioning long-standing relationships (NATO, UNESCO). Other nationalist policies included enhanced border control (the Muslim travel ban) and measures designed to limit immigration on the Mexican border.

The United States from its inception had a national identity ("American") that was inextricably intertwined with a white European worldview and white political and economic interests. Government policies were historically designed to advance white interests. Citizenship, civil rights, and social status have been and continue to be racially determined, either by law or through institutional practices. To become "American" was to assimilate into an American social and cultural "mainstream" that was shaped and defined by whiteness. It is this matrix that led Toni Morrison to conclude that "deep within the word 'American' is its association with race . . . American means white" (1992:47). Given this history, it is not surprising that many interpreted the call to "make America great again" coupled with promises of stridently nationalistic (and in some cases racialized) policies as a call to "make America *white* again." While this phrase was frequently used as a criticism of Trump's immigration policies, it also appeared on a highway billboard erected by a congressional candidate in Tennessee (WTVC 2016).

External/Internal Threat

An essential component of the new white nationalism is the emphasis on the "threat" to the United States that is posed by both external and internal actors, who are often portrayed in highly racialized ways. Threats play an important political role, providing images and story lines that are effective bases for nationalist appeals and social mobilization. Globally, the threats come from nonwhite areas—China, Iran, North Korea, ISIS/Islamic terrorists—that all pose a danger to the American way of life. The other external threat is immigration, which has been viewed as a recurring threat to the United States for two centuries. The call to secure America's borders—against Muslim terrorists and Latin American immigrants—invokes images of the racialized other and enhances white solidarity. In the period before the 2018 midterm elections, Trump and the national media repeatedly focused on the "caravan," an impromptu group of Central American refugees and migrants traveling across Mexico toward the US border. Although this group was hundreds of miles (and weeks of travel) away from the border, media coverage was akin to that of a hurricane approaching the southeast coast of the United States (Obeidallah 2018). At the same time, a campaign video focused on a Mexican immigrant convicted of killing two police officers and linked him to the "caravan" and other southern border issues (Herb, Sands, and Shortell 2018). While the ad was condemned as racist by Democrats and a few Republicans, it had a clear strategic rationale. According to Marisa Abrajano and Zoltan Hajnal (2015), whites who have negative attitudes toward immigrants are more likely to vote Republican and to change their affiliation to the Republican Party.

Equally significant to the new white nationalism are images of internal "threats" to the "American way of life." While there is no shortage of actors, including "elites," the "deep state," and "radical" college students and faculty, our focus here is on racialized threats. Certainly Trump and the Republican Party in general have continued the "law and order" rhetoric that has been directed toward African Americans for decades. And the pictures of African American professional football players kneeling during the national anthem to protest police violence (a form of protest continually criticized by Trump) became an omnipresent media image of "unpatriotic" minorities. Perhaps the most central threat incorporated in white nationalist ideology is the belief that immigration is irrevocably changing the United States from a white nation to a majority-minority nation. In the summer of 2018, conservative Fox News commentator Laura Ingraham created a controversy when she began one show with the claim that "in some parts of the country, it does seem like the America that we know and love doesn't exist anymore" and that these "massive demographic changes" were a "national emergency" (BBC 2018). And in the wake of the 2018 elections, conservative commentator and former presidential candidate Patrick Buchanan (2019), in an article titled "No This Is Not JFK's Democratic Party," decried the increasing diversity (and decline of white males) among the new representatives arriving in Congress. Indeed, newly elected New York congressional representative Alexandria Ocasio-Cortez is continually featured on the web page of Fox News as an example of the dangers posed by these changes. These claims increasingly resonate with older white Americans who grew up in a nation that was much less diverse—in the 1960s, the US was 88.8 percent white, Hispanic was not even a category in the census, the foreign-born population was at a historic low, and nine of the ten largest foreign-born groups were from Europe (Doane 2014b)—and whose sense of threat from these changes makes them receptive to nationalist appeals (McElwee and McDaniel 2017a).

To be crystal clear: the new white nationalism is driven by racism—the fear of losing a privileged position in a world that is changing, In the wake of the 2016 election, it was fashionable for pundits to claim that a key factor in determining the outcome was the shift to Trump by white working-class voters who were losing ground in an era of globalization and deindustrialization and who felt ignored by the federal government. What this portrayal ignores is that white voters in *every* income category voted for Trump over Clinton, while voters (of all races) who made less than $50,000 supported Clinton—thus undercutting the position that Trump's appeal was economic (Serwer 2017; McElwee and McDaniel 2017b). This is not a nationalist movement, it is a *white* nationalist movement (Bonilla-Silva 2019).

Increased Toleration for Racism

Another element of the new white nationalism is an increased degree of tolerance for racism. While the proscription of overt racism that is a core element of the etiquette of color-blind racial ideology remains strong—as evidenced by the attempts of Trump, Ingraham, and others to deny that their remarks were racist amid strong criticism—I believe that events of the past few years have shifted the boundaries of what will be tolerated. What was considered beyond the pale or "hate speech" has crept back into the mainstream, reminding us that the distance was not as far as had been assumed. The "Birther" movement (in which Trump played a key role) and the other elements of racialized reaction to Barack Obama's election (which from the outset was never a game changer in terms of US racism) were certainly part of this trend (Reid 2017). A solid majority of Americans—57 percent—may consider Trump a racist, including 21 percent of Republicans (Eltagouri 2018), but he was elected president by 46 percent of the population and continues to receive the support of Republican political figures. Similarly, Iowa congressional representative Steve King was broadly criticized and removed from committee assignments in early 2019 for seeming to approve of white nationalism and white supremacy, but he was also re-elected by Iowa voters in November 2018 after making statements such as "we can't restore our civilization with somebody else's babies" (Cillizza 2019). And even in the wake of his most recent comments, one Iowa voter remained supportive and stated that "people who think it's offensive need to get a damn backbone and shut the hell up" while making reference to an "invasion" on the Mexican border, while another said that "everybody slips up a little bit. I don't think he really meant what he said" (Barrett and Hillyard 2019). What needs to be emphasized here is the willingness of a significant portion of white Americans either to agree with or to overlook overtly racial statements. This is not a fringe element but ostensibly (this point needs to be researched further) 25 to 45 percent of the population!

CONCLUSIONS

In this chapter, I began with the argument that the white resistance we have seen in recent years is not new but is instead the latest manifestation of dominant group reaction to social changes and gains by oppressed groups that are seen as threatening to white supremacy. In addition, I suggested that the most recent wave of white resistance has been supported by a racial ideology that I have labeled the "new white nationalism," which in some important ways represents a significant divergence from the dominant color-blind racial ideology. I presented the "new white nationalism" as an emergent ideology that coexists and overlaps with both classical racism and color blindness. This is an important corrective for our understanding of contemporary racial politics in which analysts have tended to cordon off white supremacist ideology as limited to a small fringe of extremists (although, to be fair, they have made some connections to mainstream ideology). In contrast, I contend that the new white nationalism has a much larger segment of the population that either share its views or, like Republican politicians, are willing to tolerate them in order to achieve conservative political objectives.

What does this mean for contemporary racial politics? At the present, I do not see the new white nationalism as becoming the dominant racial ideology, but I do see it as a significant force driving US politics. Yet there is the potential for conflict. If Trump loses the presidency in 2020 and/or the Democrats regain control of the Senate, I foresee the increased assertion of white nationalism especially manifest in a rise in hate crimes and domestic white terrorism. And we know that the demographic changes that evoke feelings of threat among many whites will continue to happen. What is also dangerous is the increasing willingness of the Republican Party to move away from democracy. Tactics such as racialized voter suppression, racial gerrymandering, and rule changes by party leaders in the wake of Republican electoral losses (as happened in Wisconsin and North Carolina) indicate a preference for retaining power over a commitment to democracy. And a conservative Republican–dominated Supreme Court has shown itself increasingly willing to roll back civil rights protections (e.g., *Shelby County v. Holder*) and to tolerate violations at the state level. Recent research findings (Berlatsky 2018) draw a connection between white intolerance of other groups and support for authoritarianism. Viewed through the lens of history, this should not be surprising, for whenever whites have felt their status threatened, bad things have happened.

These developments pose challenges to both social scientists and social activists. We need a better understanding of the new white nationalism, both theoretically and empirically. This includes mapping out the ideology's contours, related discursive strategies, and mechanisms of transmission, especially the role of Fox News and the other alt-right media. It is also important to understand the emergence of the new white nationalism in an international context. There are clear parallels between developments in the US, the Brexit movement in the UK, and the rise of far right parties and/or governments in France, Germany, Italy, Poland, Hungary, Austria, and other countries. Moreover, we know that there are connections between some of these groups, one example being former Trump advisor Steve Bannon's meeting with Marine Le Pen and the National Front in France (Willsher 2018). Finally, scholars and activists concerned with social justice need to formulate strategies to counter the new white nationalism both ideologically and politically. One of the lessons of history is that when extremist thought moves into the mainstream, human tragedy inevitably follows.

REFERENCES

Abrajano, Marisa, and Zoltan Hajnal. 2015. *White Backlash: Immigration, Race, and American Politics*. Princeton: Princeton University Press.

Anderson, Carol. 2016. *White Rage: The Unspoken Truth of Our Racial Divide*. New York: Bloomsbury.

Barrett, Maura, and Vaughn Hillyard. 2019. "Steve King's Iowa Constituents Split on Support after Racist Comments." NBC News, January 17. Retrieved January 17, 2019 (https://www.nbcnews.com/politics/politics-news/steve-king-s-iowa-constituents-split-support-afterracist-comments-n960026).

BBC. 2017. "Donald Trump: 'America First, America First.'" *BBC News*, January 20. Retrieved January 18, 2019 (https://www.bbc.com/news/av/world-us-canada-38698654/donald-trump-america-first-america-first).

———. 2018. "Laura Ingraham: Demographic Changes 'National Emergency.'" *BBC News*, August 10. Retrieved August 18, 2018 (https://www.bbc.com/news/world-us-canada-45146811).

Berlatsky, Noah. 2018. "The Trump Effect: New Study Connects White American Intolerance and Support for Authoritarianism." NBC News, May 27. Retrieved October 23, 2018 (https://www.nbcnews.com/think/opinion/trump-effect-new-study-connects-white-americanintolerance-support-authoritarianism-ncna877886).

Blair, Russell. 2017. "In Some High School Gyms, the President's Name Is a Taunt." *Hartford Courant*, March 5.

Bonilla-Silva, Eduardo. 1997. "Rethinking Racism: Toward a Structural Interpretation." *American Sociological Review* 62: 465–80.

———. 2018 [2003]. *Racism Without Racists*. 5th ed. New York: Rowman & Littlefield.

———. 2019. "'Racists,' 'Class Anxieties,' Hegemonic Racism, and Democracy in Trump's America." *Social Currents* 6(1): 14–31.

Buchanan, Patrick. 2019. "No, This Is Not JFK's Democratic Party." Rasmussen Reports, January 8. Retrieved January 14, 2019 (http://www.rasmussenreports.com/public_content/political_commentary/commentary_by_pat_buchanan/no_this_is_not_jfk_s_democratic_party).

Bump, Phillip. 2016. "7 Percent of Donald Trump Supporters Think He's Racist." *Washington Post*, September 1.

Choi, Matthew. 2018. "Trump: I'm a Nationalist, But Not a White Nationalist." Politico, October 23.

Cillizza, Chris. 2018. "Half the Country Thinks Donald Trump Is a Racist. HALF." CNN, July 4. Retrieved July 4, 2018 (https://www.cnn.com/2018/07/04/politics/donald-trump-quinnipiac-poll/index.html).

———. 2019. "How in the World Is Steve King Still in Congress?" CNN, January 11. Retrieved January 11, 2019 (https://www.cnn.com/2019/01/11/politics/steve-king-iowa/index.html).

Costello, Maureen. 2016. "The Trump Effect: The Impact of the Presidential Campaign on Our Nation's Schools." Southern Poverty Law Center, November 27. Retrieved March 6, 2017 (https://www.splcenter.org/sites/default/files/splc_the_trump_effect.pdf).

Danner, Chas. 2016. "Trump Again Insists He Is Least Racist Person.'" *New York Magazine*, June 11.

Dawsey, Josh. 2018. "Trump Derides Protections for Immigrants from 'Shithole' Countries." *Washington Post*, January 12.

Desjardins, Lisa. 2017. "Every Moment in Donald Trump's Long and Complicated History with Race." PBS, *News Hour*, August 22. Retrieved September 12, 2017 (https://www.pbs.org/newshour/politics/every-moment-donald-trumps-long-complicated-history-race).

Doane, Ashley W. 2006. "What Is Racism? Racial Discourse and Racial Politics." *Critical Sociology* 32: 255–74.

———. 2007. "The Changing Politics of Color-Blind Racism." *Research in Race and Ethnic Relations* 14: 159–74.

———. 2014a. "Shades of Colorblindness: Rethinking Racial Ideology in the United States." Pp. 15–38 in *The Colorblind Screen: Television in Post-Racial America*, edited by Sarah Nilsen and Sarah E. Turner. New York: New York University Press.

———. 2014b. "Being White, Going Grey: The Racial Career of a Baby Boomer." Pp. 133–53 in *Race and the Lifecourse: Readings from the Intersections of Race, Ethnicity, and Age*, edited by Diditi Mitra and Joyce Weil. New York: Palgrave Macmillan.

———. 2017. "Beyond Color-Blindness: (Re)Theorizing Racial Ideology." *Sociological Perspectives* 60: 975–91.

Du Bois, W. E. B. 1998 [1935]. *Black Reconstruction in America, 1860–1880*. New York: Free Press.

Eltagouri, Marwa. 2018. "Most Americans Think Trump Is Racist, According to a New Poll." *Washington Post*, March 1.

Henricks, Kasey. 2018. "'I'm Principled against Slavery, but . . .': Colorblindness and the Three-Fifths Debate. *Social Problems* 65: 285–304.

Herb, Jeremy, Geneva Sands, and David Shortell. 2018. "Trump Video Accused as Racist Also Lacks Factual Basis." CNN, November 2. Retrieved November 3, 2018 (https://www.cnn.com/2018/11/02/politics/trump-video-accused-as-racist-also-lacks-factualbasis/index.html).

Kaleem, Jaweed. 2016. "'There's Nothing Wrong with Being White': Trump's Win Brings 'White Pride" Out of the Shadows." *Los Angeles Times*, November 17.

McElwee, Sean, and Jason McDaniel. 2017a. "Fear of Diversity Made People More Likely
to Vote Trump." *The Nation*, March 14.

———. 2017b. "Economic Anxiety Didn't Make People Vote Trump, Racism Did." *The Nation*, May 8.

Morrison, Toni. 1992. *Playing in the Dark*. Cambridge, MA: Harvard University Press.

Mueller, Jennifer C. 2017. "Producing Colorblindness: Everyday Mechanisms of White Ignorance." *Social Problems* 64: 219–38.

Norton, Michael I., and Samuel R. Sommers. 2011. "Whites See Racism as a Zero-Sum Game That They Are Now Losing." *Perspectives on Psychological Science* 6: 215–18.

Obeidallah, Dean. 2018. "Trump Is Trying to Whip Up Fear about the Browning of America." CNN, November 4. Retrieved November 4, 2016 (https://www.cnn.com/2018/11/04/opinions/trump-whip-up-browning-of-americaobeidallah/index.html).

Painter, Nell Irvin. 2010. *The History of White People*. New York: Norton.

Reid, Joy-Ann. 2017. "The Seeds of Trump's Victory Were Sown the Moment Obama Won." NBC News, October 20. Retrieved October 21, 2017 (https://www.nbcnews.com/think/opinion/seeds-trump-s-victory-were-sown-moment-obama-wonncna811891).

Serwer, Adam. 2017. "The Nationalist's Delusion." *The Atlantic*, November 20.

Smedley, Audrey. 2007. *Race in North America: Origin and Evolution of a Worldview*. 3rd ed. Boulder, CO: Westview.

Washington Post. 2015. "Full Text: Donald Trump Announces a Presidential Bid." *Washington Post*, June 16.

Willsher, Kim. 2018. "Steve Bannon Tells French Far-Right 'History Is on Our Side.'" *The Guardian*, March 10.

WTVC. 2016. "'Make America White Again': Tenn. Congressional Candidate's Billboard Ignites Uproar." *NewsChannel 9*, June 22. Retrieved January 18, 2019 (https://newschannel9.com/news/local/congressional-candidates-controversial-billboard-has-polkcounty-abuzz).

CHAPTER 2

THE UNBLACKENING

"White" License and the "Nice Racism" Trope

JOHNNY E. WILLIAMS

OF THE MANY social groups residing in the United States, socially defined black folks have consistently attracted the harshest and most violent structural subjection. The modern civil rights movement provided some relief from antiblack racism for a fleeting moment before systemic white racism morphed into its current more insidious form—"nice racism" or "good whites" (Thompson 2003). This iteration of white supremacy is largely unacknowledged by "whites"[1] whose antiblack racism expresses itself as racial innocence whereby they acknowledge the maliciousness of white supremacy but not their complicity in it. Though they identify as white, they do not problematize their identification, leading most whites to believe they are merely individuals whose racial identity is of little importance in a white supremacy society. Because the "good-white" iteration of white racism never decenters whiteness, it works primarily to make whites feel good about being white (Thompson 2003). Moreover, it confines thinking and action to making them aware of "race"[2] rather than eliminating white supremacy. "Nice racism" manifests as inclusive-exclusive discourse and supposedly nonracial policies and actions that are really just the substructures of systemic white racism. These racist discourses, policies, and practices assume an aura of legitimacy because self-identified whites imagine themselves and state and national politicians to be race neutral.

Unlike the commonly used term "white privilege," I use "white license" in this paper to signify how people who imagine themselves to be white wield power through social, political, and economic institutions to control and direct their own and racialized Others' behavior and attitudes. Like critical race theory, rather than accept the idea that *white* is a natural referent, white license views it as a product of *raced* social relations grounded in power (Delgado and Stefancic 2001). "White" is not an inherent characteristic of people but rather a product of social practices and the ideology of whiteness. Unlike the concept of white privilege, which is concerned only with understanding the meaning of whiteness in everyday life, my concept focuses on how the conditions of systemic white racism make white license possible. Whites secure their white license through a process of domination, acts, decisions, and policies directed at the racially oppressed (Leonardo 2004). White license revolves less around the white imaginary, or the state of being dominant, than around the directed institutional process that secures white domination and the advantages associated with it (Leonardo 2004:137). In other words, systemic white racism is not merely a manifestation of individual white privilege; it grants whites license to enact their bigoted ways of thinking. These enactments are possible because whites authorize officials to implement their racist conceptions of being in organizing the world. The point is that white license is routinized and results from intentional action to justify and legitimate the exploitation and domination of people they designate as inferior. Their whiteness as an idealized license and property manifests in material form as a tangible system of oppression—white supremacy (Harris 1993).

To clarify, "white" (a category of "race" with no biological or scientific foundation) and whiteness are social constructions with very real, tangible, and violent effects. Systemic white racism hinges on the concept of whiteness—a fiction enforced by power and violence. Whiteness constantly shifts its boundaries, separating those who are entitled to have certain license from those whose exploitation and vulnerability to violence is justified by their not being white (Kivel 2011:19). Whites hold the power to decide who is white and who is not. Whiteness is relational, existing only in relation or opposition to blackness and other fabricated racial categories created by whiteness. Whiteness often goes unnoticed by self-identified whites in ways that divert them from considering the root cause of racial oppression. In short, whiteness shapes how self-identified white people view themselves and others, and seats them in a place of structural advantage where white cultural norms and practices go unnamed and unquestioned (Frankenberg 1993). White culture, norms, and values manifest in societal institutions as natural and are used as the standard by which all other cultures, groups, and individuals are measured and consigned as inferior (Tator and Henry 2006:46–47).

In this chapter I examine how self-identified whites and white supremacy institutions use "nice racism" deflection discourse and practices to promote inclusive-exclusive policies, "white *ignore-ance*," and "perpetrator as victim" strategies to camouflage their tacit collusion in obstructing efforts to eliminate systemic white racism. "Benign" systemic white racism is subtle, mild, and at times "nice" in its expression. It is content to focus on race and racial identity without situating them in the appropriate structural contexts. As a circumlocution, "nice racism" use terms like *inclusion* to impede a systemic understanding of racial injustice and inequalities (Andersen 2001). Whites who think of white supremacy as individual acts of meanness directed at the racially oppressed are the usual purveyors of "nice racism." Their narrow interpretation of white racism excludes virtually all racially cordial whites from involvement in the social system of white racism, which socially fashioned them. Because white supremacy is a ubiquitous and central sociopolitical and economic column of the United States, no one in the nation is immune from its influence. According to historian Edward Carr:

> As soon as we are born, the world gets to work on us and transforms us from merely biological into social units. Every human being at every stage of history or pre-history is born into a society and from his earliest years is moulded by that society. The language which he speaks is not an individual inheritance, but a social acquisition from the group in which he grows up. Both language and environment help to determine the character of his thought; his earliest ideas come to him from others. As has been well said, the individual apart from society would be both speechless and mindless. (1987:31)

Given that most whites are averse to grasping how white supremacy socially and politically creates them as white, they usually do not problematize their whiteness or consider how the collective practice of systemic white racism is evident in their lives. Additionally, because "white" is normative, thus ordinary, self-identified whites have a difficult time conceding that systemic white racism is a deadly problem. When pressed to acknowledge that they are *raced* and bigoted, whites resort to benign white supremacy discourse to minimize, dismiss, and negate their involvement in systemic white racism. These denials and refusals ensure that a majority of self-identified whites are ill-disposed and ill-equipped to dismantle white supremacy.

"NICE RACISM"

Individualism is a major factor driving self-identified whites' refusal to accept the social and systemic character of white racism (Williams 2018). Individualism holds that individual bigots are causes of systemic white racism, not consequences of it. Whites holding this view refuse to consider how their collective exercise of power within a white supremacy society creates inequality (Lipsitz 1995:381). The whiteness culture in which they are immersed conditions whites as well as socially defined black folks to see systemic white racism as the manifestation of isolated individuals' personal prejudices (Lipsitz 1995; Scheruich 1993:6–7). Therefore, foregrounding the autonomous properties of systemic white racism (i.e., prejudice, individualism, ethnocentrism, xenophobia, etc.) inclines self-identified whites not to see it as an indissoluble system and structure of white power. Systemic white racism is a collective social activity, not merely an individual action. The social structures of white supremacy are products of social interaction between individuals who shape and are shaped by the racialized context in which they live (Essed 1991).

Because self-identified whites center systemic white racism as isolated autonomous properties, they usually assume that overt bigoted white people other than themselves exemplify participation in white racism. These people affix Confederate flags to automobile windows or display the design on bumper stickers or clothing, openly spew racial epithets, and are against exogamy. The "nice racism" variation of white supremacy conceptually and structurally obscures how *raced* relationships or social ties between self-identified white individuals and groups create, secure, maintain, and excuse systemic white racism. This variation ensures that most whites will not consider or acknowledge how white supremacy institutions benefit them solely on the basis of their whiteness, not their meritorious efforts.

Raising questions about what whites think they know about racism is important for them to come to grips with its real source. Systemic white racism's ideologies such as race and whiteness express narratives designed to conceal the power residing within its structures and ideas. This is why white supremacy institutions routinely use euphemistic terms like *inclusion, diversity, equity, tolerance,* and *multiculturalism* that contribute virtually nothing to approaching white racism as a systemic problem. These terms are obstacles to questioning and eliminating systemic white racism because systemic racism does not allow *inclusion* and *equity* to make a difference in ridding the world of white supremacy. For example, *multiculturalism* allows space for blackness but at the same time disempowers socially defined black people from making structural demands for change. Moreover, racial euphemistic terms and practices help to facilitate the unblackening[3] of historically white institutions. For example, the Hechinger Report on the hiring of black faculty found that 58 percent of professors at seventy-two historically black colleges and universities are black even though these institutions account for just 1.7 percent of all faculty nationwide (Krupnick 2018). The little progress that has been made at historically white colleges and universities in racially "diversifying" their teaching ranks suggests that terms like *diversity* and a host of others are no more than superficial institutional rhetoric designed to mask their efforts to remain white spaces (Krupnick 2018).

Moreover, self-identified whites use the *diversity* concept to evade confronting their whiteness problem by inserting "white" in the pantheon of "racial diversity" to avoid problematizing its nefarious sociopolitical origins and aims. Offices of Diversity, Inclusion, and Equity codify *diversity* to ensure that self-identified whites never consider structural remedies for white supremacy. These offices also attempt to equip the racially oppressed with strategies for accommodating and coping with systemic white racism rather than eliminating it. What sustains white supremacy is not merely white people's unconscious thoughts and habits that enable them to feign innocence but their active participation in creating and maintaining their white license. Hence, self-identified whites are socialized to think of white racists as people who are consciously and intentionally mean, not as members of a system of racial oppression shaping all whites. It is imperative that they grasp how their socialization into whiteness guarantees their participation in everyday systemic white racism. The only way for whites to be more aware of their collusion is for them to actively and collectively confront their whiteness. This means that it is not sufficient for whites to simply be more aware of their involvement in systemic white racism; they must be committed to terminating its systemic operation as well. They must be willing to shift from a white society to a human-centered society.

WHITE "IGNORE-ANCE"

Whiteness ensures that systemic white racism's structures are invisible not only to people who imagine themselves as white but also to those are who oppressed by them. The structures are hard to detect given the ideological hegemony of whiteness. Whiteness enables an *ignore-ance* of the working of white supremacy structures (Feagin 2001). *White ignore-ance* is "an active dynamic negation, an active refusal of information" (Mills 1997; Ellsworth

1997:57). This concept contends that whites are ignoring whiteness and white supremacy to which they are very much attuned but choose *not* to admit they are aware of. Their ignorance is a conscious choice. Given this, Ellsworth argues that white *ignore-ance* is a "social space formed and informed by historical junctures of power and social and cultural process" (1997:38). White supremacy's societal hegemony configures people's sense-making regarding white racism and race to support it through *ignore-ance* (Mueller 2017). White *ignore-ance* as an ideological strategy tends to move constantly within the closed circle of white hegemony, "producing not knowledge, but recognition of whiteness and 'race' as things we already know." It can do this with ease "because it [takes] as already established fact exactly the premises which ought to [be] . . . in question" (Hall 1982:75). Thus, when people encounter events that breach their expectations about how the world should be, they are able to ignore inconsistences because civil society institutions such as media, education, religion, and family constantly reinforce white racism ideology as common sense. For example, media use narrowly constructed racial narratives like those highlighting how individual bigots *overcome* their *personal* aversion to socially defined black, Latinx, Indigenous, and Asian folks to avert people's attention from the systemic character of white racism. Films such as *The Green Book* (2018), *The Help* (2011), *The Blind Side* (2009), *Avatar* (2009), *Crash* (2004), and *American History X* (1998) epitomize this account. These movies portray how whites overcome their racial bigotry by reassessing their conscience, instead of abolishing systemic white racism. This narrative contradicts the reality that whites are relentlessly submerged in the cultural air of white supremacy. They all internalize whiteness and act on their white supremacist worldview. White as an imagined identity and whiteness as ideology are created through the material and cultural systemic practices of white supremacy, yet most self-identified whites self-righteously claim that they are not racists. Their identities as whites in a white supremacy society makes their assertion absurd. Whites believe that their nonracist absurdity is true because of the ordinariness of whiteness and systemic white racism—how right it seems. Systemic white racism is grounded not merely in each individual white person's attempt to do harm but in their mythical racial group's collective effort to secure and preserve what they falsely believe is rightly theirs (Kendall 2013). Explicit in this work is securing white power and wealth through the social mechanism of systemic white racism—whiteness and white license. Because this effort disregards concern for human decency and the common good, it is structurally bound to undermine or kill anyone and any group that stands in the way of self-identified whites achieving their ends.

Self-identified whites generally believe that talking about whiteness signifies that they are complicit in white supremacy (DiAngelo 2011). For this reason, they prefer to frame their white identity in ethnic terms instead: identifying as Italian, Irish, or Jewish, for example. This practice suggests that whites understand that their plain undifferentiated whiteness is a "toggle between nothingness and awfulness" (Bazelon 2018; Painter 2010, 2015). On some level, whites are aware that they are racist. However, they still want to believe that they are not. The insidious delusion that they can be white in a nation with an enduring social system of white supremacy requires a willful *ignore-ance* of history to maintain. Thus, self-identified whites' affinity for individualism and supposed indifference to race telegraph their *ignore-ance* of it and is designed to make it easier for them to negate information about their complicity in racial oppression (Mills 2007). This deflection frame is hard to dislodge from the mindset of self-identified whites because it is socially rooted as common sense (Hall 1982:75). Not discussing whiteness limits whites' ability to interrogate how white supremacy systematically informs their lives. Only when they talk about whiteness is their attention drawn to it, which makes them more likely to recognize it as something significant. Therefore, they are consciously averse to labels like *white*, *racist*, and *white supremacist*—terms that do not allow them to skirt direct discussion of their whiteness. Not talking about whiteness also silences racially oppressed voices and resistance in ways that protect or enable whites to continue to operate in systemic inhuman ways.

INCLUSIVE-EXCLUSIVE

If self-identified whites are serious about ridding themselves of their whiteness problem, they need to cease their efforts to dress up white supremacy in "nice racism" discourse. Discourse is never neutral (Fiske 1994). Words convey a broad sense of meanings, and these meanings inform people's immediate social, political, and historical conditions. As Toni Morrison noted in her 1993 Nobel lecture, language has the power to humanize and dehumanize, include and exclude:

> [Language] creates us the very moment it is being created. Language gives our lives meaning; [it is in many ways] the measure of our lives. [Therefore,] oppressive language does more than represent violence; it is violence; does more than represent the limits of knowledge; it limits knowledge. Whether it is obscuring state language or the faux-language of mindless media;

whether it is the proud but calcified language of the academy or the commodity driven language of science; whether it is the malign language of law-without-ethics, or language designed for the estrangement of minorities, hiding its racist plunder in its literary cheek—it must be rejected, altered and exposed.

Similarly, terms such as *implicit bias, unconscious racism,* and *tolerance* are differentially problematic because they work to inhibit people from questioning and challenging taken-for-granted and naturalized racial epistemological, ontological, and axiological commitments and enactments (Blanton and Jaccard 2008). As such, they reinforce whiteness and systemic white racism while simultaneously dismissing, diminishing, and denying white racism's effects on the minds and bodies of whites and racial Others. White-dominated institutions wax on and on about *diversity, inclusion, social justice, equity,* and *multiculturalism,* knowing that such verbiage merely obscures their operation as white supremacy institutions. In this sense, "nice racism" discourse enables whites to boast about being racially inclusive while using this muted racial language and enacting exclusionary policies designed to ensure that there is never a critical mass of socially defined black people present in white-dominated institutions to threaten white people's racist ways of living, knowing, and thinking. In brief, "nice racism" functions as cover for their white supremacy collusion. For example, sociologist Ted Thornhill's study of white college admissions counselors at historically white colleges and universities finds that they prefer to admit apolitical or white-assimilated black high school students over activist-oriented black conscious ones (Thornhill 2018). His finding highlights the ways in which "nice racism" or "good-white" practices facilitate socially defined black students' assimilation into whiteness. In essence, "nice racism" discourse and practices mask the everyday workings of systemic white racism by not admitting or hiring racially oppressed members who force white bigots and their institutions to confront the racialized social interactions they engage in to (re)produce white supremacy. Rather than confronting the root source of systemic white racism, the chief aim of "nice racism" is to ensure its brutal effectiveness and longevity. The fact is that whites know that "nice racism" is adept at concealing their racist practices behind contorted justifications and practices. "Nice racism" is a conscious rather than unconscious effort to sanitize any talk about white racism.

Because white institutions are inclusive-exclusive insofar as they work to incorporate racial Others who accept white normativity, their "nice racism" practices seek out socially defined black folks who are well-behaved, happy, and nonthreatening respectable Negroes.[4] Socially defined black folk of this ilk have no interest in going toe-to-toe with white supremacy. They would rather accommodate and survive white supremacy, even if doing so means subjugating not only their humanity but the humanity of others for the approval of whites. Inclusive-exclusive, respectable Negroes "go along to get along" in white supremacy institutions and groups. They know that their job is to exclude any socially defined black person who refuses to perform the whiteness ethos-pathos (problematic thinking that is immoral). In this sense, "unblackening" and "nice racism" work hand in hand in that the latter facilitates the recruitment of respectable Negroes who further assist in expelling any recruits who insist on resisting white supremacy. Though the respectable Negro subterfuge is understandable, it fails to deal with the complex realities of surviving in a society that relentlessly wages a violent campaign against socially defined black people's well-being. Respectable Negroes believe they can stave off the daily brutality and violent mistreatment of whites and their system of racial oppression by making their behavior congruent with whiteness. They become enraged when other black folks refuse to contort their humanity to meet the needs of white people as they do. Their approach mandates that systemic white racism be dealt with in a civil, emotionally detached, and dehumanized way that comforts whites rather than challenges their antiblack racism.

The use of "civility," in particular, is another inclusive-exclusive deflection tactic that is deployed to pressure socially defined black people to have civil discussions with self-identified whites who have already breached the bounds of civility through attempts to dictate how black folks should respond to and resist their whiteness and systemic white racism. Being civil then imposes a burden on the racially oppressed given that our calling out self-identified white people's bigoted actions and beliefs is deemed uncivil. For respectable Negroes the social cost visited on whites by naming them bigots looms larger than the brutality and cruelty of systemic white racism on black people's bodies and minds. This is obfuscation of the highest order. Civility as a "nice racism" trope enables self-identified whites and their racially oppressed colluders to restrict contesting the ordinariness of whiteness and systemic white racism. Calls for civility then cede valuable rhetorical ground by default, demonstrating their own timidity and coddling avowed racists. This is why socially defined black folks and other racially oppressed groups should not play the civility game. Civility does not solve the problem of systemic white racism. The concept of civility is subjective, based on the values of those in power, and is consistently weaponized and deployed to silence socially defined black people (Lowe 2018).

Civility as an inclusive-exclusive white racism strategy seeks to undermine socially defined black people's solidarity and resistance by limiting the definition of white supremacy practices to supporting slavery and using racial slurs. It pretends to root out racial bigotry via civil talk about systemic white racism when in fact it does nothing to demolish white supremacy. Therefore, it is nothing. Civility turns off listening to the truths about the everyday brutality of white supremacy. Civility proponents claim that no one can hear you when you are emotional about the inhumanity of whiteness and systemic white racism. This assertion is simply incorrect: true civility is broad enough to take in heightened language, personal truths, and anger. In contrast, the fake civility of "nice racism" is simply about preventing socially defined black people from effectively asserting their interests, points of view, and humanity.

RACIST PERPETRATOR AS VICTIM

The civility ploy also facilitates shifting the blame for systemic white racism from the perpetrators to the victims. This transference enables self-identified whites to portray themselves as humane and caring devotees of humanity, not whiteness. When socially defined black and other racially oppressed people identify them as active or passive participants in systemic white racism, self-identified whites attempt to excuse their behavior by calling the victims of their bigotry racists. This deflection is usually followed by perpetrators' attempts to assert their supposed antiracism bona fides. They indignantly proclaim all the good they have done for the racially oppressed. Respectable Negroes' support of whites' denials of racism help them evade facing the truth, hindering their ability to see the all-encompassing systemic workings of white supremacy in their lives. This failure is further buttressed by the "white" people's contention that racially oppressed people lie about, exaggerate, and misinterpret their actions as bigoted. They even unreflectively express the sentiment that systemic white racism is outdated. By consigning white supremacy to the historical past, self-identified whites consciously refuse to acknowledge how they carry it within them and are still directed by it. Systemic white racism is literally entrenched in all that they do in the present.

Racist thinking informs this distorted blame logic. Commonplace racial ideology and stereotypes nurture whites' views that they are victims of supposed "black racists" instead of perpetrators of antiblack racism. Stereotypes of socially defined black folks as animalistic, brutes, and thugs help distance whites from their racial bigotry by perpetuating the myth of white victimhood at the hands of violent "black racists." Such descriptive racist language and thinking is also used to mark immigrants, especially Central American and Mexican migrants, as threats to white hegemony. For example, United States president Donald Trump, hosting a May 2018 California Sanctuary State Roundtable, told government officials: "We have people coming into the country or trying to come—we're stopping a lot of them but we're taking people of the country, you wouldn't believe how bad these people are. These aren't people, these are animals" (Austin-Hillery 2018). Deflective racist rhetoric serves to rationalize abusive, inhumane behavior and policies to deter immigration from Latinx and African and African diaspora nations. This is truly an attempt to unblacken the United States.

Not reducing white racism to a matter of good and bad people—racists bad, antiracists good—would mean a few things. It would mean that self-identified whites will stop focusing only on intentions. Too often, whites either excuse or justify a racist act by saying that no malice was involved. They refuse to recognize that white racism is as much about impact as it is about intent. Just because whites do not have racist intent does not mean that the racially oppressed are not harmed by their "nice" racist actions and beliefs. Grasping this may help self-identified whites comprehend that their inattention rather than their intent is the real driver of benign systemic white racism. This banal form of white racism appears with the face of respectability, as a form that does not necessarily involve physical violence or threatening abuse but is executed instead with a smiling face (Wahlquist 2017).

CONCLUSION

To restore their humanity, self-identified whites must confront their whiteness problem and grasp how their benign system of white supremacy works to facilitate their inattentiveness to the brutality of systemic white racism. The collective accumulation of "nice racism" thinking and acts through everyday interactions and institutional practices and policies helps facilitate institutional "unblackening." To counter this racist practice, it is imperative that whites untangle the contradictions of whiteness. They must grasp the centrality of white racism in their lives so that they can begin the consciousness-raising process necessary to see the depth of white supremacy's entrenchment in society. While engaged in this work they may come to understand and act to end systemic racial oppression. To arrive here they must first *willingly* take on the illusory nature of "nice racism" and whiteness.

The historical and contemporary record counsels that self-identified whites' addiction to white license and materialism will probably never lend itself to ending their domination and exploitation of racialized Others. Therefore, it is advisable that we, the racially oppressed, heed the advice of the late South African human rights champion Steve Biko, who says that socially defined black people

> must learn to accept that no group, however benevolent, can ever hand power to the vanquished on a plate. We must accept that the limits of tyrants are prescribed by the endurance of those whom they oppress. As long as we go to Whitey begging cap in hand for our own emancipation, we are giving him further sanction to continue with his racist and oppressive system. We must realize that our situation is not a mistake on the part of Whites but a deliberate act, and that no amount of moral lecturing will persuade [them] to "correct" the situation. The system concedes nothing without a demand, for it formulates its very method of operation on the basis that the ignorant will learn to know, the child will grow into an adult and therefore demands will begin to made. It gears itself to resist demands in whatever way it sees fit. When you refuse these demands and choose not to come to the round table to beg for deliverance, you are asking for the contempt of those who have power over you. (Coetzee and Roux 2004:96)

NOTES

1. *White* is a philosophically problematic term about human categorization. Nevertheless, the term is sociologically important because of the way it is routinely used by self-identified whites to reinforce systemic white racism.
2. "Race" is encased in quotation marks because it is a problematic cultural invention of arbitrary meaning applied to supposed (but unscientific) "natural" divisions within the human species. Rather than a biological division, race is an ideology that structures and controls discourse in support of white supremacy.
3. I take the term *unblackening* from a segment from the comedian Larry Wilmore's *The Nightly Show*, which aired on the cable TV Comedy Central Network. The term refers to the unblackening of the executive branch months before Barack Obama left office. It connotes how socially defined black people equipped with confidence and knowledge of self as a full member of humanity are systematically excluded from or weeded out of white-dominated institutions. These white supremacy institutions prefer "blacks" who are flexible enough to acquiesce to or accept the normativity of white hegemony.

4. I use "Negroes" to denote that these people want to be "white" because being "white" for them signifies being fully human. The Negro is rooted at the core of the white supremacy universe from which s/he/they need extraction. This I paraphrase from Fanon 1967.

REFERENCES

Andersen, Margaret. 2001. "Restructuring for Whom? Race, Class, Gender, and the Ideology of Invisibility." *Sociological Forum* 16: 181–201.

Austin-Hillery, Nicol. 2018. "Trump's Racist Language Serves Abusive Immigration Policies." *Human Rights Watch*. Retrieved January 4, 2019 (https://www.hrw.org/news/2018/05/22/trumps-racist-language-serves-abusive-immigration-policies).

Bazelon, Emily. 2018. "White People Are Noticing Something New: Their Own Whiteness." *New York Times*, June 13.

Blanton, Hart, and James Jaccard. 2008. "Unconscious Racism: A Concept in Pursuit of a Measure." *Annual Review of Sociology* 34: 277–297.

Carr, Edward H. 1987. *What Is History?* New York: Penguin Books.

Coetzee, P. H., and A. P. J. Roux, eds. 2004. *The African Philosophy Reader*, 2nd edition. London: Routledge.

Delgado, Richard, and Jean Stefancic. 2001. *Critical Race Theory: An Introduction*. New York: New York University Press.

DiAngelo, Robin. 2011. "White Fragility." *International Journal of Critical Pedagogy* 3: 54–70.

Ellsworth, Elizabeth. 1997. *Teaching Positions: Difference, Pedagogy, and the Power of Address*. New York: Teachers College Press.

Essed, Philomena. 1991. *Understanding Everyday Racism. An Interdisciplinary Theory*. Newbury Park, CA: Sage.

Fanon, Frantz. 1967. *Black Skin, White Masks*. New York: Grove Press.

Feagin, Joe R. 2001. *Racist America: Roots, Current Realities, and Future Reparations*. New York: Routledge.

Fiske, John. 1994. *Media Matters: Everyday Culture and Political Change*. Minneapolis: University of Minnesota Press.

Frankenberg, Ruth. 1993. *White Women, Race Matters: The Social Construction of Whiteness*. Minneapolis: University of Minnesota Press.

Hall, Stuart. 1982. "The Rediscovery of 'Ideology': Return of Repressed Media Studies." Pp. 56–90 in *Culture, Society, and the Media*, edited by Michael Gurevitch, Tony Bennett, James Curran, and Janet Woolacott. New York: Teachers College Press.

Harris, Cheryl I. 1993. "Whiteness as Property." *Harvard Law Review* 106: 1707–91.

Kendall, Francis E. 2013. *Understanding White Privilege*. New York: Routledge.

Kivel, Paul. 2011. *Uprooting Racism: How White People Can Work for Racial Justice*. Gabriola Island, BC: New Society Press.

Krupnick, Matt. 2018. "After Colleges Promised to Increase It, Hiring of Black Faculty Declined." *The Hechinger Report*. Retrieved October 3, 2018 (https://hechingerreport.org/after-colleges-promised-to-increase-it-hiring-of-black-faculty-declined).

Leonardo, Zeus. 2004. "The Color of Supremacy: Beyond the Discourse of 'White Privilege.'" *Educational Philosophy and Theory* 36: 137–152.

Lipsitz, George. 1995. "The Possessive Investment in Whiteness: Racialized Social Democracy and the 'White' Problem in American Studies." *American Quarterly* 47: 369–387.

Lowe, Naima. 2018. "I Fought Academia's Cult of Civility and All I Got Was This Lousy PTSD diagnosis." *Medium*. Retrieved October 15, 2018 (https://medium.com/@yourstrulynaima/academias-cult-of-civility-30007869d4d4).

Mills, Charles W. 1997. *The Racial Contract*. Ithaca, NY: Cornell University Press.

———. 2007. "White Ignorance." Pp. 11–38 in *Race and Epistemologies of Ignorance*, edited by Shannon Sullivan and Nancy Tuana. Albany: SUNY Press.

Morrison, Toni. 1993. "Nobel Lecture." Retrieved September 26, 2018 (https://www.nobelprize.org/prizes/literature/1993/morrison/lecture).

Mueller, Jennifer. 2017. "Producing Colorblindness: Everyday Mechanism of White Ignorance." *Social Problems* 64: 219–238.

Painter, Nell. 2010. *The History of White People*. New York: W. W. Norton.

———. 2015. "What Is Whiteness?" *New York Times*, June 21.

Scheurich, James J. 1993. "Toward a White Discourse on White Racism." *Educational Researcher* 22: 5–10.

Tator, Carol, and Frances Henry, with Charles Smith and Maureen Brown. 2006. *Racial Profiling in Canada: Challenging the Myth of "a Few Bad Apples."* Toronto: University of Toronto Press.

Thompson, Audrey. 2003. "Tiffany, Friend of People of Color: White Investment in Antiracism." *Qualitative Studies in Education* 16: 7–29.

Thornhill, Ted. 2018. "We Want Black Students, Just Not You: How White Admissions Counselors Screen Black Prospective Students." *Sociology of Race & Ethnicity*, online first. Retrieved October 3, 2018 (https://doi.org/10.1177/2332649218792579).

Wahlquist, Calla. 2017. "'Racism Can Appear with Face of Respectability.'" *The Guardian*, October 31.

Williams, Johnny E. 2018. "The Academic Freedom Double Standard: 'Freedom' for Courtiers, Suppression for Critical Scholars." *Journal of Academic Freedom* 9. Retrieved December 19, 2018 (https://www.aaup.org/sites/default/files/Williams.pdf).

CHAPTER 3

POLITICAL CORRECTNESS

A Genuine Concern for Discussion or Slippery Language Rooted in Racial Animosity

J. SCOTT CARTER AND J. MICAH ROOS

VERY FEW CONCEPTS have been as contested in the media and by the public as that of political correctness (Norton et al. 2006). The concept is often misunderstood and is often attributed to political progressives (Norton et al. 2006). However, the term "politically correct" (PC) came from the conservative right to describe spaces created on university campuses to improve sensitivity toward marginalized groups. The term was and continues to be a pejorative used by conservatives signifying that liberals are too sensitive and that their own, dissenting voices are being oppressed and silenced by the minority (Sue 2016; Weigel 2016). Weigel adds that no one would ever call oneself politically correct because the term connotes that the speaker is acting in bad faith and hiding the truth from the audience.

The term originally gained currency when discussed by political pundits Roger Kimball in *Tenured Radicals* (1990) and Dinesh D'Souza in *Illiberal Education* (1991) in the early 1990s. The term was used minimally in newspapers and magazines before 1990 (Weigel 2016). In describing the rising hegemony of the politically correct, Richard Bernstein wrote in the *New York Times* in 1990 that "'politically correct' has become a sarcastic jibe used by those, conservatives and classical liberals alike, to describe what they see as a growing intolerance, a closing of debate, a pressure to conform to a radical program or risk being accused of a commonly reiterated trio of thought crimes: sexism, racism and homophobia." Bernstein goes on to describe the forces of political correctness as being so strong that they have successfully removed subjects such as affirmative action and homosexuality from civil debate.

In light of violent outbreaks related to police shootings, concerns over illegal immigration, the rise of the Black Lives Matter movement, and continued acts of domestic terrorism, conservatives and conservative pundits have renewed a call to end political correctness. *Huffington Post* blogger and author BJ Gallagher (2017) recently wrote that "While the original intent of political correctness may have been good (to encourage tact and sensitivity to others' feelings around issues of gender, race, religion, sexual orientation, physical abilities, and such), the *effect* of political correctness has been to make everyone avoid these topics altogether—thereby hindering our ability to get comfortable in living and working with those who are different from us." Gallagher strongly states that political correctness has actually become a bigger problem than the original problem it was meant to fix.

This anti-PC stance has especially been promoted by President Donald Trump. In reference to the travel ban for Muslims, he stated that opponents who cried out in outrage were simply being too "politically correct" (Weigel 2016). After the Pulse mass shooting was labeled a terrorist attack, Trump stated unequivocally, "I refuse to be politically correct" (Weigel 2016) in raising concern over Islamic terrorism. Trump has also raised concern over the impact of political correctness regarding other issues, including illegal immigration and inner-city violence in Chicago. In response to sexist remarks he made about women in the past, Trump doubled down on his fight against political correctness in a presidential debate held in Cleveland Ohio by stating, "I think the big problem this country has is being politically correct" (Weigel 2016). Donald Trump is not the only one raising concern about the PC culture. Comedians such as Chris Rock and Dave Chapelle have done the same. Silman (2015) has stated that more and more comedians are coming out against the PC culture because they feel that their comedic freedom is being threatened by overly sensitive audiences.

Many scholars in the social sciences are not sold on the explanation that political correctness problematically shuts down meaningful debate and blocks freedom of speech (Bonilla-Silva 2018; Sue 2016; Wikstrom 2016). For instance, Wikstrom posed that the label of "PC" is an "othering" technique used to "question the legitimacy of their values, to dispute their integrity, or to accuse them of intellectual dishonesty" (2016:59). Wikstrom further posed that espousing an anti-PC stance, particularly when referring to racial issues, is akin to "verbal jiu jitsu" whereby the dominant group attempts to flip the argument and portray themselves as the victims of oppression where they or their free speech is being silenced (2016:138). Sue (2016) further adds that by using political correctness as a complaint, whites are able to express less-than-genuine reactions that silence talking back among minorities and promote the dominate narrative of whiteness. Bonilla-Silva (2018) similarly argued that whites use such slippery language to deflect any notion of racism while highlighting cultural explanations of racial differences to maintain their dominant racial position. In this light, both Sue and Bonilla-Silva see eschewing political correctness as a mechanism to maintain inequality and the racial status quo. As such, we pose that the anti-PC movement simply reflects a whitelash against growing diversity and change, where many whites (and some nonwhites) attempt minimize the plight of marginalized groups and whites' role in reproducing the marginalized groups' problems.

With that said, the purpose of our study is two-fold: First, we use nationally representative data from the American National Election Studies 2016 pilot study to assess whether objections to political correctness are genuine and rooted in conservative principles. Scholars in the *principled objection* camp pose that issues related to politics in general and racial politics in particular can be and are often based in true conservative ideals rather than any persistent racial animosity (Sniderman and Carmines 1997; Sniderman, Crosby, Howell 2000). This is particularly true for President Trump, who insists, "I am not a racist, in fact, I am the least racist person that you've ever encountered" (Fisher 2016). Second, because many of the calls for ending political correctness leading up to the 2016 election related to racial issues (e.g., illegal immigration; the policing of Chicago; banning of Muslims from entering the country), we then assess whether this call is rooted in racial animosity. That is to say, is the impact of conservatism significantly explained away by racial animosity? We define racial animosity as negative feelings and views toward an out-group based on their race. Some argue that President Trump's plea for ending political correctness was done less to promote understanding and more to pander to constituents who hold similar views and to deflect attention from problematic narratives that reproduce the racial status quo.

While pundits and scholars have questioned the genuineness of calls to end political correctness, very little research has examined factors that predict these calls. One reason for this omission is possibly a lack of national data looking particularly at resistance to PC language. This research will remedy this problem and provide insights into anti-PC stances.

LITERATURE REVIEW

Calls to end political correctness expose different principled positions for the political Right and Left. With respect to the Right, the concern lies in the notion that discourse is being repressed and that anyone willing to speak the truth will be called out as being racist or sexist or whatever the context may bring (Kimball 1990: D'Souza 1991). While reflecting on liberal studies at universities (e.g., African American studies), Kimball argues that such academic interests amount to liberal politics that threaten the foundations of America in general and American universities in particular. Kimball also bemoans the politics of victimhood.

Conversely, the concern among minorities and more progressive whites on the left is that those requesting the end of political correctness are not being genuine in advocating debate and open-mindedness. Rather, liberals fear that the call to end political correctness is really an attempt to bully others and to conceal intolerant viewpoints. Sue (2016) states that by playing the victim and decrying political correctness, whites are able to express less-than-genuine reactions and to silence back talk among minorities, thus promoting the dominant narrative of whiteness. Decrying political correctness may also prevent meaningful debate on issues of inequality and discrimination that could benefit members of oppressed groups.

This concern over genuineness among politicians and in public opinion regarding attitudes in general and racial attitudes in particular is not a new phenomenon. Beginning in the 1950s, a series of papers published in *Scientific American* expressed very optimistic views toward the future of race relations and racial attitudes in the US (Hyman and Sheatsley 1956, 1964; Greeley and Sheatsley 1971; Taylor, Sheatsley, and Greeley 1978). Using more contemporary data from the General Social Survey and the American National Election Study, more contemporary research has provided further evidence that whites in America may be growing more and more racially progressive over time (Carter, Corra, et al. 2014; Schuman et al. 1997). Bonilla-Silva (2018) posed that such a view paints a very optimistic view of the state of race relations.

However, several issues and concerns still haunt the study of racial attitudes and race relations in the US today. One, the seeming liberalization of white attitudes toward principles of racial equality has not significantly reduced the disadvantages experienced by African Americans (Jones, Schmitt, and Wilson 2018). Two, while whites' attitudes toward principles of racial equality have become more progressive over time, their views toward ameliorative racial policies have not (Bobo and Smith 1994; Carter and Carter 2014; Carter and Corra 2012; Carter, Steelman, et al. 2005; Carter, Corra, and Jenks 2016; Schuman et al. 1997). For instance, when attitudes toward policies such as affirmative action are assessed, whites' views are much less supportive than their attitude toward abstract principles, and this discrepancy has remained stable since early public opinion polls in the 1970s (Carter, Steelman, et al. 2005).

A small but vocal camp of scholars maintain a "principled objection" position and pose that politics of race and this principle/implementation gap are not necessarily dictated by negative racial attitudes. Rather, citizens today can maneuver through the affective components of racial policies and issues and form valid opinions based largely on conservative ideas (Sniderman and Carmines 1997; Sniderman, Crosby, and Howell 2000). For instance, Sniderman and Carmines posed that anti-affirmative action attitudes are affected less by racial animus than by the general belief that such polices are unfair and unjust to whites. In this sense, whites are able to make a "principled objection" to policies that are racial in nature and that redistribute resources because they see them as violating traditional values of individualism. Thus, while racism may continue be prevalent in US society, its role in dictating views toward racial policy is negligible at best.

Although the "principled objection" perspective finds some degree of support in the literature, scholars have consistently found evidence that race in general and negative racial attitudes in particular play a significant role in policy attitudes even when controlling for conservative ideals. Indeed, Bobo and Tuan (2006) posed that given the extensive history between the races and the insidious role race has played in US politics, the notion that racism does not affect policy views is confounding and should be put to rest. Within the literature on politics and race, scholars have consistently connected such lack of support for racial policies to negative racial attitudes outside of conservative principles. The dominant perspective poses that this view is rooted in a new and "less obtrusive" racism that attacks minority cultures. This form of racism has been termed differently by various scholars, including color-blind racism (Bonilla-Silva 2018); laissez-faire racism (Bobo, Kluegel, and Smith 1997), symbolic racism (Kinder and Sears 1981), modern racism (McConahay 1986), or racial resentment (Kinder and Sanders 1996; Tuch and Hughes 2011). This ideology differs greatly from the dominant ideology under Jim Crow, which maintained that blacks were biologically inferior to whites (Bonilla-Silva 2018).

Bonilla-Silva (2018) more critically posed that we live in a racist system where color-blind ideology is used to explain current-day racial inequality in seemingly nonracial ways. Whites are able to rely on several frames that minimize past and current racial discrimination, including *abstract liberalism*, *naturalizations*, *cultural frames*, and *minimization of racism*. These frames enable whites (and some nonwhites) to minimize the "race problem" and attack the minority cultures even in the face of persistent and debilitating racial inequality. Bonilla-Silva argued that this new ideology is more slippery and dangerous than old-fashioned racism, where racial oppression was overt. Relevant to this chapter, the call to end political correctness would be a color-blind, abstract liberal argument made by conservatives, and those with neoliberal perspectives, in an attempt to shut down concerns over racist rhetoric. Bonilla-Silva viewed abstract liberalism as a tactic to maintain the racial hierarchy through laissez-faire, neoliberal economics and rhetoric. In fact, he termed abstract liberal rhetoric as "reasonable racism," where negative racial views can resemble rational and moral views.

While, according to Bonilla-Silva, negative racial animosity is not required to espouse color-blind techniques such as the call to end political correctness, the purpose of this project is to assess whether calls against political correctness are indeed rooted in more than just conservative zeal. That is to say, does racial animosity play a significant role among conservatives who advocate ending political correctness? Scholars in the principled objection camp would argue that conservative responses like this (ending PC stances) are mainly rooted in conservative ideals. Race scholars, such as Bonilla-Silva (2018), argue that such a proposition is highly unlikely given the racial nature of the calls (e.g., zero-tolerance policy on immigration) made by Trump, conservative politicians, and pundits alike.

DATA SOURCES

Data for this project was obtained from the 2016 American National Election Study (ANES) pilot study to assess whether the call for political correctness is rooted not only in conservative ideals but in racial resentment. The ANES is biannually administered to a randomly selected nationally representative sample of noninstitutionalized adults over the age of eighteen in the United States. Data is primarily collected through face-to-face interviews, although mixed modes (i.e., face-to-face and telephone) have been utilized in some years.

Outcome Variable

We provide two different ways to measure attitudes about the rejection of PC speech. The Politically Correct (PC) Rejection variable was generated by combining two items with slightly different wording. The two versions of the item are as follows:

> There's been a lot of talk lately about "political correctness." Some people think that the way people talk needs to change with the

> times to be more sensitive to people from different backgrounds. Others think that this has already gone too far and many people are just too easily offended. Which is closer to your opinion?

and

> Some people think that the way people talk needs to change with the times to be more sensitive to people from different backgrounds. Others think that this has already gone too far and many people are just too easily offended. Which is closer to your opinion?

Both items used the same response categories:

The way people talk needs to change a lot	[coded as 1]
The way people talk needs to change a little	[coded as 2]
People are a little too easily offended	[coded as 3]
People are much too easily offended	[coded as 4]

We tested whether the different wording changed the results, and we found no difference, so we combined the two versions for our analyses.

Explanatory Variables

The primary explanatory variable being used in this project was the level of political conservatism. As noted above, we assessed whether political conservatism independently affected the rejection of political correctness in general. We used a self-report measure of political conservatism, in which participants were asked to select the position on a seven-item Likert scale that best represented their political leanings, from "very liberal" to "very conservative" with "neither liberal nor conservative" as the middle category.

Potential Mediator Variable: Racial Resentment

Although we expected some independent and significant impact of political conservativism on rejection of political correctness, the primary purpose of our chapter is to assess whether these views are partially explained by racial resentment. Kinder and Sanders (1996) defined racial resentment as a new, more subtle racism (relative to traditional racism) that is rooted in anti-black affect and beliefs that blacks are violating ethics of hard work and individualism.

While the concept of racial resentment is abstract and difficult to measure, it has been of particular interest to race scholars over the past five decades (Kinder and Sanders 1996; Roos, Hughes, and Reichelmann 2018). The ANES includes several questions that have been labeled in past research as indicating degree of racial resentment. These questions include the following, with possible responses ranging from agree strongly (1) to disagree strongly (5):

Tryhard: "It's really a matter of some people not trying hard enough; if blacks would only try harder they could be just as well off as whites."
Irishup: "Irish, Italians, Jewish and many other minorities worked their way up, blacks should do the same without special favors."
Slavery: "Generations of slavery and discrimination have created conditions that make it difficult for blacks to work their way up."
Deserve: "Over the past few years, blacks have gotten less than they deserve."

Racial Resentment is specified as a confirmatory factor analytic (CFA) model in the structural equation modeling framework. What this means is that we take the degree to which the four indicators of racial resentment hang together as the true measure of racial resentment. This is similar to, but not exactly, what one would do if they had several thermometers in various parts of their yard and wished to estimate a *true* measure of the yard's temperature. The CFA model is one of a family of latent variable models that separate the shared covariance of the indicator responses from measurement error, resulting in a measure with less error and potentially less bias.

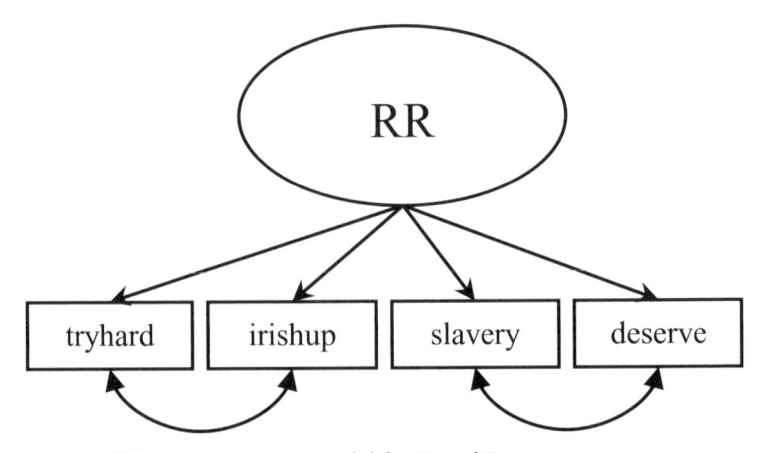

FIGURE 3.1. CFA measurement model for Racial Resentment

Other Explanatory Variables

In some models we also include a number of explanatory demographic variables that have been shown to affect racial attitudes in the past (Carter, Steelman, et al. 2005; Carter, Corra, et al. 2014), including the following:

Age: respondent age, in years

Gender (self-report): created as a dummy variable, where self-reported gender of female = 1 and male = 0

Family Income: coded as the midpoint of sixteen binned categories: less than $10,000, $10,000–19,999, $20,000–29,999, $30,000–39,999, $40,000–49,999, $50,000–59,999, $60,000–69,999, $70,000–79,999, $80,000–$99,999, $100,000–$119,999, $120,000–$149,999, $150,000–$199,999, $200,000–$249,999, $250,000–$349,999, $350,000–$499,999, and $500,000 or more

Educational Attainment: coded as highest degree obtained, with the following categories: no high school, high school graduate, some college, two-year college degree, four-year college degree, postgraduate (some or complete)

RESULTS

Table 3.1 presents results (standardized estimates and z-scores) for four regression models, using the full ANES pilot sample. Models 1 and 2 are without controls (age, gender, education, family income), and models 3 and 4 add controls. Model 1 presents the association between conservative self-identification and rejection of political correctness. Given the outspoken rhetoric against PC culture used by the current president and others and the arguments made by principled objection scholars, we would expect conservative self-identification to independently and significantly predict lower levels of support for political correctness even when relevant control variables are included. Indeed, we do find support for this independent relationship. A standard-deviation increase in conservative self-identification is associated with a 0.429 SD increase in rejection of political correctness. Thus, relative to those that identify as more liberal, conservatives are more likely to reject political correctness.

This project also assesses whether the relationship between level of conservatism and PC rejection is partially predicted by racial resentment. Principled objection scholars pose that conservatives can indeed hold conservative ideals related to racial policies that are not compromised by racial animus.

TABLE 3.1. Self-report conservatism and Racial Resentment predicting PC rejection, with and without controls

	M1	M2	M3	M4
CONSERVATISM	0.429***	.074*	.408***	.109***
RACIAL ANIMUS	—	.585***	—	.540***
AGE (YEARS)	—		.083**	.037
FEMALE (MALE AS REFERENCE)	—		−.075**	−.076***
EDUCATION (HIGHEST DEGREE)	—		−.019	.028
FAMILY INCOME (LOGGED)	—		.053	.053
R^2	0.184	.400	.199	.390

Standardized estimates; N = 1200; *p < .05. **p < .01. ***p < .001.

While political correctness is not inherently racial in tone, in the past and currently, problems with political correctness have been distinctly associated with issues of race and ethnicity, such as immigration. Accordingly, model 2 adds racial resentment as a predictor of PC rejection, and this results in a sizable reduction—by nearly 83 percent—in the standardized effect of conservative self-identification. Comparing models 3 and 4 yields a similar pattern, with a reduction of 73 percent in the standardized effect of conservative self-identification on PC rejection. These findings demonstrate that the conservatism effect is not independent and is partially predicted by racial animosity held by these respondents.

Table 3.2 presents identical models to those in table 3.1, but with the participants restricted to only those that self-identify as being white. The overall sample drops from 1200 to 875, yet the pattern is unchanged. Models 5 and 6 demonstrate a reduction in the bivariate relationship between conservative self-identification and PC rejection by just over 83 percent, and models 7 and 8 (with controls) demonstrate a reduction of over 78 percent in this effect. In models 3, 4, 7, and 8 controls tend to have minimal effects. The R^2 figure in the tables represents the percentage of the variance in the outcome the model explains—this ranges from 0 to 1, and higher values are better (1 being perfect prediction). Overall, models with racial resentment included explain twice of the variance or more in the rejection of PC speech; this is further evidence that PC rejection is more closely associated with racial animosity than with conservative self-identification, providing strong evidence against the "principled objection" argument.

TABLE 3.2. Self-report conservatism and Racial Resentment predicting PC rejection, with and without controls, among whites

	M5	M6	M7	M8
CONSERVATISM	0.454***	.076*	.439***	.094**
RACIAL ANIMUS	—	.603***	—	.597***
AGE (YEARS)	—		.040**	−.004
FEMALE (MALE AS REFERENCE)	—		−.065*	−.067*
EDUCATION (HIGHEST DEGREE)	—		−.046	.022
FAMILY INCOME (LOGGED)	—		.035	.073*
R^2	0.206	.428	.214	.429

Standardized estimates; N = 875; *p < .05. **p < .01. ***p < .001.

CONCLUSIONS

Without a doubt, the call to end political correctness is being waged by the current conservative presidential administration, politicians, and pundits. President Trump has repeatedly called for the end of PC tactics that, he argues, prevent debate and even discussion on sensitive topics such as undocumented immigration and Islamic extremism. This attack on political correctness has also found a home in prominent media outlets and among segments of the population who support greater reform on these issues. It is also apparent that Trump and conservative pundits use the term *politically correct* as a slur against liberals and progressives who are concerned about policies proposed and set in place by this administration, which appears to be anti-immigration, anti-Muslim, and possibly racist. The PC label acts as a defensive technique that places conservatives as the victims and liberals as perpetrators of a technique that blocks debate on sensitive yet critical issues affecting the US. This victimhood frame has been a prominent technique used by factions opposed to policies meant to alleviate racial inequality (Bobo and Tuan 2006; Carter and Lippard 2015).

In line with prominent scholars in this book, the anti-PC stance generally speaking reflects a broader pushback (or whitelash) among elite Republicans and mostly conservative white (and some nonwhite) citizens. In line with the arguments of Bonilla-Silva, anti-PC views enable many whites and others to use slippery language that has a color-blind ring to it to explain away racial matters in nonracial ways. Bonilla-Silva goes on to say that such rhetorical mechanisms play a powerful role in the production and reproduction of the racist system characteristic of the US today. Thus, anti-PC rhetoric is meaningful for the dominant group who attempts to maintain control in a world growing more diverse daily as well as for marginalized groups who continue to struggle against persistent racism and discrimination.

REFERENCES

Allison, Paul D. 2012. "Handling Missing Data by Maximum Likelihood." Keynote presentation at the SAS Global Forum, April 23, Orlando, FL. Retrieved May 11, 2020 (https://85d.26c.myftpupload.com/wp-content/uploads/MissingDataByML.pdf?time=1588979985).

Bernstein, Richard. 1990. "The Rising Hegemony of the Politically Correct." *New York Times*, October 28.

Bobo, Lawrence, James R. Kluegel, and Ryan A. Smith. 1997. "Laissez-Faire Racism: The Crystallization of a Kinder, Gentler, Antiblack Ideology." Pp. 23–25 in *Racial Attitudes in the 1990s: Continuity and Change*, edited by Steven A. Tuch and Jack K. Martin. Westport, CT: Praeger.

Bobo, Lawrence, and Ryan A. Smith. 1994. "Antipoverty Policy, Affirmative Action, and Racial Attitudes." Pp. 365–95 in *Confronting Poverty: Prescriptions for Change*, edited by Sheldon H. Danziger, Gary D. Sandefur, and Daniel H. Weinberg. Cambridge, MA: Harvard University Press.

Bobo, Lawrence, and Mia Tuan. 2006. *Prejudice in Politics: Group Position, Public Opinion, and the Wisconsin Treaty Rights Dispute*. Cambridge, MA: Harvard University Press.

Bonilla-Silva, Eduardo. 2018. *Racism without Racists: Color-Blind Racism and the Persistence of Racial Inequality in America*. Lanham, MD: Rowman & Littlefield.

Carter, J. Scott, and Shannon K. Carter. 2014. "Place Matters: The Impact of Place of Residency on Racial Attitudes among Regional and Urban Migrants." *Social Science Research* 47: 165–77.

Carter, J. Scott, and Mamadi Corra. 2012. "Beliefs about the Causes of Racial Inequality: The Persisting Impact of Urban and Suburban Locations?" *Urban Studies Research*, June 21. Retrieved May 11, 2020 (https://doi.org/10.1155/2012/242741).

Carter, J. Scott, Mamadi Corra, Shannon K. Carter, and Rachael McCrosky. 2014. "The Impact of Place? A Reassessment of the Importance of the South in Affecting Beliefs about Racial Inequality." *Social Science Journal* 51(1): 12–20.

Carter, J. Scott, Mamadi Corra, and David Jenks. 2016. "In the Shadows of Ferguson: The Role of Racial Resentment on White Attitudes toward the Use of Force by Police." *International Journal of Criminal Justice Sciences* 11: 114–31.

Carter, J. Scott, and Cameron Lippard. 2015. "Group Positioning, Threat and Immigration: The Role of Elite Actors and Interest Groups in Setting the 'Lines of Discussion.'" *Sociology of Race and Ethnicity* 1(3): 394–408.

Carter, J. Scott, Lala Steelman, Lynn Mulkey, and Casey Borch. 2005. "When the Rubber Meets the Road: The Differential Effects of Urbanism and Region on Principle and Implementation Measures of Racial Tolerance." *Social Science Research* 34(2): 408–25.

Cokorinos, Lee. 2003. *The Assault on Diversity: An Organized Challenge to Racial and Gender Justice.* Lanham, MD: Rowman & Littlefield.

D'Souza, Dinesh. 1991. *Illiberal Education: The Politics of Race and Sex on Campus.* New York: Free Press.

Fisher, Marc. 2016. "Donald Trump: 'I am the least racist person.'" *Washington Post*, June 10.

Gallagher, BJ. 2017. "The Problem with Political Correctness." *The Blog*: Huffington Post, February 25, 2013, updated December 6, 2017.

Greeley, Andrew M., and Paul B. Sheatsley. 1971. "Attitudes toward Racial Integration." *Scientific American* 225(6): 13–19.

Hyman, Herbert H., and Paul B. Sheatsley. 1956. "Attitudes toward Desegregation." *Scientific American* 195(6): 35–39.

———. 1964. "Attitudes toward Desegregation." *Scientific American* 211(1): 16–23.

Jones, Janelle, John Schmitt, and Valerie Wilson. 2018. "50 years after the Kerner Commission: African Americans Are Better Off in Many Ways but Are Still Disadvantaged by Racial Inequality." Economic Policy Institute.

Kimball, Roger. 1990. *Tenured Radicals: How Politics Has Corrupted Our Higher Education.* New York: Harper and Row.

Kinder, Donald R., and Lynn M. Sanders. 1996. *Divided by Color: Racial Politics and Democratic Ideals.* Chicago: University of Chicago Press.

Kinder, Donald R., and David O. Sears. 1981. "Prejudice and Politics: Symbolic Racism versus Racial Threats to the Good Life." *Journal of Personality and Social Psychology* 40(3): 414–31.

McConahay, John B. 1986. "Modern Racism, Ambivalence, and the Modern Racism Scale." Pp. 91–125 in *Prejudice, Discrimination, and Racism*, edited by John F. Dovidio and Samuel L. Gaertner. San Diego: Academic Press.

Norton, Michael I., Samuel R. Sommers, Evan P. Apfelbaum, Natassia Pura, and Dan Ariely. 2006. "Color Blindness and Interracial Interaction: Playing the Political Correctness Game." *Psychological Science* 17(11): 949–53.

Roos, J. Micah, Michael Hughes, and Ashley V. Reichelmann. 2018. "A Puzzle of Racial Attitudes: Is Racial Resentment a Measure of Racial Policy Attitudes?" Paper presented at the 81st annual meeting of the Southern Sociological Society, "Racial Theory, Analysis, and Politics in Trump America," April 4–7, New Orleans, LA.

Schuman, Howard, Charlotte Steeh, Lawrence Bobo, and Maria Krysan. 1997. *RACIAL attitudes in America: Trends and Interpretations.* Cambridge, MA: Harvard University Press.

Silman, Anna. 2015. "10 Famous Comedians on How Political Correctness Is Killing Comedy: 'We are addicted to the rush of being offended.'" *Salon*, June 11.

Sniderman, Paul M., and Eward G. Carmines. 1997. *Reaching beyond Race*. Cambridge, MA: Harvard University Press.

Sniderman, Paul M., Gretchen C. Crosby, and William G. Howell. 2000. "The Politics of Race." Pp. 236–79 in *Racialized Politics*, edited by David O. Sears, Jim Sidanius, and Lawrence Bobo. Chicago: University of Chicago Press.

Sue, Derald Wing. 2016. *Race Talk and the Conspiracy of Silence: Understanding and Facilitating Difficult Dialogues on Race*. Hoboken, NJ: John Wiley and Sons.

Taylor, D. Garth, Paul B. Sheatsley, and Andrew M. Greeley. 1978. "Attitudes toward Racial Integration." *Scientific American* 238(6): 42–49.

Tuch, Steven A., and Michael Hughes. 2011. "Whites' Racial Policy Attitudes in the Twenty-First Century: The Continuing Significance of Racial Resentment." *Annals of the American Academy of Political and Social Science* 634(1): 134–52.

Weigel, Moira. 2016. "Political Correctness: How the Right Invented a Phantom Enemy." *Guardian*, November 30.

Wikstrom, Peter. 2016. "No One Is 'Pro-Politically Correct': Positive Construals of Political Correctness in Twitter Conversations." *Nordic Journal of English Studies* 15(2): 159–70.

CHAPTER 4

DIVERSITY REGIMES

*How University Diversity Initiatives Shape
White Race Consciousness*

JAMES M. THOMAS

What does it mean to be race conscious? I define race consciousness as the recognition of race's continued significance in social, political, and cultural life. Race consciousness is not an inherent disposition. The social sciences are now largely in agreement that we do not come into this world *seeing* race. We learn race's meaning and significance through interactions and interactional contexts. For many racial and ethnic minorities, race consciousness becomes a core part of their identity as they enter adulthood and are forced to confront the realities of a racialized social structure (Banton 1997). Many whites, meanwhile, are often blind to these realities precisely because of the advantages they derive from their position within the racialized social structure (Bonilla-Silva 2013; Doane 2014). These advantages are so commonplace that many whites accept them as normal.

Nevertheless, there are race-conscious whites (DiTomaso, Parks-Yancy, and Post 2011; Taylor 2011). So, what accounts for their race consciousness? In this chapter I focus on white race consciousness within the university setting to theorize how a university's diversity initiatives shape white race consciousness. In previous work, I theorized the rise of *diversity regimes*: a set of meanings, practices, and actions that cultivate benign celebrations of difference but do little to fundamentally challenge racial inequality (Thomas 2018a). Here, I emphasize the organizational and interactional contexts of diversity regimes in structuring white race consciousness. My analysis identifies five hegemonic race-conscious archetypes that arise from a university's diversity regime: the Privilege Checker, the Problem Solver, the Cool Consumer, the Distant Observer, and the Pessimist. While not exhaustive, my typology helps map the cultural terrain produced by a diversity regime and provides a framework for discerning how the organization and deployment of diversity produces complacency and contradictions.

Benign commitments to multicultural ideals are a hallmark of contemporary racial discourse (Bell and Hartmann 2007; Berrey 2011; Hartmann 2015). These commitments provide important cultural resources from which whites construct and enact race consciousness (DiTomaso, Parks-Yancy, and Post 2011; Hartmann and Bell 2011). Yet it is unclear whether cultural resources derived from benign commitments to diversity and inclusion help dismantle racial rule or reproduce it. By attending to the relationship between diversity regimes and whites' race consciousness, my analysis helps reveal how the cultural resources for combatting white supremacy become co-opted for its maintenance.

LITERATURE REVIEW

Contemporary racial ideology is defined by and through the paradigms of color blindness and hollow, or trivial, multiculturalism (Bell and Hartmann 2007; Bonilla-Silva 2013; Forman 2004). Meanwhile, scholarship on contemporary diversity ideology (Embrick 2011) has shown how it perpetuates race-based inequalities by condensing race with less meaningful forms of difference, thereby minimizing race's role in shaping race-based outcomes (see Edelman, Fuller, and Mara-Drita 2001). While multiculturalism, color blindness, and diversity ideology are not synonymous, they are products of a similar discursive shift whereby racial inequality is fashioned as a particular kind of problem to be solved by symbolic and public commitments to abstract equality, market individualism, and inclusive civic nationalism (Melamed 2011). This new language of race does not challenge unequal relations between differently defined racial groups. Instead, unequal outcomes among racialized groups are framed as moral matters (Melamed 2011; Myers 2005; Ryan 1976). As this new language of race materializes, it restitches the significance of race into the social fabric of our society, from racial discrimination in housing, education, and employment to increasing wealth inequality between whites and nonwhites (Desmond and Gershenson 2016; Dettling et al. 2017; Reardon and Owens 2014; Shapiro, Meschede, and Osoro 2013).

The new language of race and our social order are mutually reinforcing. Race's meaning "is defined and contested in both collective action and personal practice" (Omi and Winant 2014:61). Collective action transforms, destroys, and then reforms racial categories, investing meaning into those racial categories and their relationships (Omi and Winant 2014:64). People use these meanings to craft their understandings of the world, including how they fit into it. Thus, race is an important tool through which people forge their sense of self and marshal themselves toward the worlds in which they live.

For several decades, scholars have examined the themes, frames, ideas, and imagery whites use to marshal race and a sense of self (Giroux 1997; Hartigan 2008; McDermott and Samson 2005). The anthropologist Ruth Frankenberg found that white women draw on color-and power-evasive discourses to "describe and comprehend their positions in the racial order" (1993:20). Elsewhere, the sociologist Eduardo Bonilla-Silva finds several dominant frameworks through which whites explain away race's continued significance (Bonilla-Silva 2013:8). Meanwhile, the sociologist Eileen O'Brien (2001) illuminates the organizational schemas that whites within two antiracist organizations draw on in fashioning their antiracist praxis and their sense of self. These analyses fit a trending focus on whiteness as a situated activity "whose meaning is imparted by the particular context in which white actors are located" (McDermott and Samson 2005:249).

My analysis serves as a complement. I frame the American university as a key organizational context that provides its members with cultural and symbolic resources to (1) invest meaning in racial categories and their relationships with one another and (2) craft their understandings of the world, including how they fit into it. Colleges and universities are well recognized as important agents of socialization. Over the past forty years, colleges and universities have increasingly endorsed the ideals of multiculturalism. Today, the American university is a "cosmopolitan canopy" where people of different racial and ethnic backgrounds often coexist in the same living spaces, learning spaces, and public spaces (see Anderson 2012). Yet the university is also a site where whiteness is entrenched within the very fabric of the institution and where whites continue to hold disproportionate levels of power and decision making relative to their populations (Carnevale and Strohl 2013). Studying this particular context where multicultural values and whiteness are simultaneously ubiquitous can help us better understand the limits of the former for dismantling the latter.

Diversity initiatives are now commonplace among American universities. Many, however, fail to fundamentally challenge racial inequality (Thomas

2018, 2019). If the dominant way of talking about race today minimizes or dismisses its significance in structuring people's everyday lives, then this approach likely affects antiracist praxis, including how whites construct race-conscious selves. I argue that a university's *diversity regime* creates the cultural and discursive conditions for hollow race consciousness (see also Ahmed 2012).

CONTEXT AND METHODOLOGY

My analysis draws on two years of ethnographic fieldwork at an institution I'll call Diversity University (DU), a public, flagship university in the American South. As a university with a history steeped in racial conflict, DU is similar to many other American colleges and universities in that the legacies of white supremacy remain inscribed in its traditions and its campus landscape (Wilder 2013). DU's recent investments in diversity infrastructure situate it squarely within a larger trend within American higher education (Sturm 2007). DU shares many of the same conditions common to other large, public, flagship universities, including public disinvestment, rising tuition costs, the increased difficulty in securing federally backed student loans, and the pressure to recruit "high-dollar" students and increase overall enrollment (Newfield 2011).

From December 2013 to the spring of 2016, I attended over thirty meetings, campus workshops, events, and activities in which diversity and inclusion were the focus. I also conducted twenty-six formal interviews with students, faculty, staff, and administrators plus dozens of field interviews and informal conversations. In campus workshops and other events I observed many well-meaning whites engage their nonwhite peers in discussions on power, privilege, and inequality. Interviews with diversity workers on campus helped me better understand their challenges in performing diversity work on a campus whose student body is approximately 76 percent white. These insights are the empirical material from which a typology of whites' race consciousness emerged.

My analysis follows a grounded approach (Charmaz 2006). I began by reviewing field notes and interview data to identify how social actors, and whites in particular, attempted to make sense of the continued significance of race in social, political, and cultural life. I then began to formulate codes, themes, and categories that helped give order to my observations. Subsequent field notes and interviews helped establish patterns in my data, while disconfirming others. Over time, a story emerged that revealed a typology of white race consciousness and its connections to my concept of a *diversity regime*.

THE ARCHETYPES OF WHITE RACE CONSCIOUSNESS

In what follows, I sketch the five race-conscious archetypes I developed: the Privilege Checker, the Problem Solver, the Cool Consumer, the Distant Observer, and the Pessimist. My typology approximates a particular range of whites' race consciousness within the college setting. These archetypes help explain how a diversity regime gives rise to hollow, or trivial, multiculturalism.

The Privilege Checker

The Privilege Checker is committed to contesting the racialized social structure, yet they understand it almost entirely through a lens of privilege: as something that confers to whites certain benefits and advantages over nonwhites. Consequently, the Privilege Checker seeks to hold other whites accountable for their lack of race consciousness. They invoke the platitude "Check your privilege" in order to police the racial indiscretions of others, such as when a white student or colleague seeks to minimize or deny the persistence of everyday racism. Policing racial indiscretions reinforces the Privilege Checker's own sense of race consciousness and demonstrates their "wokeness" in comparison to other whites. Yet because Privilege Checkers view the racialized social structure mostly through the lens of privilege, their race consciousness is confined to personal and interpersonal contexts. The Privilege Checker struggles to understand white supremacy's locus of power: a set of historical and social processes—or racial projects—that over time consolidate racial power and racial meanings (Strmic-Pawl 2015; see also Omi and Winant 2014).

Pamela is a black woman and assistant director for DU's Department of Residential Life. She also adjuncts as an instructor for DU's required freshman experience course, of which there are dozens of sections offered each semester. In our interview Pamela discusses how she incorporates diversity and inclusion into her classroom:

> As part of our curriculum, [DU] gives you a standard outline and they do want you to do something on diversity and inclusion so I had two days set aside. I brought in [a guest speaker] and we did some work with her. And then I brought in one of my graduate students and we did the privilege walk lesson.

The privilege walk consists of having students line up next to each other in the middle of a classroom with plenty of space to move around. They start out holding hands, and then the instructor reads several statements aloud. If the statement applies to the student, they take one step forward or backward according to the instructions. These statements include the following:

- If you are right-handed, take one step forward.
- If English is your first language, take one step forward.
- If you constantly feel unsafe walking alone at night, take one step back.
- If you have ever been profiled by someone else using stereotypes, take one step back.

After all of the statements are read aloud, participants take stock of where they are in the room in relation to others and take stock of the advantages they maintain relative to others.

I asked Pamela how students responded to this exercise: "I had a student, a white young lady, she said this is the most she's ever learned about race since she was born." Pamela continues:

> We talked a lot about privilege and class as opposed to race. Race came up a couple of times because I had them read the book about the atomic bomb. I can't remember the name of it and I had them do presentations and I broke them up in groups. One of the topics was about women during World War II and one was about minority women so basically black Americans, Asians, and all that. And I had a few people up there crying during their presentation which was not my intent but they had realized how bad it was and how people had to live and what they had to go through and what women couldn't do during that time. I was like well that's the whole point of this project: for you to get it.

Privilege is centered in Pamela's classroom. Yet this centering of privilege comes at the expense of consideration of power, and the consideration of racism as a *structuring* phenomenon. The privilege walk frames disadvantages from racism as "interpersonal" and flattens those disadvantages alongside human differences disconnected from structural inequality. Without emphasizing race, the privilege walk conveys *some* awareness of race. Yet students' reactions to discussions of privilege suggest a limited ability to make connections between discriminatory practices of the past and the present. Students cried, according to Pamela, because of "what women couldn't do *during that time*" (emphasis mine).

From workshops on implicit bias to a curriculum that includes exercises like the privilege walk, DU's diversity efforts discursively represent racism as something seated at the individual level. This "personalizing" of racism has dire consequences. There is no evidence that implicit bias training or exercises like the privilege walk have improved retention rates for black faculty, improved recruitment and retention rates for black students, or redistributed power and decision making toward minority faculty, staff, and students. The focus on teaching white students to recognize, or "check," their privilege fails to properly diagnose the underlying conditions that maintain racial inequality. The idea of checking one's privilege functions to obscure, rather than clarify, white supremacy as a political, economic, and social order.

The Cool Consumer

Writing in mid-nineteenth century Paris, Charles Baudelaire describes the *flâneur* as a particular type of character belonging to its emergent cosmopolitan scene: "For the perfect *flâneur*, for the passionate spectator, it is an immense joy to set up house in the heart of the multitude, amid the ebb and flow of movement, in the midst of the fugitive and the infinite" (1995:4 and 9). Later, the German intellectual Walter Benjamin theorized Baudelaire's *flâneur* as a late-capitalist consumer type semidetached in their engagement with the crowds and commodities of the modern metropolis (Benjamin 1997, 2002). The *flâneur* reflects important shifts in the political economy, self-regulation, new modes of communication, and the growing commodification of social relationships (Featherstone 1998; Giulianotti 2002; Harvey 2009).

Like the *flâneur*, the Cool Consumer is semidetached from the realities of everyday racism. Their partial detachment is a reflection not of their lack of personal investment in reducing inequality but rather of their self-investment. The Cool Consumer seeks casual knowledge of everyday racism. This casual knowledge functions as cultural capital. The Cool Consumer is only race conscious insofar as an awareness of everyday racism can be exchanged for opportunities and advancement. Remaining semidetached, the Cool Consumer can stroll in and out of diversity programming without having to commit to doing the work of dismantling white supremacy. For the Cool Consumer, opportunities for multicultural competency represent opportunities for self-advancement.

Following an incident of racial violence on its campus, the outgoing director for diversity and multicultural affairs within DU's student government penned an editorial reflective of the Cool Consumer archetype. In it, this white male student argued for diversity's importance, stressing that "it is essential we learn to communicate with people from other cultures if we expect to compete in the global job market . . . General Electric, Boeing, Walgreens, and Bank of America know that creating inclusive environments can improve the bottom line." Though racial violence serves as the backdrop to this editorial, the author uses it as an opportunity to reimagine cross-cultural contact as an investment opportunity for entrepreneurial students seeking to strengthen their individual market positions. Diversity is fashioned into an intangible asset that facilitates new modes of sociality. Social interactions with nonwhite students are reconfigured as human capital acquisitions (see Thomas 2019). Superficial diversity allows for the Cool Consumer to remain semidetached from the material consequences of existing racial inequality and oppression yet overwhelmingly benefit from the opportunity to leisurely stroll through the university's "marketplace of difference."

The Problem Solver

The Problem Solver is a pragmatist who seeks to distill the complexity of racial inequality into easy-to-recognize and easier-to-fix sets of problems. The Problem Solver acknowledges everyday racism yet remains only ever focused on the present moment. Attempts to place racial inequality in historical, institutional, or global contexts are eschewed. Instead, the solution to everyday racism is in improving "race relations."

In 2012, DU elected its first black woman as student body president. Two weeks later, a white student confronted her with racial slurs in the downtown entertainment district. She filed harassment charges and initiated DU's student judicial process. During this process, a white administrator encouraged her to follow a reconciliation model with the perpetrator because the judicial process could result in his expulsion and would do little to "open his mind." She ultimately dropped the charges and pursued reconciliation, with the white administrator serving as mediator. This event was a watershed moment, as DU soon shifted its organizational framework for dealing with racial harassment—later termed bias incidents—toward a reconciliation model. The student judicial process remains intact. Now, however, victims of bias incidents are encouraged to meet with the accused and help "open their minds."

DU's institutional embracing of racial reconciliation reduces racial harassment and racial violence to isolated interactions and advocates finding common ground with perpetrators. The factors that give rise to racial violence and conflict are minimized and cast as irrelevant or counterproductive to achieving reconciliation. Indeed, during a panel discussion on racism across campus, one panelist dismissed an audience question on power's relevance because "power is too vague of a concept and doesn't give us any practical ways to solve our problems here on the ground." Their response reflects both the archetype of the Problem Solver and the tendency within diversity programming to embrace the Problem Solver model.

The rise of chief diversity officers (CDOs) in higher education is well documented (Gose 2006) and reflects colleges' and universities' tendency to embrace the Problem Solver model. While some CDOs have academic backgrounds, most are practitioners. At DU, for example, there is significant emphasis on logic models that convert everyday racism into a set of operationalized problems to be solved through increasing students' intercultural competencies and raising their awareness of "minority issues." Elsewhere, we see universities embracing "bystander antiracism" as an "essential element of antiracist social policy" (Nelson, Dunn, and Paradies 2011:264). Bystander training asks individual students, faculty, and staff to "change the social norms toward the intolerance of racism" (Nelson, Dunn, and Paradies 2011: 265).

The Distant Observer

Distant Observers fancy themselves above the fray. While their structural position in the racial hierarchy affords them such a vantage point, their membership in the academy enables naive objectivity. Distant Observers are social scientists in training. Their analysis of everyday racism diagnoses the racialized social structure but offers little in the way of a prescription. Indeed, once the problem is revealed, the Distant Observer is only ever likely to recommend its further study. Calls for more resources to study that which is already known by men and women of color square neatly with the university's mission to promote free inquiry. Like the Cool Consumer, the Distant Observer is semidetached from everyday racism. Yet while the Cool Consumer's detachment enables them to capitalize on casual knowledge of everyday racism, the Distant Observer's detachment enables a posture of objectivity that enhances their self-righteousness.

At the end of the academic year DU's chancellor gave his State of Campus report to the full faculty body. He mentioned a violent racist incident from the previous year and the steps the university was taking to ensure that nothing similar ever again transpired. He characterized the event as isolated. Upon the conclusion of the meeting, three women social scientists—two of whom are African American—approached him and challenged his characterization. They pointed to the disproportionate service they give to minority students who are confronted with everyday racism. One of the women described her own personal encounter with racism on campus. The chancellor's response was incredulous: "Prove it."

An elderly white man telling these three women to prove their lived experiences is expected given DU's organizational context. The chancellor is aware of DU's institutional data showing disproportionate retention and degree completion rates for African Americans compared with their white peers. He is also aware of institutional data showing minority underrepresentation across faculty ranks. Embodying the Distant Observer, however, the chancellor insists that the problem is far from fully understood. He can call for further study in perpetuity because doing so fits squarely with the mission of the university as a purveyor of knowledge.

The Pessimist

The Pessimist is the most tragic of white race-conscious archetypes. Unlike the Distant Observer, the Pessimist eschews the pretenses of value-neutral objectivity and willingly steps into the "Darkwater" of everyday racism. Yet once submerged in the Darkwater, Pessimists become overwhelmed (see Du Bois 1999). Their earnest attempts to reckon with the complexity of the color line in the twenty-first century often lead them to conclude that racial rule is unbending. How can a university openly committed to diversity produce this cynicism?

The organizational structure of diversity work diminishes its capacity to address racial inequality (Thomas 2018). Diversity work is often organized in a way that exemplifies what I term *decentralization* (see also Weick 1976, 1982). Decentralization entails a combination of five structural features:

- a lack of coordination or slow coordination;
- relative absence of regulations or the inability to properly enforce existing regulations;
- unresponsiveness;
- poor observational capabilities; and
- a shared belief that no matter what organizational actors do, the same outcome persists.

These features need not be impediments to organizational goals so long as those goals have a degree of clarity and consensus. The problem is that attaining clarity and consensus within an organizational setting is never a straightforward process. Organizational actors have to work out agreements and understandings in response to the everyday contingencies of their social settings (Hall 1987:6). Yet there is little consensus on what diversity means, and the lack of clarity affects how diversity is put into practice.

Decentralization is both an organizational context *and* a set of actions that reproduces that context—a dialectic between the negotiated order of social actions and the contexts within which those actions unfold. The end result is confusion, frustration, and even defeatism. As Gail, the director of DU's Institute for Racial Justice, conveyed, "One of the biggest obstacles on this campus is that everybody assumes nothing is being done. So nothing begets nothing, and people are tired and become instantly fatigued when they think they have to start from zero." Time and again, diversity workers spoke of "uphill battles" with the administration and of feeling that their efforts were undervalued and often futile. Decentralization, then, bears responsibility for the Pessimist's understanding of everyday racism. Decentralization produces fatalism as race-conscious whites try to chip away at the existing power structure with little to no guidance or support from their institution.

TWENTY-FIRST-CENTURY DIVERSITY REGIMES AND HOLLOW RACE CONSCIOUSNESS

My analysis identifies five archetypes of white race consciousness: the Privilege Checker; the Problem Solver; the Cool Consumer; the Distant Observer; and the Pessimist. The differences between these archetypes are matters of kind, not degree. While these archetypes are by no means exhaustive, they are hegemonic—they shape the central qualities of all race-conscious identities and practices within the university setting.

Yet these archetypes cannot be understood outside of the organizational context within which they operate. Contemporary racial ideology exists in a dialectic relationship to social structure: it is socially constitutive of social structures and categories while at the same time shaped by and constrained by the very things it constructs (Fairclough 1993:64). The late sociologist Peter Hall reminds us that social organization cannot be understood apart from how it is enacted. Meanwhile, its very formation conditions that enactment (Hall and McGinty 2012:423). Diversity regimes are the result of larger discursive and social forces that minimize, deny, and subsequently reproduce the racial order within organizational spaces. Consciousness is not independent of social structure and action; it is constituted by it. In a vicious cycle, diversity regimes lead to hollow forms of race consciousness that minimize, evade, or deny existing racial inequality, ultimately entrenching it.

How can universities and other organizations committed to the ideals of multiculturalism and inclusivity avoid producing hollow race consciousness? First, universities and other organizations must reorganize their efforts around contesting racial inequality rather than around the more abstract principles of diversity and multiculturalism. This requires redefining diversity from a matter of generic human difference to one of racial equity. Second, there needs to be a fundamental realignment of departments, divisions, and resources, and racial equity must be centralized. Each department and division should be held accountable for demonstrating its steps toward racial equity. My research and the research of others finds that minority women and men perform a disproportionate amount of diversity work. Centralizing diversity work can lead to a more equitable division of labor as units with fewer racial and ethnic minorities can no longer "outsource" this labor or place its burden on one or two people of color.

Diversity programming also needs to reject benign celebrations of difference in favor of meaningful discussions on how power, resources, opportunities, and decision making are distributed. Instead of opportunities for human capital investment, diversity programming should offer opportunities for full campus involvement in realigning resources in order to meet the goals of racial equity. Universities can also tether their general education modules on multiculturalism to service-learning requirements, putting the ideals of racial equity into practice within the university and its surrounding communities. These suggestions can reorient the actions of faculty, students, and staff toward a critical race consciousness that recognizes the centrality of racial inequality in everyday life and also provide opportunities to contest it in everyday practice.

REFERENCES

Ahmed, Sara. 2012. *On Being Included: Racism and Diversity in Institutional Life*. Durham, NC: Duke University Press.

Anderson, Elijah. 2012. *The Cosmopolitan Canopy: Race and Civility in Everyday Life*. New York: W. W. Norton & Company.

Banton, Michael. 1997. *Ethnic and Racial Consciousness*. 2nd edition. London: Routledge.

Baudelaire, Charles. 1995. *The Painter of Modern Life and Other Essays*. 2nd edition. London: Phaidon Press.

Bell, Joyce M., and Douglas Hartmann. 2007. "Diversity in Everyday Discourse: The Cultural Ambiguities and Consequences of 'Happy Talk.'" *American Sociological Review* 72(6): 895–914.

Benjamin, Walter. 1997. *Charles Baudelaire: A Lyric Poet in the Era of High Capitalism*. Translated by Harry Zohn. London: Verso Books.

———. 2002. *The Arcades Project*. Translated by Howard Eiland and Kevin McLaughlin. 3rd edition. Cambridge, MA: Belknap Press.

Berrey, Ellen. 2011. "Why Diversity Became Orthodox in Higher Education, and How It Changed the Meaning of Race on Campus." *Critical Sociology* 37(5): 573–96.

Bonilla-Silva, Eduardo. 2013. *Racism without Racists: Color-Blind Racism and the Persistence of Racial Inequality in America*. 4th edition. Lanham, MD: Rowman & Littlefield.

Carnevale, Anthony P., and Jeff Strohl. 2013. "Separate and Unequal: How Higher Education Reinforces the Intergenerational Reproduction of White Racial Privilege." Washington, DC: Georgetown Public Policy Institute, Georgetown University.

Charmaz, Kathy. 2006. *Constructing Grounded Theory: A Practical Guide through Qualitative Analysis*. Thousand Oaks, CA: Sage.

Desmond, Matthew, and Carl Gershenson. 2016. "Housing and Employment Insecurity among the Working Poor." *Social Problems* 63(1): 46–67.

Dettling, Lisa, Joanne W. Hsu, Lindsay Jacobs, Kevin B. Moore, and Jeffrey P. Thompson. 2017. "Recent Trends in Wealth-Holding by Race and Ethnicity: Evidence from the Survey of Consumer Finances." FEDS Notes. Washington, DC: Board of Governors of the Federal Reserve System.

DiTomaso, Nancy, Rochelle Parks-Yancy, and Corinne Post. 2011. "White Attitudes toward Equal Opportunity and Affirmative Action." *Critical Sociology* 37(5): 615–29.

Doane, Ashley "Woody." 2014. "Shades of Colorblindness: Rethinking Racial Ideology in the United States." Pp. 15–38 in *The Colorblind Screen: Television in Post-Racial America*, edited by Sarah Nilsen and Sarah E. Turner. New York: NYU Press.

Du Bois, W. E. B. 1999. *Darkwater: Voices from within the Veil*. Mineola, NY: Dover.

Edelman, Lauren B., Sally Riggs Fuller, and Iona Mara-Drita. 2001. "Diversity Rhetoric and the Managerialization of Law." *American Journal of Sociology* 106(6): 1589–1641.

Embrick, David G. 2011. "The Diversity Ideology in the Business World: A New Oppression for a New Age." *Critical Sociology* 37(5): 541–56.

Fairclough, Norman. 1993. *Discourse and Social Change*. Cambridge: Polity Press.

Featherstone, Mike. 1998. "The Flâneur, the City, and Virtual Public Life." *Urban Studies* 35(5–6): 909–25.

Forman, Tyrone A. 2004. "Color-Blind Racism and Racial Indifference: The Role of Racial Apathy in Facilitating Enduring Inequalities." Pp. 43–66 in *The Changing Terrain of Race and Ethnicity*, edited by Maria Krysan and Amanda E. Lewis. New York: Russell Sage Foundation.

Frankenberg, Ruth. 1993. *White Women, Race Matters: The Social Construction of Whiteness*. London: Taylor & Francis.

Giroux, Henry. 1997. "Rewriting the Discourse of Racial Identity: Towards a Pedagogy and Politics of Whiteness." *Harvard Educational Review* 67(2): 285–321.

Giulianotti, Richard. 2002. "Supporters, Followers, Fans, and Flaneurs: A Taxonomy of Spectator Identities in Football." *Journal of Sport and Social Issues* 26(1): 25–46.

Gose, Ben. 2006. "The Rise of the Chief Diversity Officer." *Chronicle of Higher Education*, September 29, 2006.

Hall, Peter M. 1987. "Presidential Address: Interactionism and the Study of Social Organization." *Sociological Quarterly* 28(1): 1–22.

Hall, Peter M., and Patrick J. W. McGinty. 2012. "Social Organization across Space and Time: The Policy Process, Mesodomain Analysis, and Breadth of Perspective." Pp. 421–37 in *The Meta-Power Paradigm: Impacts and Transformations of Agents, Institutions, and Social Systems—Capitalism, State, and Democracy in a Global Context*, edited by Tom R. Burns and Peter M. Hall. New York: Peter Lang.

Hartigan, John. 2008. "Establishing the Fact of Whiteness." *American Anthropologist* 99(3): 495–505.

Hartmann, Douglas. 2015. "Reflections on Race, Diversity, and the Crossroads of Multiculturalism." *Sociological Quarterly* 56(4): 623–39.

Hartmann, Douglas, and Joyce M. Bell. 2011. "Race-Based Critical Theory and the 'Happy Talk' of Diversity in America." Pp. 259–77 in *Illuminating Social Life: Classical and Contemporary Theory Revisited*, 5th edition, edited by Peter Kivisto. Los Angeles, CA: Sage.

Harvey, David. 2009. *Social Justice and the City*. Athens: University of Georgia Press.

McDermott, Monica, and Frank L. Samson. 2005. "White Racial and Ethnic Identity in the United States." *Annual Review of Sociology* 31(1): 245–61.

Melamed, Jodi. 2011. *Represent and Destroy: Rationalizing Violence in the New Racial Capitalism*. Minneapolis: University of Minnesota Press.

Myers, Kristen. 2005. *Racetalk: Racism Hiding in Plain Sight*. Lanham, MD: Rowman & Littlefield.

Nelson, Jacqueline K., Kevin M. Dunn, and Yin Paradies. 2011. "Bystander Anti-Racism: A Review of the Literature." *Analyses of Social Issues and Public Policy* 11(1): 263–84.

Newfield, Christopher. 2011. *Unmaking the Public University: The Forty-Year Assault on the Middle Class*. Cambridge, MA: Harvard University Press.

O'Brien, Eileen. 2001. *Whites Confront Racism: Antiracists and Their Paths to Action*. Lanham, MD: Rowman & Littlefield.

Omi, Michael, and Howard Winant. 2014. *Racial Formation in the United States*. 3rd edition. New York: Routledge.

Reardon, Sean F., and Ann Owens. 2014. "60 Years after Brown: Trends and Consequences of School Segregation." *Annual Review of Sociology* 40(1): 199–218.

Ryan, William. 1976. *Blaming the Victim*. New York: Vintage.

Shapiro, Thomas, Tatjana Meschede, and Sam Osoro. 2013. "The Roots of the Widening Racial Wealth Gap: Explaining the Black-White Economic Divide." Waltham, MA: Institute on Assets and Social Policy, Brandeis University.

Strmic-Pawl, Hephzibah V. 2015. "More Than a Knapsack: The White Supremacy Flower as a New Model for Teaching Racism." *Sociology of Race and Ethnicity* 1(1): 192–97.

Sturm, Susan P. 2007. "The Architecture of Inclusion: Interdisciplinary Insights on Pursuing Institutional Citizenship." *Harvard Journal of Law and Gender* 30 (October): 409–24.

Taylor, Jared. 2011. *White Identity: Racial Consciousness in the Twenty-First Century*. Oakton, VA: New Century Books.

Thomas, James M. 2018. "Diversity Regimes and Racial Inequality: A Case Study of Diversity University." *Social Currents* 5(2): 140–56.

———. 2019. "The Economization of Diversity." *Sociology of Race and Ethnicity* 5(4): 471–85.

Weick, Karl E. 1976. "Educational Organizations as Loosely Coupled Systems." *Administrative Science Quarterly* 21(1): 1–19.

———. 1982. "Administering Education in Loosely Coupled Schools." *Phi Delta Kappan* 63(10): 673–76.

Wilder, Craig Steven. 2013. *Ebony and Ivy: Race, Slavery, and the Troubled History of America's Universities*. New York: Bloomsbury.

PART II

THE REENTRENCHMENT OF WHITE SUPERIORITY IN AMERICAN INSTITUTIONS

CHAPTER 5

INSTITUTIONAL RACISM REVISITED

How Institutions Perpetuate and Promote Racism through Color Blindness

CHARLES A. GALLAGHER

WE ARE LIVING in extremely paradoxical times regarding race and race relations in the United States. The rise in overt racism by neo-Nazis, white nationalists, and right-wing extremist groups under the banner of Alt-Right has emerged at a time when color blindness, which is understood ideologically as a shorthand for perceived racial equality, is now the national narrative of race relations. Overt racism in speech and action and the view that we are now a color-blind society share the same stage in the media and American political and cultural life. While this color-blind ideological perspective has been decades in the making and has been researched extensively (Gallagher 2003, 2015; Doane 2014; Forman and Lewis 2015; Moore 2008), what is different today is that color blindness as a way of framing race relations is now a thoroughly embedded narrative in all of our nation's institutions.

In 1954 the Supreme Court's *Brown v. Board of Education* decision made the doctrine of "separate but unequal" unconstitutional and charged our nation's institutions the following year with integrating our public schools with "all deliberate speed." To segregate children by color and subject them to unequal educational resources and, by extension, to deny any societal resources by race was, as Supreme Court Justice Earl Warren told America in 1954, "inherently unequal." While this educational mandate and goal were never achieved because public schools continue to be extremely segregated

(Orfield and Frankenberg 2014), what did take root was a narrative of *aspirational* color blindness that would become our national story line on race relations. This first wave of color blindness was ostensibly embedded in the aspirational ideals of classic Lockean political liberalism, in which society is obliged to afford equal rights to all individuals regardless of group membership. By the 1950s, color blindness was a bold societal assertion, suggesting that all men and women are created equal. It was also extremely well timed, with the triumph over fascism in World War II, the rise of the modern civil rights movement, and the geopolitics of the cold war making this mantra of race-based equality exceptionally appealing as a national narrative in the United States and abroad.

Among moderates and those who believed in the principle of color blindness, the narrative transformed once it became evident that to address centuries of embedded institutional racism, the government would need to use *group* membership as the mechanism to address racial inequality. The glaring economic and social inequities between whites and people of color could be made "whole" again only by taking group membership into account and reallocating resources along racial lines. The call to integrate public schools and public facilities (such as pools, parks, and recreational centers); civil rights legislation to end discrimination in voting, housing, and jobs; the heated debates around "forced" busing; and affirmative action policies were all by definition group-based racial projects (Omi and Winant 1994) intended rectify past wrongs.

However, moving from the ideal of equality to the actual dismantling of institutional racism was short lived and met resistance from multiple constituencies from the start, most notably from Dixiecrats and those who wished to maintain the white supremacist status quo. Color blindness was an aspiration that all people in the abstract should be treated equally but morphed quickly into a belief that using race to remedy past injustices was, in and of itself, racist. This sacrosanct sentiment of individual over group rights is summed up by US Supreme Court Justice Clarence Thomas before his appointment. In 1991, Thomas stated, "America was founded on a philosophy of individual rights, not group rights. I believe in compensation for actual [victims of discrimination but] not for people whose only claim to victimization is that they are members of a historically oppressed group" (cited in Swain 2002:164). A zero-sum game was born in which whites came to see themselves as the victims of antiwhite bias. Color blindness today has mutated into an ideological narrative that claims "reverse racism," commonly understood to mean discrimination against whites, because racial groups matter in understanding inequality.

Over the last decades, color blindness has gone from an ideal to a normative, formalized practice embedded in every major institution's organizational structure. This ideological perspective shapes how institutions perceive, construct, articulate, and disseminate the widely held belief that racial equality has been achieved in the United States. Institutional color blindness is the guiding principle that structures the mission and culture of organizations and that connects workers to, and ideologically embeds them in, the organizational goals of the institution where they work, are schooled, are entertained, worship, or read or view current events. Each institution has its own internal logic and discursive practices that create, establish, support, and justify the belief that racist acts are aberrations or anomalies and that color blindness is organizationally normative.

Today, a primary reason whites so readily embrace a color-blind narrative, as indicated in numerous surveys on racial attitudes and perceptions of mobility, is that most major institutions provide variations on some theme of color blindness. Each institution has its own ideological message, mission statement, vocabulary, and tropes that normalize how and why our nation has achieved color blindness and describe the role the institution has had in that narrative. Whites have been socialized into color blindness through their connections to and involvement in the institutions they inhabit. While the institutional logics and story lines vary among and often within specific institutions (legislation, the courts, mass media, education, corporations, and so on), the overarching narrative is that institutional racism no longer plays a role in reducing life chances, limiting socioeconomic mobility, or discriminating against racial minorities. However, colorblindness in institutions could hurt whites if misused or abused.

WHITE RACIAL FRAMES AND MISSING RACISTS

Wingfield and Feagin point out that "the dominant form of racial framing that typically comes through in the U.S. media, schools, and other institutions is a solid and well-legitimated *white racial frame*" (2012:144). Eduardo Bonilla-Silva's theory of "color-blind racism" with its four theoretical frames understands contemporary racial oppression as an ideology that "rationalizes the status of minorities as the product of market dynamics, naturally occurring phenomena, and their alleged cultural deficiencies" (Bonilla-Silva and Dietrich 2011:191). Abstract liberalism, naturalization, cultural racism, and the minimization of racism are Bonilla-Silva's (2014) ideological principles that explain how and why whites see a meritocratic system for all regardless of race and the cultural and political cover whites use to reject any challenges to white privilege.

What appears to be different now, if one is to take polling data at face value, is a majority of whites do believe that the United States is a meritocracy, that white privilege is in the past, and that racism, regardless of what appears on YouTube, reflects the sentiments of an unrepresentative white fringe. Bonilla-Silva and Feagin's theories of "racism without racists" and "white racial frames" are incredibly accurate anchors of how whites now frame race relations and whites' ability to claim that racial inequality is the result of nonexistent or race-neutral factors. Also, what is different today is that a sizable part of the white population truly believes this last point: that race no longer shapes life chances even though every objective, empirical record shows otherwise.

Today, the view that racial inequality is the result of nonracial factors is not a dodge to maintain white privilege or a knowing, sarcastic, white-to-white wink to preserve white supremacy or dismiss racial discrimination. This type of color-blind racism, one where whites' views of society are decoupled from what is happening throughout America, is the result of being steeped in institutions where color blindness is endorsed as a crucial, well-articulated, and central position. Daily, whether it is in church, at school, during work hours, interacting with social media, or watching a Netflix series, whites are endlessly bombarded with various versions of how and why the US is now a color-blind nation. Most white Americans already mistakenly believe that they are a numerical minority (Gallagher 2015), and within this space, right-wing political rhetoric tells white America that they are under siege by immigrants and people of color. For many white Americans, President Trump is "taking back America" and presumably giving it back to white people. There is no shortage of successful people of color whites can point out to affirm their view that we are a color-blind nation. Indeed, the Obama presidency cemented the color-blind narrative in the white imagination since a black man was able to reach the US presidency.

Now, Trump has emboldened some whites to evoke their color as both a badge of honor and the cause of their perceived socioeconomic oppression. Those animated by racism draw on color blindness to promote identity politics grounded in white resentment and economic loss. This group believes that discrimination against whites is as big a problem as discrimination against racial minorities. Many racist whites believe that racial minorities stand equally to whites in the eyes of the law and access to employment and public resources. For many of these "color blinders," not only is institutional racism a practice of the past but race politics and "political correctness" have swung the pendulum too far left. They believe that accommodating the demands of racial minorities has led to whites being subject to institutional racism and discrimination, even though according to the idea of color blindness, being white (or any race) should not matter (Norton and Sommers 2011).

Individuals are embedded in various institutions and are socialized into norms and ideologies of color blindness through constant, repetitious institutional exposure. These institutions deploy the idea of color blindness in different ways across various social settings for similar ideological and instrumental purposes. The result is, however, the same. The color-blind narrative coming out of these institutions frames institutional racism and white privilege as nonexistent while presenting race as a benign and neutral social category. This chapter examines how we arrived at this particular moment and briefly summarizes the role institutions play in maintaining and promoting a color-blind view of race relations, specifically in the context of the courts, and suggests future lines of research.

MIXED MESSAGES: COLOR BLINDNESS AS THE NEW NORM AS RACISM INCREASES

On the one hand, overt acts of racism are on the rise. According the Center for the Study of Hate and Extremism, hate crimes in the nation's ten largest cities increased by over 12 percent in 2017 (Levin and Reitzel 2018). Surfing YouTube produces hundreds of uploaded acts of racist violence by whites against people of color. These videos include racist and xenophobic rants by whites at Walmart; politicians, teachers, and preachers caught off guard using racist slurs; racist road rage incidents; and, tragically, white officers shooting unarmed black men. One can watch the spectacle of hate that played out in Charlottesville, Virginia, as neo-Nazis and white separatists came together at a "Unite the Right" rally, wearing their Nazi outfits, carrying tiki torches, and chanting, "Jews will not replace us." The rally culminated with James Alex Fields Jr. mowing down Heather Heyer with his car as she demonstrated against the white supremacists.

The modern version of the panopticon evident through a cell phone camera has brought these horrific images to the world, actions that many whites in the past would have denied or discounted as one-off acts of racism that do not reflect white majority behaviors. Cell phones have also brought to light the practice where whites call 911 (the police) when people of color use public spaces that whites believe are the exclusive domain of whites. "Living while black" is now a familiar media exploit of black folks trying to go about their business—at Starbucks, golfing, barbecuing, and so on—and having the police called on them. The perspective of the whites engaging in this behavior is that black people have no right to be in this public (white) space and thus must be up to some criminal or socially disruptive activities. The sociologist Elijah Anderson tried to explain this occurrence: "When the anonymous black person enters the white space, others there immediately try to make sense of him or her—to figure out 'who that is,' or to gain a sense of the nature of the person's business and whether [the whites] need to be concerned" (2015:13). Thus, the presence of someone black or brown becomes a cause for "concern," even if the presence is a routine and normal behavior such as pushing a child in a stroller or leaving an Airbnb lodging. Given the hundreds of cell phone–recorded instances of racist behavior shown over and over in the media, why do white Americans not yet acknowledge these acts of racist violence as a sign that our society is still quite racist?

But they do not. This view that racism still infects many parts of society and the countervailing belief that we have transcended race is evident in nationally representative polling data. For example, a 2015 CNN poll found that 81 percent of whites believed that blacks have as good a chance of getting a job as whites, 43 percent that most or all of the goals of the civil rights movement had been achieved, and close to half, 49 percent, that the criminal justice system treats whites and blacks equally (Struyk 2017). A Pew study in 2016 also found that although a majority of whites (53 percent) believe that "our country needs to continue making changes to give blacks equal rights with whites," close to four out of ten (38 percent) believe that the country has already made the changes "to give blacks equal rights with whites." This Pew study also found that a significant number of white Americans (41 percent) believe that "too much" attention is paid to race relations in our country. An NBC poll found that a majority of whites (59 percent) believe that people are *not* judged by the color of their skin.

An additional twist to the situation has been ushered in by decades of believing in color blindness. While much of white America has come to believe that "Jim Crow" racism has significantly decreased, a sizable number of whites (57 percent) in a 2015 poll by the Public Religion Research Institute believe that "discrimination against whites is as big a problem as discrimination against blacks and other minorities." In other words, white Americans view themselves as the new target of American racism. The 2016 study by Pew found that 70 percent of whites viewed discrimination as based on individual prejudice while only 19 percent felt that it was "built into laws and institutions." As an ideological position regarding the nature of US race relations, color blindness is "the tendency to claim that racial equality is the norm, while simultaneously ignoring or discounting the real and ongoing ways in which institutional racism continues to disadvantage racial minorities . . . and reflects the fact that most whites, as expressed in national polling data, now view race as a benign social marker that has little or no bearing on an individual's or group's educational, economic or occupational mobility" (Gallagher 2015:40). This position is not to suggest that white people do not see color. Color is the reason whites call 911 when racial minorities occupy "white spaces." Color is part of the equation when whites decide to live in all-white neighborhoods; color determines who ascends to the upper ranks of management. Race continues to matter for the everyday decisions large and small that whites make, but color blindness, from the white perspective, means that race plays a minimal role, if any, in racial minorities' social standing or treatment in society.

This color-blind perspective is especially true for younger Americans who see nothing but successful people of color throughout their media consumption. In 2019, traditional-aged college students were raised in a climate full of societal cognitive dissonance, where color blindness and outright racism inhabit the same social space but where the conflict between these two narratives tends to gravitate toward color blindness. The formative years of most college students had them watching, listening to, and being led by a president who was black and the first African American to hold this office. Eight years of a black man running the executive branch of government set in motion a cultural narrative in social media, the press, and among conservative opinion makers that the United States had entered into an era of color blindness and postracism. A 2014 survey found that 64 percent of white millennials "believe that having a Black President demonstrates that racial minority groups have the same opportunity as white people" (DBR 2014).

As color blindness became the established story line for race, young people were also watching extreme depictions of racist violence. The typical twenty-year-old today, thanks to a 24/7 news cycle and ubiquitous social media, watched over and over the death of, to name just a few, Laquan McDonald, Eric Garner, Sean Bell, and Michael Brown, all black men killed by the police. They have watched race riots take place in Ferguson, Missouri, in 2014, Baltimore, Maryland, in 2015, and Milwaukie, Wisconsin, in 2016. In 2015, ninety-three unarmed individuals were killed by the police, and thirty-seven of them were black men (Lowery 2016)—a percentage far higher than their percentage in the US population. College students today came of age seeing the rise of the Black Lives Matter movement, a social protest that emerged to bring public attention to police brutality and systemic racism. However, this has had little to no impact on young American views of institutional racism. For example, white millennials polled suggested that racism is wrong and is a problem in today's society. However, like older generations, they also believe that it is significant problem for both whites and people of color (Hobbes 2019). Therefore, rather than recognizing the discord between the rise of white supremacy and its promotion of color blindness, white America routinely discounts institutional racism and privileges a narrative of color blindness in that it is now everyone's problem, not just something that plagues people of color.

BRINGING INSTITUTIONS AND INSTITUTIONAL RACISM BACK IN

The question now should be why color blindness is so pervasive as to cloud views of racism. I contend that the institutional narratives that whites have been socialized into throughout much of their lives have color blindness as the common denominator. Each institution in the United States has now some version of color blindness that undergirds its organizational mission. The judicial system, media, corporate America, our public schools, and the entertainment industry all embrace some version of color-blind race neutrality through their mission statements and institutional practices. These views structure the organizations' mission and culture and connect and ideologically embed workers to the goals of the institution where they work. For example, it may take the form of discussions about diversity, or calling itself an inclusive institution, or appeals to equality by chief diversity officers, or corporate mission statements affirming a commitment to diversity and inclusion so that they can, in many ways, be current and attract all people to their product offerings. While each institution plays a role in socializing whites into color blindness, I focus the rest of this chapter primarily on the role of the courts.

Color Blindness in Court

Race scholars have examined how institutions use color-blind racist practices to maintain the white spaces and racial status quo in law schools (Evans and Moore 2015; Moore 2008), public high schools (Lewis and Diamond 2015), political discourse (López 2013; Wingfield and Feagin 2012; Gallagher 2015), the Internet (Daniels 2015), television news (Shah and Yagagami 2015), and immigration (Douglas, Saenz, and Murga 2015). This list is far from exhaustive. However, when one steps back and looks at this web of color-blind narratives, what becomes obvious is that these institutions are all using similar color-blind scripts. The courts are perhaps the most important institution to shape the general contours and provide the ideological language of America's color-blind narrative, particularly how the Supreme Court has framed color blindness through the tenets of race neutrality.

One can draw a line from Justice John Marshall Harlan's dissent in *Plessy v. Ferguson* in 1886, the case that affirmed the doctrine of "separate but equal," to the *Brown* decision in 1954, delivered by Chief Justice Earl Warren. Justice Harlan wrote in his dissent on *Plessy*, "our Constitution is colorblind and neither knows nor tolerates classes among citizens.... The law regards man as man and takes no account of his surroundings or of his color when his civil rights as guaranteed by the supreme law of the land are involved." Justice Warren concluded "that in the field of public education the doctrine of 'separate but equal' has no place. Separate educational facilities are inherently unequal." These ideals of an aspirational color blindness were voiced at time when lynchings, Jim Crow statutes, and institutional racism defined US race relations. Between 1877 and 1950 there were 3,959 lynchings in twelve southern states. If the *Brown* decision and the civil rights legislation of the 1960s could be viewed as a pivot toward a color-blind nation where equal opportunity was afforded to all, it was in reality a pivot in name only and was extremely short lived. In 1964 Barry Goldwater honed the idea of a color blindness that was blind to using race to remedy racial inequality by stating, "It has been well-said that the Constitution is color-blind ... and so it is just as wrong to compel children to attend certain schools for the sake of so-called integration as for the sake of segregation" (qtd. in López 2013:85).

Color blindness as a narrative continued to morph ideologically to where using race as a legal remedy to racial inequality gets defined as a form of racism. *Regents of the University of California v. Bakke* overturned racial admissions quotas in higher education, and subsequent cases also embraced race "neutrality." The role of race in admissions has been diminished and is now subject to constant debate where its use must be very narrowly tailored. We now inhabit a time when the courts view any use of race as a violation of the sacrosanct belief that all matters of social and political life be race neutral. Ian Haney López argues that in the 1978 *Bakke* decision, Justice Powell essentially argued that "the constitutional harm occurred the moment the government took express notice of race ... if the state expressly mentioned race—common almost exclusively in affirmative action programs—then the Court would review the legislation with extreme skepticism" (2013:87). Some twenty years later, *Hopwood v. Texas* (1996) basically took race out of the admissions equation altogether because its use was viewed as a form of "reverse discrimination." López concludes that color blindness redefined was "quick to condemn all corrective uses of race, but blind to racial discrimination against minorities" (2013:87).

The Supreme Court, particularly under John Roberts, has taken a race-neutral—that is, a color-blind—approach to all matters of law and is loath to make remedies that attempt to address social problems at the group level. We are witnessing a retreat from race in the Supreme Court that is simply unprecedented, as indicated by Chief Justice Roberts's vapid, ahistorical, and tone-deaf observation regarding school integration. He argues in the 2007 *Parents Involved* decision that "the way to stop discrimination on the basis of race is to stop discriminating on the basis of race." Race neutrality—that is, color blindness—is thought of as the norm, and data showing race-based inequities are simply a byproduct of past wrongs that have been righted. The 2013 ruling that invalidated preclearance conditions in the Voting Rights Act on the grounds that racial parity in southern federal districts had been achieved is one example of how color blindness is used to frame current race relations. Justice Roberts's observation that the act's voting provisions had been "based on 40-year-old facts having no logical relationship to the present day" suggests that racism in the form of voter suppression in the South is over; color-blind egalitarianism has been achieved, and to maintain preclearance, as Justice Scalia suggested, is a form of "racial entitlement." In the 2013 decision, which eviscerated the Voting Rights Act, Chief Justice Roberts summed up the move to a color-blind perspective by writing, "Our country has changed." As Justice Roberts saw it, voting discrimination and voter suppression were actions of the past.

Describing how color blindness is a "founding fantasy of modern American law," legal scholar Sora Han argues that this "fantasy of colorblindness is essential to maintaining a constitutional split between the social particularities of civil rights and the declaration of universal equality founding American democracy . . . [it] both confounds and gives language to a national desire to make general assessments about the direction of legal reform" (2015:1). The sociologist and legal scholar Wendy Moore makes a similar observation in her analysis of white spaces in elite law schools. She writes, "The post–civil rights legal frame, which is based on abstract liberalism that confines racial analysis to the level of the individual completely disconnected from the racial social structure, has stalled the progressive legal reforms that may have dismantled white supremacy" (Moore 2008:29). This disconnection from existing racial structures, and the decoupling of whites from seeing or acknowledging the structural reasons for ongoing racial inequality, is exactly what makes institutional color blindness so pernicious and malignant. Indeed, the disconnect has become easier, to quote Bonilla-Silva's idea of having "racism without racists," because the instructional structures have become so sophisticated and routinized at endlessly promoting a narrative of color blindness that most whites now believe that any real aspects of racism, particularly at the institutional level, are gone. Moreover, when racism comes back from the "dead," then it is probably because of "old" white racists holding on to the past, or racism is out to attack a new target that includes whites.

CONCLUSIONS

Color blindness is a story line told over and over in most parts of the media while race riots rage and white supremacy groups are on the rise. This is the social paradox I referenced in the opening: a nation ostensibly moving toward color blindness while racist and xenophobic acts throughout the country happen with greater frequency. The largely false premise that occupational mobility is now the same for everyone regardless of race (or gender, religion, or sexual orientation) and that institutionalized racism and discrimination is a practice of the past has become the new narrative of race relations in the United States. Color blindness as a way of seeing and understanding race relations and the racial hierarchy that continues to allocate resources based on color rests on certain core beliefs that have their root in cherished American ideals.

There are then two competing narratives about how far we have come in relation to racial equality and social mobility in the United States. We live in a country that is increasingly multiracial and multiethnic, but our institutions are disproportionately white. As of 2016 the non-Hispanic white population in the United States was 62 percent. All things being equal—that is, if the playing field were truly level—we should see major institutions staffed and controlled with numbers that reflect the US population. In other words, whites should be in control of no more than 62 percent of the organizations and institutions that reflect power, prestige, and avenues to wealth. What we see, however, is that whites are still vastly overrepresented in the halls of power and in the most desirable occupations; in 2016, 83 percent of the US Congress was white, as were 90 percent of all elected officials, 95 percent of all elected prosecutors, 96 percent of all Fortune 500 CEOs, 75 percent of all doctors, 87 percent of all college presidents, and 82 percent of full and 75 percent of associate professors. We are at a crossroads regarding race relations that is unlike any other in American history. There is a belief, borne out in many examples, that people of color are making great strides. Compared to a hundred years ago, this is true. But on many social and economic fronts, progress has stalled, and in some instances, like school integration, it has actually reversed. We have a vision of our nation, one that neatly conforms to a deeply held conviction on equality, that coexists with systemic institutionalized racism and, most recently, the rise of far-right political and social movements.

REFERENCES

Anderson, Elijah. 2015. "The White Space." *Sociology of Race and Ethnicity* 1(1): 10–21.
Bonilla-Silva. 2014. *Racism without Racists: Color-Blind Racism and the Persistence of Racial Inequality in America*. Lanham, MD: Rowman & Littlefield.
Bonilla-Silva, Eduardo, and David Dietrich. 2011."The Sweet Enchantment of Color-Blind Racism in Obamerica." *Annals of the American Academy of Political and Social Science* 634: 190–206.
Clement, Scott. 2017. *Millennials Are Just as Racist as Their Parents. Washington Post*, April 7.
Daniels, Jessie. 2015. "My Brain Database Doesn't See Skin Color": Color-Blind Racism in the Technology Industry and in Theorizing the Web." *American Behavior Scientist* 59(11): 1377–93.
DBR. 2014. "MTV Bias Survey." [San Francisco]: David Binder Research.
Doane, Ashley. 2014. "Shades of Colorblindness: Rethinking Racial Ideology in the United States." Pp. 15–38 in *The Colorblind Screen: Television in Post-Racial America*, edited by Sarah Nilsen and Sarah Turner. New York: NYU Press.
Douglas, Karen Manges, Rogelio Saenz, and Aurella Lorena Murga. 2015. "Immigration in the Era of Color-Blind Racism." *American Behavioral Scientist*: 1429–51.
Dover, Tessa L., Brenda Major, and Cheryl R. Kaiser. 2016. "Diversity Policies Rarely Make Companies Fairer, and They Feel Threatening to White Men." *Harvard Business Review*, January 4.
Evans, Louwanda, and Wendy Leo Moore. 2015. "Impossible Burdens: White Institutions, Emotional Labor, and Micro-Resistance." *Social Problems* 62: 439–54.
Forman, Tyrone A., and Amanda E. Lewis. 2015. "Beyond Prejudice? Young Whites' Racial Attitudes in Post–Civil Rights America, 1976 to 2000." *American Behavior Scientist* 59(11): 1394–1428.
Gallagher, Charles. 2003. "Color-Blind Privilege: The Social and Political Functions of Erasing the Color Line in Post-Race America." *Race, Gender and Class* 10(4): 22–37.
———. 2010. "In-Between Racial Status, Mobility and the Promise of Assimilation: Irish, Italians Yesterday, Latinos and Asians Today." Pp. 10–21 in *Multiracial Americans and Social Class: The Influence of Social Class on Racial Identity*, edited by Kathleen Korgen. New York: Routledge.

———. 2015. "Color-Blind Egalitarianism as the New Racial Norm." Pp. 40–56 in *Theories of Race and Ethnicity: Contemporary Debates and Perspectives*, edited by Karim Murji and John Solomos. Cambridge, UK: Cambridge University Press.

Gallup. 2018. "Race Relations." In Depth: Topics A to Z. Retrieved May 12, 2020 (https://news.gallup.com/poll/1687/race-relations.aspx).

Han, Sora Y. 2015. *Letters of the Law: The Fantasy of Colorblindness in American Law*. Stanford, CA: Stanford University Press.

Hartmann, Douglas, Paul R. Croll, Ryan Larson, Joseph Gerteis, and Alex Manning. 2017. "Colorblindness as Identity: Key Determinants, Relations to Ideology, and Implications for Attitudes about Race and Policy." *Sociological Perspectives* 60(5): 866–88.

Hobbes, Michael. 2019. "Turns Out White Millennials Are Just as Conservative as Their Parents." *Huffpost*, June 2.

Hughley, Matthew W., David G. Embrick, and Ashley "Woody" Doane. 2015. "Paving the Way for Future Race Research: Exploring the Racial Mechanisms within a Color-Blind, Racialized Social System." *American Behavioral Scientist* 59(11): 1347–57.

Levin, Brian, and John David Reitzel. 2018. "Report to the Nation: Hate Crimes Rise in U.S. Cities and Counties in Time of Division and Foreign Interference." May. Center for the Study of Hate & Extremism, California State University, San Bernardino.

Lewis, Amanda, and John Diamond. 2015. *Despite the Best Intentions: How Racial Inequality Thrives in Good Schools*. New York: Oxford University Press.

López, Ian Haney. 2013. *Dog Whistle Politics: How Coded Racial Appeals Have Reinvented Racism and Wrecked the Middle Class*. New York: Oxford University Press.

Lowery, Wesley. 2016. "Study Finds Police Fatally Shoot Unarmed Black Men at Disproportionate Rates." *Washington Post*, April 7.

Moore, Wendy. 2008. *Reproducing Racism: White Space, Elite Law Schools, and Racial Inequality*. New York: Rowman & Littlefield.

Mueller, Jennifer C. 2017. "Producing Colorblindness: Everyday Mechanisms of White Ignorance." *Social Problems* 64: 219–38.

Norton, Michael, and Samuel Sommers. 2011. "Whites See Racism as a Zero-Sum Game That They Are Now Losing." *Perspectives on Psychological Science* 6(3): 215–18.

Omi, Michael, and Howard Winant. 1994. *Racial Formation in the United States: From the 1960s to the 1990s*. New York: Routledge.

Orfield, Gary, and Erika Frankenberg, with Jongyeon Ee and John Kuscera. 2014. "Brown at 60: Great Progress, a Long Retreat, and an Uncertain Future." The Civil Rights Project, University of California Los Angeles.

Pew Research Center. 2016. "Views of Race Relations." In *On Views of Race and Inequality, Blacks and Whites Are Worlds Apart*. June 27. Retrieved January 19, 2019 (http://www.pewsocialtrends.org/2016/06/27/2-views-of-race-relations/).

Shah, Hemant, and Mai Yamagami. 2015. "Color Blind Racism in Television News and Commentary: The Redemption of Shirley Sherrod." *Howard Journal of Communications* 26: 193–205.

Struyk, Ryan. 2017. "Blacks and Whites See Racism in the United States Very, Very Differently." CNN Politics Data, August 18. Retrieved January 19, 2019 (https://www.cnn.com/2017/08/16/politics/blacks-white-racism-united-states-polls/index.html).

Swain, Carol. 2002. *The New White Nationalism in America*. Cambridge: Cambridge University Press.

Wingfield, Adia Harvey, and Joe Feagin. 2012. "The Racial Dialectic: President Barack Obama and the White Racial Frame." *Qualitative Sociology* 35: 143–62.

CHAPTER 6

PRISON IN THE STREET

What Market-Based Bipartisan Reform Means for Racial Stratification

KASEY HENRICKS AND BETHANY NELSON

WHAT DO BARACK OBAMA and Donald Trump, two opposing political figures, have in common? Both agree the US criminal justice system is broken. In his last few days of public office, President Obama (2017) advanced a fifty-five-page case for criminal justice reform in the *Harvard Law Review*, highlighting how the executive branch can promote prison alternatives and touting his own use of clemency power to commute prison sentences. More than a year of "law and order" rhetoric later, even President Trump was making good on Obama's recommendations. In June 2018, for example, he authorized the release of a sixty-three-year-old woman, Alice Marie Johnson, who was serving a life sentence for a nonviolent drug conviction and whom her warden described as having been a model prisoner for two decades (BBC 2018). Trump has further endorsed legislation that permits prisoners to finish their sentences under house arrest so long as they complete rehabilitation programs (the First Step Act) and stated he would overrule any efforts of the then attorney general Jeff Sessions to hinder prison reform (see George 2018).

An emerging bipartisan coalition has the potential to reverse America's status as the world's leader in incarceration, inspiring some analysts to believe that a new era of prison reform is within reach (e.g., Dagan and Teles 2016; Green 2015), but how is such a coalition possible during a moment of profound political polarization? Democrats and Republicans can hardly agree on any political issue, whether that be race and discrimination, the social safety net, immigration and border control, same-sex marriage, tax reform, or global warming and environmental regulation, to name a few. According to the Pew Research Center (2017), Democrats and Republicans disagree so deeply on these issues that the magnitude of this party divide is much larger than other demographic differences like education, religion, gender, age, and even race and has only grown larger under the presidency of Donald Trump.

When it comes to the politics of prison reform, stances between parties are often treated as a conflict with clearly defined battle lines. Liberals are framed as preferring policies that are lenient and rehabilitative, whereas conservatives are associated with "get tough" stances on crime and punishment (Murakawa 2014). This kind of Manichaean framing paints clear boundaries as though partisan stances are fixed and oppositional. Under these circumstances, the commonalities that bind them together—which reflect the totalizing features of broader ideologies rooted in social categories like race—become unquestioned, overlooked, and taken for granted (Bonilla-Silva 2003). Identifying these commonalities, however, helps clarify how a bipartisan coalition is possible. As the sociologist Amanda Lewis explains, it helps clarify how differently positioned social actors, ranging from "golf-club-membership-owning executives, suburban soccer moms, urban hillbillies, antiracist skinheads, and/or union-card-carrying factory workers," come together in politico-historical moments to promote shared interests (2004:634).

What explains the conservative-liberal convergence when it comes to the divisive issue of prison reform? We argue that a market-inspired racial project, one that centers around public finance, holds some answers. By the concept "racial project," we draw from Michael Omi and Howard Winant to mean *"simultaneously an interpretation, representation, or explanation of racial dynamics, and an effort to reorganize and redistribute resources along particular racial lines"* (1994 [1986]:56, emphasis original). Posing questions like "What kind of returns do prisons have for public investment?," liberals and conservatives embrace a market framework to problematize "mass imprisonment" as though it is a business failure—one that is deeply racialized. Similar to narratives of welfare racism, where government expenditures seen as disproportionately spent on people of color are framed as costly, inefficient initiatives paid out of pocket by whites' "hard-earned tax dollars" (see Sears and Citrin 1982), both sides claim that entirely too many taxpayer dollars are "wasted" on an ineffective corrections system.

In this chapter, we narrow our analysis to arguments advanced by the liberal American Civil Liberties Union (ACLU) and the conservative Right on Crime (RoC) movement on their official websites, www.aclu.org/issues/mass-incarceration and http://rightoncrime.com. The ACLU and RoC are suitable focal points because each is emblematic of criminal justice reforms advanced across the partisan spectrum, and both have high-profile signatories within the Democratic and Republican Parties. The ACLU has a long-standing liberal history, having been formed shortly after World War I to safeguard civil liberties during the Red Scare. The RoC movement was formed in 2010 by the Texas Public Policy Foundation in conjunction with the American Conservative Union Foundation and Prison Fellowship. Despite the fact that the ACLU and RoC tend to be associated with different political parties, we identify patterned ways these organizations share common market logics to advance prison reforms that have deep implications for racial inequality.

We argue that the market-driven logics these organizations deploy around prison reform indicate proactive, strategic, and seemingly race-neutral policies that expand the carceral state and entrench white racial domination within social institutions. Dividing our analysis into three parts, we first show that both organizations portray prisons as a wasteful but necessary expression of punishment that holds criminality accountable. Second, we find that labels of deservingness for alternative forms of justice are coded attempts to expand new forms of surveillance. Finally, we posit that justice policies centered around personal responsibility and costliness place an undue burden on those in the justice system.

PRISON AS A NECESSARY EXPRESSION OF PUNISHMENT

While liberals and conservatives may concede that prisons are flawed, we suggest that both still see prisons as occupying a virtuous place in the public imagination. It is a place of justifiable punishment for a broad range of unlawful misdeeds, reserved for the undesirables of America, people who are frequently seen without sympathy or compassion through a lens of racial threat (Beckett, Reosti, and Knaphus 2016).

Part of the reason organizations like the ACLU and RoC see prisons as a justifiable modality of punishment, we contend, is that they take for granted the category of crime. Both organizations treat crime as though it is an objective state of deviance. Rather than reflect on the underlying factors that lead to only some actions being labeled as criminal, and how what is labeled as criminal changes over time, we observe that the ACLU and RoC narrow their focus to what occurs after someone becomes involved with the justice system. What these organizations label as punishable crime is not seen as what the criminologist Michael Hallett describes as "a de facto shift toward the penal regulation of urban poverty" (2012:215), where people of color are increasingly locked away due to a shift from a welfare state to a security state.

When Jennifer Turner, a representative from the ACLU, describes prison as "a waste of human life and public resources that could be much better spent" (2013:¶6), she does so by decrying the use of lifetime prison sentences without parole for nonviolent criminal offenses. This ACLU affiliate highlights that more than three thousand people in the US will spend the remainder of their lives in prison, sometimes for crimes as petty as a ten-dollar sale of marijuana due to laws like "three strikes." Turner argues that a more sensible solution would be to provide offenders with the drug treatment and mental health resources they need. As compelling as Turner's case may be, her proposition will do little to alleviate the waste of human life and resources: low-level drug-offenders represent only a quarter of America's prison population (Forman 2012). Even if all these people were set free, the US would still account for the largest incarcerated population in the world.

RoC affiliate Rebecca Hagelin likens the waste of prisons to a horror film without end. "Society isn't protected," she writes, "tax dollars are wasted and the guilty are punished but largely not 'corrected'" (2018:¶6). She argues that prison creates self-reinforcing patterns of disadvantage. Those convicted of crime serve their time and return to the community with few prospects. Former inmates are often stripped of their right to vote, are excluded from public assistance, and face decreased job opportunities. Hagelin goes on to ask, rhetorically, "Instead of warehousing criminals, relegating them to endless hours of watching television or arts-and-crafts classes, what if we used that time to teach them useful trades? Or taught them how to be ready to obtain and hold a job? Or treated their substance addictions and negative behaviors?" (2018:¶12).

According to both these arguments, one liberal and the other conservative, the problem with prison is not the prison itself; it is that prisons yield diminishing returns on public investment. While each organization takes positions that argue, to varying extents, for more prison alternatives and fewer paths to incarceration, both sides lead their audiences to believe that prisons exist in their rightful place to punish criminality. These organizations argue for the continued use of prison without questioning whether crime has any intrinsic meaning. Neither one questions the problematic ideas they advance about the majority of those behind bars (i.e., "they're criminals"), nor do they push back against the underlying idea of criminality and the origins of crime. While plenty of elites commit *white*-collar crime and create mass social destruction in the process (Chambliss 1988 [1978]), they often receive probation. Sometimes there are no laws to even label their actions as criminal. Accordingly, who gets policed, what punishments they face, and the severity of sentences are all filtered through race-making processes where people of color are criminalized at levels that whites simply are not (Muhammad 2011).

Historically speaking, stereotypes that frame people of color as deviant, shiftless, and violent have been so pervasive throughout justice processes in America that "crime" is often code speak for blackness (Russell-Brown 2009 [1998]). We observe RoC members to be silent on the role race plays in the hypercriminalization of certain groups, insisting rather that the problem of "overcriminalization" is one of excess regulation that interferes with "free enterprise." Unlike the RoC, the ACLU does acknowledge racial bias in the justice system. However, it frames racial bias as a psychological problem. For instance, in support of the Preventing Tragedies Between Police and Communities Act, a congressional bill designed to end tragic police-involved killings of young black Americans, they treat racialized bias as though it is a product of individualized, irrational behavior of "bad apple" police officers. Moreover, this act's proposed solution to police violence is to have officers complete more training on better-policing methods. The ACLU clarifies: "If passed, the Preventing Tragedies bill would require officers to use non-lethal and de-escalation tactics and use the lowest level of force possible—the safest means—to deal with an identified threat" (2018:¶5).

Not only do the ACLU and RoC justify the need for carceral protection and surveillance, but they inoculate the racially biased practices of policing, adjudication, and punishment from scrutiny altogether. Returning to the ACLU's suggestion that training is the solution to police-involved killings, for example, the organization frames police brutality as some deviation from standard operating procedure. A focus on more training treats police brutality as a technical problem in need of tinkering, not a larger problem in need of overhaul. This incremental reform requires officers to follow additional procedures when interacting with the public, an approach suggesting that policing can be immunized from racial patterns of personalized sentiment (e.g., intergroup hostility, affective involvement) or broader policy decisions (e.g., "stop and frisk," "broken windows"). "More training" ignores the question of what "threats" define criminality and whether the problem with policing is policing itself (Correia and Wall 2018; Vitale 2017). This reform does not consider whether police violence is not a deviation but, instead, its governing procedure, and it remains silent on how the justice system was designed as "the avant-garde of white supremacy" (Martinot and Sexton 2003) as well as an institution built to protect "whiteness as property" (C. Harris 1993).

BRINGING PRISON TO THE STREETS

Four decades ago, the criminologist Stanley Cohen (1979) warned against reforms that attempted to replace pathways to incarceration with alternatives that expanded "community" control (see also Beckett and Murakawa 2012). He claimed that "'alternatives' become not alternatives at all but new programs which supplement the existing system or else expand it by attracting new populations" (Cohen 1979:347). We argue that this kind of carceral expansion is what we are now seeing as a consequence of prison reforms like those advanced by the ACLU and RoC.

The ACLU and RoC call for expanding prison alternatives with probation, parole, and reentry programs. Such programs are needed, the RoC organization argues, because "a state will have spent money to incarcerate and release an offender without making any effort to limit his or her potential to re-offend. This would not serve public safety interests, and it would be a waste of taxpayer dollars" (N.d.c:¶1). Stressing principles of managerial improvement (e.g., "loss prevention"), the logic of reform contends that public money would be better invested in ways that transform offenders into law-abiding citizens.

When signatories from RoC argue for reintegrating individuals into their communities after prison, they have in mind a particular type of parole and/or reentry programming. The organization identifies low-level offenders as worthwhile candidates for early prison release, so long as these offenders are placed under "proper monitoring" upon their reentry (RoC N.d.c:¶3). By proper monitoring, the organization means electronic surveillance and alcohol-detecting bracelets. The idea is that routine supervision holds ex-inmates accountable for keeping steady employment, stable housing, or participating in services designed to prepare people for both.

"These services should aid the offender's reentry into his or her community," the RoC explains, "with an objective of having someone become a productive citizen rather than a re-offender" (N.d.c:¶3). A presumption underlying reforms that require ongoing surveillance is that offenders are unproductive citizens until proven otherwise, deserving of blame for their own "senseless" choices of criminal behavior. Not only does this emphasis look inward toward behavioral pathology, but it lends itself to drastically different conclusions about what factors lead to imprisonment and how to approach reentry (Miller 2014). Rather than question structural circumstances that have unraveled alongside the prison boom, this "culture of poverty" style of damnation locates the problem of crime within the individual.

Labeling individuals as makers of their own destiny without consideration of the structural circumstances they inherit fits within the hallmarks of color-blind ideology. Color blindness acknowledges that racial inequalities persist but attributes them to personalized decisions having nothing to do with systemic patterns of racial bias and discrimination (Bonilla-Silva 2003). To say that crime has to do with personal irresponsibility is to legitimize a place in the American public imagination for coded "race speak," where people of color are intrinsically caricatured in stereotypical ways that make them deserving of suspicion and surveillance.

Rather than withdraw public dollars from the carceral state altogether, recommendations by liberals and conservatives for expanded parole and reentry build from a common foundation of penal logics intended to manage criminogenic risk that is inherently racialized (see also Van Cleve, Gonzalez, and Mayes 2015). These alternatives may symbolize a retreat from using the prison as a catchall form of punishment, but they do not translate into investments in community infrastructure that are known to be inversely linked to crime. These investments include things like employment that pays a living wage, affordable health care and housing developments, public education with adequate staff and resources, and programs aimed at poverty reduction generally.

Prison reforms offered by the ACLU and RoC do not upend the carceral state as much as they repackage alternative forms of racialized social control. These alternatives to prison are an administrative shuffle that expands shell institutions, like law enforcement agencies and community corrections initiatives, under a guise that Katherine Beckett and Naomi Murakawa describe as "submerged, serpentine forms of punishment" (2012:224). These reforms actually sharpen the carceral machinery available to the justice system's disposal and entrench a broader net to different forms of punishment. Because the increased use of parole and reentry programs multiplies the number of intersecting roads with the justice system, these reforms increase the possibilities for people to be incarcerated. In effect, this masks racial inequality in the justice system by shifting punishment away from the most visible hand of the carceral state.

Conservative and liberal organizations agree that the prison system requires significant investment, consuming limited government resources that could be better spent elsewhere. According to a report titled *Smart Reform Is Possible*, the ACLU argues the following:

> Reforms that rely less on incarceration have long made economic sense, but dramatically declining state revenues are making changes to the criminal justice system more urgent. (2011:6)

The RoC echoes these words when it frames prison reform, and government more broadly, within a common language of business:

> At a time of tight budgets in state capitols and households alike, it is time for innovative policy approaches that maximize the public safety return on our investment of taxpayers' dollars. (N.d.a:¶3)

The liberal ACLU and conservative RoC alike emphasize returns on investment, fiscal constraint, and general economics.

What if market-driven arguments from the ACLU and RoC win the political day, such that reforms are achieved simply because prison is too financially costly for public consumption? One logical conclusion is that these reforms will fundamentally transform the point of punishment. Rather than approach punishment with the conventional purposes of deterrence, rehabilitation, or incapacitation in mind, these reforms increasingly approach prison reform in business terms of profitability. No longer is the justice system expected to merely consume public dollars; instead, punishment is seen as something that can be lucrative for the state.

One pathway for generating income is to commodify crime through extraction processes brought to fruition by practices like cash bail (Page 2017) or court fines and fees (A. Harris 2016). Revenues from these sources grew by over 650 percent between 1977 and 2012 with inflation held constant, amounting to as much as $15.7 billion in 2012 (Henricks and Harvey 2017). Those locales with higher shares of minority residents, especially black folks, are much more likely to rely on these revenues for state finance, net other factors like community poverty levels and crime rates, than are predominantly white communities (Henricks and Harvey 2017; Sances and You 2017).

Although revenues from bail, fines, and fees are spent in ways that are indistinguishable from tax dollars, those individuals who pay these financial obligations are not referred to as "taxpayers." They are not considered to be financiers who make the justice system possible. Instead, they are referred to by more "colorful" names, ones that are often racialized, such as "criminals" (Harris, Evans, and Beckett 2011). Labeling people in this way is to say that they are deserving of such punishment, as though they ought to literally compensate for their own misdeeds (Parent 1990). Those labeled as criminal are collateralized to foot the bill, in part, because their social standing counters any lobby that can otherwise advocate on their behalf. Using these revenues to offset the operating expenses of the justice system, as well as to finance services offered by the state in general, is to provide hidden subsidies to those who benefit from the law (e.g., the protection of private property) but otherwise avoid it (Henricks and Seamster 2017). It permits them to withdraw their resources from a common pool of revenue and "tax" dollars. More fundamentally, the arrangement redistributes the responsibility for state finance.

When punishment takes the form of cash bail or fines and fees, as opposed to incapacitation, crime can be redefined in consumptive terms. Breaking the law comes with an exchange value that is paid as a literal price. This change is consistent with the broader retreat from a welfare orientation of the liberal state, where investment in corrections is seen as counterproductive for making individuals more self-reliant and personally responsible. Having people pay for crime, and perhaps the sheer participation in the justice system, draws on market logics of consumption to define citizenship. The actions of making bail, securing legal representation, and satisfying legal debts are likened to consumer patronage, as though criminalized offenders are purchasing justice system services of their own volition. The pay-to-participate logic represents a shift away from the "social contract" and more humanistic concerns, like civic belonging, and toward financial considerations.

Both the ACLU and RoC argue against practices like cash bail so long as costs exceed revenues. Citing how 60 percent of the jail population awaits trial behind bars because they cannot make bail, Katie Greer from the RoC estimates that "pretrial incarceration is costing the nation roughly $13.6 billion every year" (2017:¶2). Meanwhile, Udi Ofer from the ACLU says, "There's a better way towards justice" (2017:¶9). Pointing to states that have already initiated reform measures, like New Jersey, he argues for policy changes that ensure that "judges make informed decisions for each individual they see and exhaust all other alternatives before ever resorting to money bail" (Ofer 2017:¶9). Both organizations are critical of imposing financial punishments on those who are too poor to pay, but neither sees cash bail as bankrupt to its core or as a conflict of interest among institutions that constitute the system (Bannon, Nagrecha, and Diller 2010; Beckett and Harris 2011; Katzenstein and Nagrecha 2011; Martin 2018).

Rather than aspire to a neutral, value-free rule of law, the commodification of crime through practices like cash bail or fines and fees transforms the justice system into the originator and beneficiary of its own revenue stream. This financial arrangement creates vested interests among those who work within these institutions (Page 2011). Regardless of whether those employed within the justice system are well intentioned or desire progressive penal reform, their livelihood is tied to the collection of revenues that help pay for their own salaries, in addition to cycling people in and out of the system. These employees are positioned to weigh their material interests against their morals in an era of precarious labor, where their occupational security provides ample incentive to participate in practices of monetary punishment but little reason to act to the contrary. The ACLU and RoC do not critique the practices of cash bail or fines and fees in this way. They do not make an argument that these sanctions are a perverse incentive for the justice system to prioritize revenue generation over due process, public safety, and the general rule of law. All the while, people of color are disproportionately left to the pay the price.

CONCLUSIONS

There is a tendency to understand racial inequality, and all the mechanisms like mass imprisonment that produce it, not as something in which everyone participates—liberals and conservatives alike (Bonilla-Silva 2003). Rather than hold a structural viewpoint that implicates the entire social system, eyes can become fixated on the incendiary sins of the style of racism that is endorsed by white nationalist groups, the Ku Klux Klan, and to some extent the Republican Party. Focusing attention in such narrow ways glosses over all the well-meaning, well-intentioned liberals who otherwise promote interests that maintain the status quo of racial inequality. It turns a (color-)blind eye to liberalism so that "liberal agendas become contrast background, glossed quickly and presumed virtuous" (Murakawa 2014:10). So long as partisanship is crudely cast in these bifurcated terms, scholars fail to explicate the complicit and active roles that conservatives and liberals play together in creating the problems associated with mass imprisonment.

Today may seem like a moment when America stands at a political crossroads. Following the election of Barack Obama, the nation's first black president, was the election of Donald Trump—a man who has denied Obama's claim to American citizenship, has generalize Mexicans as criminals, drug users, and rapists, and has called for banning all Muslim entry into America. Liberal pundit Van Jones described the 2016 election result as a "whitelash" signifying a stark division between reactionary white conservatives and a multiracial liberal coalition. Even Jones, however, is among those liberal supporters who has worked with the RoC on prison reform, joining forces with the likes of conservative power players ranging from Trump to the Koch Brothers to say: "When you've got more than 2 million people behind bars, I'll fight alongside anybody to change those numbers" (qtd. in Ball 2015:49).

In the shadow of the current political polarization stands bipartisan movement on prison reform that unites what otherwise seems like strange bedfellows. What makes this bipartisanship possible, we suggest, is a common scaffolding of a market-inspired racial project. Behind the political divide that separates liberal organizations like the ACLU and conservative ones like RoC rests a common assessment of the situation: that prisons are a failure because they do not aspire to market values of cost efficiency, financial stability, and economic vitality. When market logics are recognized as the centerpiece of bipartisan agendas of prison reform, we argue that the permutation of mass imprisonment, not its resolution, can be seen as a logical outcome. By stressing market principles, liberals and conservatives are de-emphasizing questions of racial justice in favor of seemingly race-neutral matters related to the market.

REFERENCES

American Civil Liberties Union. 2011. *State Reform Is Possible: States Reducing Incarceration Rates and Costs while Protecting Communities.* New York: American Civil Liberties Union. Retrieved June 1, 2018 (https://www.aclu.org/sites/default/files/field_document/smartreformispossible_web.pdf).
———. 2018. "End the Culture of Warrior Policing." New York: American Civil Liberties Union. Retrieved May 15, 2018 (https://action.aclu.org/petition/stop-police-killing-communities?ms=web_160711_criminallawreform_racialjustice_preventtragedies).
Ball, Molly. 2015. "Do the Koch Brothers Really Care about Criminal-Justice Reform?" *Atlantic*, March 3.
Bannon, Alicia, Mitali Nagrecha, and Rebekah Diller. 2010. *Criminal Justice Debt: A Barrier to Reentry.* New York: Brennan Center for Justice.

BBC. 2018. "Alice Johnson Freed after Trump Grants Clemency Plea." *BBC News*, June 7. Retrieved October 1, 2018 (https://www.bbc.com/news/world-us-canada-44390737).

Beckett, Katherine, and Alexes Harris. 2011. "On Case and Conviction: Monetary Sanctions as Misguided Policy." *Criminology and Society* 10(3): 509–37.

Beckett, Katherine, and Naomi Murakawa. 2012. "Mapping the Shadow Carceral State: Toward an Institutionally Capacious Approach to Punishment." *Theoretical Criminology* 16(2): 221–44.

Beckett, Katherine, Anna Reosti, and Emily Knaphus. 2016. "The End of an Era? Understanding the Contradictions of Criminal Justice Reform." *Annals of the American Academy of Political and Social Science* 664(1): 238–59.

Bonilla-Silva, Eduardo. 2003. *Racism without Racists: Color-Blind Racism and the Persistence of Racial Inequality in America.* Lanham, MD: Rowman & Littlefield.

Chambliss, William J. 1988 [1978]. *On the Take: From Petty Crooks to Presidents.* Bloomington: Indiana University Press.

Cohen, Stanley. 1979. "The Punitive City: Notes on the Dispersal of Social Control." *Contemporary Crises* 3(4): 339–63.

Correia, David, and Tyler Wall. 2018. *Police: A Field Guide.* Brooklyn, NY: Verso.

Dagan, David, and Steven Teles. 2016. *Prison Break: Why Conservatives Turned against Mass Incarceration.* New York: Oxford University Press.

Davis, Angela Y. 2003. *Are Prisons Obsolete?* New York: Seven Stories Press.

Feagin, Joe R. 2000. *Racist America: Roots, Current Realities, and Future Reparations.* New York: Routledge.

Forman, James, Jr. 2012. "Racial Critiques of Mass Incarceration: Beyond the New Jim Crow." *New York University Law Review* 87(1): 101–46.

George, Justin. 2018. "How Jeff Sessions Is Undermining Trump's Prison Reform Agenda." *The Marshall Project*, October 25. Retrieved October 27, 2018 (https://www.themarshallproject.org/2018/10/25/how-jeff-sessions-is-undermining-trump-s-prison-reform-agenda).

Green, David A. 2015. "US Penal-Reform Catalysts, Drivers, and Prospects." *Punishment and Society* 17(3): 271–98.

Greer, Katie. 2017. "Listen: Money Bail and Pretrial Detention." Austin, TX: Right on Crime. Retrieved June 1, 2018 (http://rightoncrime.com/2017/11/listen-money-bail-and-pretrial-detention/).

Hagelin, Rebecca. 2018. "Prison Reform and Redemption Act Offers Hope for Former Prisoners." Austin, TX: Right on Crime. Retrieved May 30, 2018 (http://rightoncrime.com/2018/04/prison-reform-and-redemption-act-offers-hope-for-former-prisoners/).

Hallett, Michael. 2012. "Reentry to What? Theorizing Prisoner Reentry in the Jobless Future." *Critical Criminology* 20(3): 213–28.

Harris, Alexes. 2016. *A Pound of Flesh: Monetary Sanctions as a Punishment for the Poor.* New York: Russell Sage Foundation.

Harris, Alexes, Heather Evans, and Katherine Beckett. 2011. "Courtesy Stigma and Monetary Sanctions: Toward a Socio-Cultural Theory of Punishment." *American Sociological Review* 76(2): 234–64.

Harris, Cheryl I. 1993. "Whiteness as Property." *Harvard Law Review* 106(8): 1707–91.

Henricks, Kasey, and Daina Cheyenne Harvey. 2017. "Not One but Many: Monetary Punishment and the Fergusons of America." *Sociological Forum* 32(S1): 930–51.

Henricks, Kasey, and Louise Seamster. 2017. "Mechanisms of the Racial Tax State." *Critical Sociology* 43(2): 169–79.

Katzenstein, Mary Fainsod, and Mitali Nagrecha. 2011. "A New Punishment Regime." *Criminology and Public Policy* 10(3): 555–68.

Lewis, Amanda E. 2004. "What Group? Studying Whites and Whiteness in the Era of 'Color-Blindness.'" *Sociological Theory* 22(4): 623–46.

Martin, Karin D. 2018. "Monetary Myopia: An Examination of Institutional Response to Revenue from Monetary Sanctions for Misdemeanors." *Criminal Justice Policy Review* 29(6–7): 630–62.

Martinot, Steve, and Jared Sexton. 2003. "The Avant-Garde of White Supremacy." *Social Identities* 9(2): 169–81.

Miller, Reuben J. 2014. "Devolving the Carceral State: Race, Prisoner Reentry, and the Micro-Politics of Urban Poverty Management." *Punishment and Society* 16(3): 305–35.

Moynihan, Daniel P. 1965. *The Negro Family: The Case for National Action.* Washington, DC: Office of Policy Planning and Research, US Department of Labor.

Muhammad, Khalil Gibran. 2011. *The Condemnation of Blackness: Race, Crime, and the Making of Modern Urban America.* Cambridge, MA: Harvard University Press.

Murakawa, Naomi. 2014. *The First Civil Right: How Liberals Built Prison America.* New York: Oxford University Press.

Obama, Barack. 2017. "The President's Role in Advancing Criminal Justice Reform." *Harvard Law Review* 130(3): 811–66.

Ofer, Udi. 2017. "We Can't End Mass Incarceration without Ending Money Bail." New York: American Civil Liberties Union. Retrieved May 25, 2018 (https://www.aclu.org/blog/mass-incarceration/smart-justice/we-cant-end-mass-incarceration-without-ending-money-bail).

Omi, Michael, and Howard Winant. 1994 [1986]. *Racial Formation in the United States: From the 1960s to the 1990s.* New York: Routledge.

Page, Joshua. 2011. "Prison Officer Unions and the Perpetuation of the Penal Status Quo." *Criminology and Public Policy* 10(3): 735–70.

———. 2017. "Desperation and Service in the Bail Industry." *Contexts* 16(2): 30–37.

Parent, Dale. 1990. *Recovering Correctional Costs through Offender Fees.* Washington, DC: National Institute of Justice.

Pew Research Center. 2017. *The Partisan Divide on Political Values Grows Even Wider: Sharp Shifts among Democrats on Aid to Needy, Race, Immigration.* Washington, DC: Pew Research Center.

Right on Crime. N.d.a. "The Conservative Case for Reform." Austin, TX: Right on Crime. Retrieved May 15, 2018 (http://rightoncrime.com/the-conservative-case-for-reform/).

———. N.d.b. "Overcriminalization." Austin, TX: Right on Crime. Retrieved May 15, 2018 (http://rightoncrime.com/category/priority-issues/overcriminalization/).

———. N.d.c. "Parole and Reentry." Austin, TX: Right on Crime. Retrieved May 15, 2018 (http://rightoncrime.com/category/priority-issues/parole-and-re-entry/).

Russell-Brown, Katheryn. 2009 [1998]. *The Color of Crime.* New York: New York University Press.

Ryan, William. 1971. *Blaming the Victim.* New York: Pantheon Books.

Sances, Michael W., and Hye Young You. 2017. "Who Pays for Government? Descriptive Representation and Exploitative Revenue Sources." *Journal of Politics* 79(3): 1090–94.

Sears, David O., and Jack Citrin. 1982. *Tax Revolt: Something for Nothing.* Cambridge, MA: Harvard University Press.

Turner, Jennifer. 2013. "What a Waste." New York: American Civil Liberties Union. Retrieved June 6, 2018 (https://www.aclu.org/blog/mass-incarceration/what-waste).

Van Cleve, Nicole Gonzalez, and Lauren Mayes. 2015. "Criminal Justice through 'Colorblind' Lenses: A Call to Examine the Mutual Constitution of Race and Criminal Justice." *Law and Social Inquiry* 40(2): 406–32.

Vitale, Alex S. 2017. *The End of Policing.* Brooklyn, NY: Verso.

CHAPTER 7

SETTLER CULTURE AND WHITE PROPERTY
From the Bundy Ranch Standoff to the West Virginia Coalfields

REBECCA R. SCOTT

WHAT DO THE Bundys have in common with grassroots environmentalists in West Virginia, or a big green organization like the Sierra Club? In this chapter, I explore such instances of "white" protest to illustrate how individualism and private property (i.e., in land) connect different forms of white resistance in a settler logic of alienation, appropriation, and domination. The hegemony of color blindness and hyperindividualism prevailing in white American political culture from the 1980s through the early twenty-first century has discouraged group- and community-based protests. Class has long been an absent discourse in American political culture and is often referenced through a language of race, which normalizes white wealth against the poverty of racialized others (Bettie 2014). Biological, genetic, and physical differences have been referenced to explain poverty and justify social exclusion (Wray 2006). Neoliberalism has only exacerbated this tendency, with culture and racialization increasingly standing in for all social differences in the absence of economic critique (Omi and Winant 2015; Du Bois 1998 [1935]). Even when inequality is the focus of a campaign, as it was for Bernie Sanders in 2016, the complaint is often focused on injured "ordinary Americans" who are perceptibly coded as white and male (Branigin 2017).

A resurgence of overt racism since the 2016 election has brought with it an increasing weaponization of the postracial claims of neoliberalism (Omi and Winant 2015; Takei 2018). An example is the Trump administration's attack on Native American sovereignty couched in the language of individual responsibility, bent on transforming Native American nations into another group of racial outsiders looking for special treatment (Diamond 2018). This attack reflects both the entitlement at the heart of US white liberalism and the disavowal at the heart of settler colonialism (Bruyneel 2013). On the one hand, whiteness depends on a foundational alienation—a refusal of relationship with racialized others—while on the other hand, it depends on a disavowal of this alienation (Dyer 1997). I argue that because of this disavowed rejection, white protest is often posed in the form of race-based injury, which represents a return of the repressed, whether that be "reverse racism," a problematic claim of commonality with racialized others, or both. A common example is a claim to Native American identity, especially Cherokee identity (Sturm 2011).

However, the disavowal at the heart of the settler complex also depends on an assumption of white entitlement, innocence, and agency constructed against disempowered others, which makes coalitional work difficult (Cole 2012; Wolfe 2013). This chapter will consider how these complexities shape the collective claims of injury on the part of several "white" groups in the US. The examples of Cliven Bundy family's protests, the Sierra Club's environmentalism, and grassroots activism in Appalachia will illustrate the settler complex that ties together these diverse instances of white protest.

THEORETICAL BACKGROUND: FROM WHITENESS TO THE SETTLER COMPLEX

White identity in the United States is determined by property and property relations. The desire to appropriate, protect, and conserve white property is at the heart of US racial politics (Lipsitz 1998). The acquisitive individualism characteristic of liberal subjectivity, personified by the white male property owner, has been enshrined in US law and culture as the best form of relation to place and nature (Hardin 1968; Harris 1993). Native American collective relations to place are not understood as representing a civil claim to property rights or to represent an "improvement" of land as dictated by Lockean property theory (Kazanjian 2003; Shiva 2015). This doctrine of *terra nullius* justified the expropriation and genocide of Native people across the continent. US government policies such as the Homestead Acts and the Dawes Act segmented the western US into tracts of private property, public land, and reservations, many of which were further segmented into allotments assigned to individual Native men or heads of households. These allotments were an attempt to rewrite indigenous land relations on the model of patriarchal liberal individualism, as well as a method of expropriation, as the small allotments often ended up in the hands of wealthier and more powerful white owners (Miner 2013; Taylor 2016).

This material and discursive connection between whiteness and property necessitates an understanding of white political and rights-seeking behavior that accounts for the specific ways in which white culture relates to land and nature. Property is at the center of rights and justice in the US legal system, and rights to property are favored over other forms of rights not related to property ownership (Fry, Briggle, and Kincaid 2015; Radin 1982).

Denying Kin

The settler complex is based on a historically derived legal and cultural alienation (or refusal of relationship) from other humans in the form of enslavement of African people and expropriation of Native land. Property ownership was central to European conceptions of self-rule and democratic citizenship from the late eighteenth century (Goldberg 2001). This exclusive property- and class-based claim to citizenship is very likely behind many settlers' drive to immigrate to the so-called New World, which appeared to offer "a constant supply of new territory with which to satisfy the proprietary aspirations" of the oppressed people of Europe (Wolfe 2013; Finney 2014; Howard 1992).

A second alienation, or refusal of relationship, occurs when land is transformed into abstract property. As property, land is divided in ways indifferent to place and ecology for the ease of individual ownership or in the name of national territory (Schneider 2013; J. Scott 1999). The abstraction of land into property is a refusal of the human relationship with nature, other living things, and landforms. For example, the US-Mexico border disrupts the livelihood of thousands of species struggling to accommodate settler-made obstructions (Carswell 2017). The reduction of people and nonhuman things to chattel breaks the web of interconnectivity recognized in many Native American worldviews (LaDuke 1999; Schneider 2013).

This abstract logic of equivalence, which reduces place to natural resources to exploit or protect, sees space, landforms, and living beings as generic equivalents that are subjected to sale, exploitation, or conservation, but not as representing a specific set of relationships or community. This follows the logic of colonization, which emphasizes the differences and minimizes the interconnections between subjects and objects, where agency and will reside entirely in the subject, or master, position (Plumwood 1994). The market becomes the lens through which the land is viewed, and the subjects of law become those most fully realized humans who control property to exploit or protect, rendering unintelligible any claims to rights such as clean water, air, or other nonmarket values (LaDuke 2005; Lucas 2004).

Difficulties in the Fight for Justice

The division of land into abstract units of equivalence, and of species into resources to exploit or protect, generates many irrationalities (Latour and Porter 1993). These include climate change, global radiation drift, persistent organic pollutants in breast milk, fights over rights to hunt traditionally when industrialization has endangered the game, and oceans of plastic waste (Alaimo 2016; Latour and Porter 1993; Lucas 2004; Schneider 2013). The inability to gather the collective will to tame these monsters is related to the prominence of discourses of privatization, personal responsibility, and especially acquisitive individualism. While the problems are collective in nature, the proposed solutions are almost always individualist (Cuomo 2011).

Neoliberalism, beginning in the late 1970s in Britain and combining in the US with a racial reaction to the collective social movements of the civil rights era, has performed a massive redistribution of wealth upward since the mid-twentieth century (Harvey 2007; Omi and Winant 2015). The racial code words that helped dismantle the gains of the civil rights movement were also effective at dismantling the programs helping disadvantaged whites (Omi and Winant 2015; Edsall and Edsall 1992). Neoliberalism's hegemony of individualism and personal responsibility has become so pervasive that group-based protests like Black Lives Matter evoke charges of racism, and any gathering to protest injustice is seen as equivalent to the activity of organized hate groups (Bennett 2017; Merica 2017).

The identification of proper citizenship with private, entrepreneurial individualism, homeownership, and a biopolitics of self-care enables the eruption of protest to be interpreted as the problem (Guthman 2011; Huber 2013). In such instances, the aggrieved person is identified as the source of the trouble (Ahmed 2005). Considering the normative identification of white people as the winners, as the successful subjects of neoliberalism, and as the "ordinary" American taxpayers to whom politics are addressed, the experience of real and perceived injustice can bring about some complex and contradictory political claims.

This chapter traces the connections between three disparate examples of "white" protest. First, the sovereign citizen movement of the Bundy Ranch standoff and Malheur Wildlife Refuge occupation used settler narratives of the frontier in combination with appropriations from the civil rights movement, a contradictory articulation perhaps prompted by the election of a nonwhite president. Cliven and Ammon Bundy interpreted public land management as infringing on the sovereignty and "civil rights" of the ideal, independent American of Turner's frontier thesis. Next, mainstream environmental organizations such as the Sierra Club promote a politics of consumption, liberal sentimentality, and the white savior complex that tends to disavow or minimize white victimization, and to frame environmental problems as distinct from social issues. This leads to some shaky coalitions with environmental groups such as the anti–mountaintop removal (MTR) activists in the West Virginia coalfields. The last example considers how in the fight against coal, oil, and gas in Appalachia, extraction is seen as threatening a white version of indigenous inhabitation. Underlying all of these cases is a form of abstracted individualism that denies history, interconnection, and kinship (Bennett 2010). Each of the following examples illustrate how whiteness and the settler colonial complex impedes real progress toward social justice in the US.

THIS LAND IS OUR LAND

In 2014 sovereign citizen Cliven Bundy claimed injury in his dealings with the US Bureau of Land Management (BLM). The BLM tried to seize Bundy's cattle from land he had been using, without paying the required grazing fees, for decades. Bundy claimed a preexisting right to the resources and denied the US government's right to own any land. The armed standoff that arose to defend Bundy's cattle included hundreds of armed militiamen defying the federal government. This incident occurred against the backdrop of President Obama's second term in office and his expansion in several cases of national monument status to BLM land (Varinsky 2017). Bundy's militancy, therefore, can be interpreted as a rebellion of sovereign (white) citizens against an overreaching, racialized, big government (Reeve 2012). Bundy's triumphant postacquittal "press conference," among friends with whom he had just shared steak, is a full-throated claim to white settler privilege. Establishing his status as a "maker, not a taker" (Klein 2012), Bundy expressed the hope that his guests had enjoyed the steaks he'd provided, exclaiming, "I'd like everybody in the world to enjoy . . . good food. I harvest that with my cattle, [and] my cattle convert that into an edible commodity" (Anon. 2018).

Extolling "freedom for a man to be able to produce and provide and be happy," which he considered enshrined in the Constitution, a "blue print for this type of life," Bundy claimed that "we the people" are the government and that no central government has any legitimacy over Clarke County, Nevada (Anon. 2018). Repeating that he had no contract with the federal government or any other government, he blamed his fellow citizens for thinking they must deal with the federal government at all. Borrowing both vocabulary and logic from John Locke, he proclaimed that his "improving" of the land gave him rights to the land, and that this right in fact stemmed from "the pioneers . . . the first one to come in here . . . [and] the first drop of water [his team of horses] drank." His right to the water, and presumably the land, thus stems from the "first pioneers . . . creating a beneficial use of a renewable resource," thus gaining "preemptive rights" (Anon. 2018).

There was a stark inequality in the delicate treatment the armed ranchers and allies received in their 2014 demonstration and standoff compared to the treatment of demonstrators in Ferguson, Missouri, the same year, who were met with tanks, teargas, and rubber bullets for protesting the murder of Michael Brown. The white privilege of the ranchers was underlined by an aggressively claimed whiteness. For instance, Bundy asserted that today "[Black people] have nothing to do." He thought they were better off in slavery, picking cotton. This opinion underlines the irony of his defense, in which his attorney argued that Bundy and his allies were participating in an American tradition of protest harkening back to the protests in Selma, Alabama (Mencimer 2017).

In 2016 Cliven's son Ammon, his brothers, and many of their sympathizers invaded and occupied the Malheur Wildlife Refuge in Oregon. Ammon Bundy declared, "This land belongs to the people. We must get our government [under] control and back to benefiting the people." This statement made no mention of the Northern Paiute, who have never ceded the land (Keeler 2016). The occupiers rummaged through Northern Paiute artifacts held in the refuge and used large equipment to dig latrines in the middle of culturally significant sites (Keeler 2016; Killgrove 2016). However, the Bundys' perception of their own victimhood led the family to offer to send help to Standing Rock, North Dakota, during the pipeline protest, in an apparent attempt to coalesce with Native water protectors (Allard 2016). The Bundys' literal trampling of Native land is a forthright claim of settler entitlement. However, the fundamental amorality of this claim compels them to use the language of racial injustice and indigenous oppression in justifying their protest.

EXPLORE, ENJOY, AND PROTECT

No group could be more seemingly opposed to the Bundys than the Sierra Club. One of the largest green organizations in the US, it is generally associated with Democratic politics and an embrace of environmental regulation. Nonetheless, the same settler complex that defines the Bundys' claim to preemptive rights to Nevada land underlies the Sierra Club and its white American environmental ethos (Wolfe 2013). The idealized wilderness that the Sierra Club was founded to preserve is a product of nineteenth-century industrialization and the closing of the American frontier (Cronon 1995). In the zoning of the American landscape into property, specific places were rendered interchangeable as cities, wilderness, farmland, or ranchland, creating a functionally equivalent abstraction divorced from Native American relationships to places and specific ecologies. In other words, for settlers, exploitation and conservation are two sides of the same coin (Schneider 2013). Land should be "returned" to the people for exploitation or "saved" from the people.

John Muir, the founder of the Sierra Club, thought of wild nature as a sacred natural cathedral, capable of sustaining the spirit of an educated observer. He considered the Native inhabitants as not removed enough from nature to properly enjoy it (Merchant 2003). The dualism of humanity and nature is instrumental to the objectification of nature not simply as ranchland to exploit but also as a pristine collector's object in the hands of wilderness preservationists. Both reflect the commodification of nature, as expressed in the Sierra Club's website slogan "Explore, enjoy, protect" (Sierra Club n.d.b).

The dualism of human and nature allows for a good-and-evil perspective that puts the blame for environmental harms on (bad) humans or too many (of the wrong) humans. Sierra Club California's struggles with their membership and board over questions of immigration and overpopulation in the US reflects this tendency to focus on an idealized wilderness and to neglect the specific histories of human groups interacting with places and ecologies (Cone 1998). This mainstream environmentalist orientation blames environmental problems on overfishing, illegal logging and mining, and other small resource users instead of on industrialization and overconsumption (Rutherford 2011).

In the early years of the twenty-first century, the Sierra Club's West Virginia office allied themselves with grassroots groups fighting mountaintop removal (MTR) coal mining in the state. When I interviewed one of the activists working for the Sierra Club in 2004, we both acknowledged that the organization had not had an active environmental justice policy until that time. However, at the height of the Sierra Club's Beyond Coal Campaign in West Virginia, celebrity activist Darryl Hannah joined many others in a highly publicized demonstration in front of Marsh Fork Elementary School, which was located below a dam holding back billions of tons of coal slurry (Nilles and Hitt 2009). Nonetheless, mountaintop removal has continued its massive expansion in the state. Local activists claim they've been abandoned by the celebrities and the Sierra Club; as one coalfield activist put it, "Most of them have left and moved on and are now fighting other issues with more funding. I don't understand why they didn't complete the job and end mountaintop removal" (qtd. in Biggers 2016). The website for the Beyond Coal Campaign currently focuses on the retirement of coal-burning power plants as its main objective while including the general goal of "keeping it in the ground" (Sierra Club n.d.a).

There is a sad sense of inevitability to the coalfield activists' charges of betrayal by the Sierra Club. The presence of humans, many of them dependent on the mining industry in the affected area, complicates mainstream white environmentalism. As one activist put it, "mountaintop removal is not an accident" (qtd. in Biggers 2016). The intensity of local conflict over the issue, combined with the overall economic depression and associated prescription drug abuse epidemic, paints a picture far from the Sierra Club's usual pristine wilderness backdrop (Bell 2016). This failure of coalition building reflects some of the challenges of fighting environmental damage from within a "settler colonial complex" (Wolfe 2013). The settler colonial complex divides environmental issues from social issues, leaving big green environmental organizations ill equipped for the nuances of the role of environmentalism in building community and social justice (Taylor 2016).

ENVIRONMENTAL JUSTICE AND "WHITE" PEOPLE TRYING TO GET IT RIGHT

The coalfield activists fighting mountaintop removal occupy a unique position in America's racial landscape. White Appalachians have been considered "our contemporary ancestors" or "unadulterated" Anglo-Saxons, but they are also decried as hillbillies, welfare dependents, and generally ignorant people (Scott 2010). Poor, disempowered, and generally marginalized white Appalachians are often invoked to deny the existence of white privilege. The Sierra Club and various celebrities' involvement in the anti-MTR movement was perceived in retrospect by local activists as a kind of exploitation for publicity. The failure of this coalition clearly reflects class- and region-based inequalities. However, the language of privilege or lack thereof can mask the real working of whiteness, or what might be termed the settler complex, in US political culture.

As Wolfe argues, "in the contradictory tension between desiring and rejecting the Native, ambivalence emerges as a primary settler affect" (2013:8). This is clear in white Appalachians' contradictory claims of both whiteness and indigeneity. White Appalachians associate themselves with Native Americans in a variety of ways, including identifying with the experience of losing their land though (internal) colonialism, identifying with the land-based lifestyle and place-based identity of Native Americans, and forming coalitions with Native Americans (Scott 2010). However, this identification represents an appropriation of the concept of colonialism as well as a problematic claim of white setter indigeneity in Appalachia (Pearson 2013).

This problematic identification represents a weak link in environmental coalition building between white settlers and indigenous and nonindigenous people of color. For example, in an interview from 2004, a coalfield resident and anti-MTR activist said, "Look at this face; look at these cheekbones. We've been in these mountains forever." The accuracy of this claim to genetic indigenous heritage is less important than the fact that this person's activism or political identity was not otherwise explicitly related to being Native American. The claim seems to function as an appeal to indigenous authenticity in order to make a stronger claim to the land than is possible from a settler identity (Tallbear 2013).

Similarly, another activist explicitly compared the struggle against MTR to the theft of Native land:

> This is a colony. It has been for over 130 years. They call it King Coal and that shows that it's a colony. The people of this area have a lot in common with people of color. Unlike the Indians, who knew what was happening to them, Appalachians don't seem to know what is happening, or they don't want to know. (Scott 2010:213–14)

There are many things going on in this short utterance. It underlines the whiteness of Appalachians and the community the activist represents while erasing the original colonization of the area that predates the coal industry's occupation of 130 years. "King Coal" also identifies colonialism itself with white settlers' "anticolonial" struggle against the British monarchy. This framing allows white Appalachians simultaneous identification with Anglo-American settlers and with the indigenous people they displaced. Anti-MTR activists in Appalachia are perhaps among the most educated white people in America about issues of environmental injustice, yet because their energies are consumed with the crisis that is MTR, the coalitions they build have often been as calculated as they perceived the Sierra Club's was with them.

A last illustration comes from a related movement in West Virginia against the natural gas fracking and pipeline boom. In a beautiful spot that would be destroyed by a planned pipeline, a property owner showed me a billboard describing the dangers of the new, larger pipelines, which carve a 150-foot-wide right-of-way through the landscape, with a potential impact radius of a mile in case of an explosion. Tiny crosses marked the "graves" of the species that would be affected. A plot of sacred corn represented the contribution of "the Indian guys who was in North Dakota." He said that some people from Standing Rock "came . . . had a ceremony and prayed." Although he saw the connection between the struggles, his main appreciation was for the tribal members' contribution to the protection of his property and the environment in West Virginia. My question about coalitions was answered with a description of a coalition between West Virginia counties all dealing with this pipeline. Most likely despite the intentions of the visitors from Standing Rock, their intervention seemed to have little impact on his imagination of the struggle.

However, many Appalachian activists and more radical organizations did participate in the Standing Rock protests and educated themselves on settler colonialism at the same time (Anon. 2016; Dodson 2016). In the fight for environmental justice, white protestors need to recognize and combat their settler complex in order to comprehend the reality and roots of our current environmental crisis, as well as a political crisis. These examples represent both the limitations and the potential of environmental justice coalitions among white Appalachians and groups of people of color, including indigenous groups. A real coalition must address the disavowed injustice at the heart of settler culture as well as current environmental destruction.

CONCLUSIONS AND POLICY IMPLICATIONS

The distance between the Bundy ranchers and Appalachian residents trying to preserve life in the mountains is vast, but they are connected by a commitment to the righteousness and morality of the US white settler state and its property structure. Those who actually seek environmental justice must get beyond preserving their own privilege in order to make effective coalitions with indigenous people and other people of color that do not replicate the settler complex of denial and disavowed relations. Currently President Trump is leading a resurgence of the claim of whiteness and settler privilege by declaring that "our ancestors tamed a continent" (Le Miere 2018), by attempting to reduce sovereign indigenous nations to racial minorities, and by embracing white nationalism and violence (Merica 2017; Gessen 2018)

At a water protectors workshop held in 2018 at an Appalachian university, four speakers discussed how they, as mothers, worked to protect water for their children and future generations. Two were white women from Appalachia, working in legal and other organizational capacities to protect water from fossil fuel extraction. Two were Native American, one with a tribal identity and a specific landscape at the heart of her organizing, and the other an activist at large working on various causes in the Eastern US.

Emergent from their panel discussion was an uncomfortable theme—politics as usual and the system set up by various environmental protection agencies—that is increasingly revealed as a road that leads in only one direction: the frack pad, the pipeline, the mine. In other words, the discussion pointed to the (white settler) legal and political system as being *designed* to encourage and enable the exploitation of resources, the extraction of fossil fuels, and the desecration of ecological systems and the natural commons. As one panelist put it, "the chickens have come home to roost." The political, economic, and legal structures of settler culture are responsible for the powerlessness of communities in the pathway of fossil fuel extraction and transport.

One member of the audience asked how to take white supremacy into account in environmental organizing, but ensuing discussion from the audience revealed that color blindness was in force as several people commented on "our common struggles." The Native American panelist who had previously identified her tribal affiliation gently took the gathering to task for using indigenous people as tokens, and the other Native woman pointed out the overwhelming whiteness of the audience itself. Another audience member asked how effective coalitions could be made, in light of the issues that were becoming apparent. Panelists called for practical action in support of people, which could in turn build real relationships that increase trust and community—all steps that could decolonize environmentalism and other social justice work.

Environmentalists interested in environmental justice and other antiracist white social movements need to clearly differentiate themselves from the Bundys on more than a surface or aesthetic level, which means coming to terms with white supremacist settler histories that underlie claims to land and the general presumption of innocence of the US government and legal processes based on the fundamental alienation of the property relation. Organizers must root out white supremacist ideas of acquisitive individualism in favor of solidarity and connection. However, as the panelists' discussion subtly made clear, doing so may require moving beyond the established protest scaffolding that the settler state provides.

In conclusion, white people need to get their shit together. White environmental activists need a fuller recognition of history and of the settler complex that undermines environmental politics. Settler culture makes kin out of people with vastly different goals, like the Sierra Club and the Bundys, who share a possessive, abstract, frontier orientation to the American landscape, while alienating potential allies for an environmental justice–based coalition that could bring about real, substantive change.

REFERENCES

Ahmed, Sara. 2005. *The Cultural Politics of Emotion.* Edinburgh: Edinburgh University Press.

Alaimo, Stacy. 2016. *Exposed: Environmental Politics and Pleasures in Posthuman Times.* Minneapolis: University of Minnesota Press.

Allard, Ladonna Bravebull. 2016. "Why Do We Punish Dakota Pipeline Protesters but Exonerate the Bundys?" *Guardian*, November 2.

Anon. 2016. "Solidarity with Standing Rock! #nodapl." *Appalachia Resist!* Retrieved March 7, 2018 (https://appalachiaresist.wordpress.com/solidarity-with-standing-rock-nodapl/).

Anon. 2018. "Video: Cliven Bundy—First Press Conference." *Redoubt News*, January 10. Retrieved February 2, 2018 (https://redoubtnews.com/2018/01/video-cliven-bundy-first-press-conference/).

Bell, Shannon Elizabeth. 2016. *Fighting King Coal: The Challenges to Micromobilization in Central Appalachia.* Cambridge, MA: MIT Press.

Bennett, Abbie. 2017. "Republican Senator Dan Bishop Compares Black Lives Matter, Supremacists." *News and Observer* (Raleigh, NC), August 14. Retrieved March 9, 2018 (http://www.newsobserver.com/news/politics-government/state-politics/article167141422.html).

Bennett, Jane. 2010. *Vibrant Matter: A Political Ecology of Things.* Durham, NC: Duke University Press.

Bettie, Julie. 2014. *Women without Class: Girls, Race, and Identity.* Oakland: University of California Press.

Biggers, Jeff. 2016. "Mountaintop Removal Never Ended: Coal River Mountaineers Fight On." *Common Dreams*, October 19. Retrieved March 2, 2018 (https://www.commondreams.org/views/2016/10/19/mountaintop-removal-never-ended-coal-river-mountaineers-fight).

Branigin, Anne. 2017. "Why Some Black and Brown People Can't Trust Bernie Sanders, in 1 Quote." *The Root*, October 31. Retrieved April 26, 2018 (https://www.theroot.com/why-some-black-and-brown-people-cant-trust-bernie-sande-1820017450).

Bruyneel, Kevin. 2013. "The American Liberal Colonial Tradition." *Settler Colonial Studies* 3(3-4): 311–21.

Carswell, Cally. 2017. "Trump's Wall May Threaten Thousands of Plant and Animal Species on the U.S.–Mexico Border." *Scientific American*, May 10.

Cole, Teju. 2012. "The White-Savior Industrial Complex." *Atlantic*, March 21.
Cone, Marla. 1998. "Sierra Club to Remain Neutral on Immigration. *Los Angeles Times*, April 26.
Cronon, William, ed. 1995. *Uncommon Ground: Toward Reinventing Nature*. New York: W. W. Norton.
Cuomo, Chris J. 2011. "Climate Change, Vulnerability, and Responsibility." *Hypatia* 26(4): 690–714.
Dodson, Willie. 2016. "Appalachians against the Dakota Access Pipeline." *Appalachian Voices*, December 14. Retrieved March 7, 2018 (http://appvoices.org/2016/12/14/appalachians-no-dapl/).
Du Bois, W. E. B. 1998 (1935). *Black Reconstruction in America, 1860–1880*. New York: Free Press.
Dyer, Richard. 1997. *White: Essays on Race and Culture*. New York, NY: Routledge.
Edsall, Thomas Byrne, and Mary D. Edsall. 1992. *Chain Reaction: The Impact of Race, Rights, and Taxes on American Politics*. New York: W. W. Norton.
Finney, Carolyn. 2014. *Black Faces, White Spaces: Reimagining the Relationship of African Americans to the Great Outdoors*. Chapel Hill: University of North Carolina Press.
Fry, Matthew, Adam Briggle, and Jordan Kincaid. 2015. "Fracking and Environmental (In)Justice in a Texas City." *Ecological Economics* 117.
Gessen, Masha. 2018. "Elizabeth Warren Falls for Trump's Trap—and Promotes Insidious Ideas about Race and DNA." *New Yorker*. October 16.
Goldberg, David Theo. 2001. *The Racial State*. Malden, MA: Wiley-Blackwell.
Guthman, Julie. 2011. *Weighing In: Obesity, Food Justice, and the Limits of Capitalism*. Berkeley: University of California Press.
Hardin, Garrett. 1968. "The Tragedy of the Commons." Originally published in *Science*, December 13.
Harris, Cheryl I. 1993. "Whiteness as Property." *Harvard Law Review* (8): 1707–91.
Harvey, David. 2007. *A Brief History of Neoliberalism*. New York: Oxford University Press.
Howard, Ron, dir. 1992. *Far and Away* (film). Imagine Films Entertainment and Universal Pictures.
Huber, Matthew. 2013. *Lifeblood: Oil, Freedom, and the Forces of Capital*. Minneapolis: University of Minnesota Press.
Kazanjian, David. 2003. *The Colonizing Trick*. Minneapolis: University of Minnesota Press.
Keeler, Jacqueline. 2016. "'It's So Disgusting': Malheur Militia Dug Latrine Trenches among Sacred Artifacts." *Indian Country Media Network*, February 17. Retrieved May 12, 2020 (https://indiancountrytoday.com/archive/it-s-so-disgusting-malheur-militia-dug-latrine-trenches-among-sacred-artifacts-FmyMoFlQokalIRhBNbOCyw).
Killgrove, Kristina. 2016. "Bundy Militia Compared to ISIS for Pawing through Native American Artifacts, Destroying Sites." *Forbes*, January 21.

Klein, Ezra. 2012. "Romney's Theory of the 'Taker Class,' and Why It Matters." *Washington Post*, September 17.

LaDuke, Winona. 1999. *All Our Relations: Native Struggles for Land and Life*. Minneapolis: University of Minnesota Press.

———. 2005. *Recovering the Sacred: The Power of Naming and Claiming*. Cambridge, MA: South End Press.

Latour, Bruno, and Catherine Porter. 1993. *We Have Never Been Modern*. Cambridge, MA: Harvard University Press.

Le Miere, Jason. 2018. "Donald Trump Says 'Our Ancestors Tamed a Continent' and 'We Are Not Going to Apologize for America.'" *Newsweek*, April 25.

Lipsitz, George. 1998. *The Possessive Investment in Whiteness: How White People Profit from Identity Politics*. Revised and expanded edition. Philadelphia: Temple University Press.

Lucas, Anne E. 2004. "No Remedy for the Inuit: Accountability for Environmental Harms under U.S. and International Law." Pp. 191–208 in *New Perspectives on Environmental Justice: Gender, Sexuality, and Activism*. New Brunswick, NJ: Rutgers University Press.

McNeil, Bryan T. 2013. *Combating Mountaintop Removal: New Directions in the Fight against Big Coal*. Urbana: University of Illinois Press.

Mencimer, Stephanie. 2017. "Cliven Bundy's Lawyer Compares His Armed Resistance to the Selma Marchers." *Mother Jones*, September 29.

Merchant, Carolyn. 2003. "Shades of Darkness: Race and Environmental History." *Environmental History* 8(3): 380–94.

Merica, Dan. 2017. "Trump: 'Both Sides' to Blame for Charlottesville." CNN, August 15. Retrieved March 9, 2018 (https://www.cnn.com/2017/08/15/politics/trump-charlottesville-delay/index.html).

Miner, Dylan A. T. 2013. "Tikibiing Booskikamigaag: An Indigenous History and Ecology of Flint, Michigan." [Grand Rapids, MI: Issue Press.] Retrieved March 9, 2018 (https://www.academia.edu/4412716/Tikibiing_Booskikamigaag_An_Indigenous_History_and_Ecology_of_Flint_Michigan).

Nilles, Bruce, and Mary Ann Hitt. 2009. "From the Senate to the WV Coalfields, a Pivotal Week for Mountaintop Removal." Sierra Club, June 25. Retrieved March 2, 2018 (http://blogs.sierraclub.org/compass/2009/06/from-the-senate-to-the-wv-coalfields-a-pivotal-week-for-mountaintop-removal.html).

Omi, Michael, and Howard Winant. 2015. *Racial Formation in the United States*. 3rd edition. New York: Routledge.

Pearson, Stephen. 2013. "'The Last Bastion of Colonialism': Appalachian Settler Colonialism and Self-Indigenization." *American Indian Culture and Research Journal* 37(2): 165–84.

Plumwood, Val. 1994. *Feminism and the Mastery of Nature*. London: Routledge.

Radin, Margaret Jane. 1982. "Property and Personhood." *Stanford Law Review* 34(5): 957.

Reeve, Elspeth. 2012. "Just How Racist Is the 'Obama Phone' Video?" *Atlantic*, September 27.

Rutherford, Stephanie. 2011. *Governing the Wild*. Minneapolis: University of Minnesota Press.

Schneider, Lindsey. 2013. "'There's Something in the Water': Salmon Runs and Settler Colonialism on the Columbia River." *American Indian Culture and Research Journal* 37(2): 149–64.

Scott, James C. 1999. *Seeing like a State: How Certain Schemes to Improve the Human Condition Have Failed*. New Haven, CT: Yale University Press.

Scott, Rebecca. 2010. *Removing Mountains: Extracting Nature and Identity in the Appalachian Coalfields*. Minneapolis: University of Minnesota Press.

Shiva, Vandana. 2015. *Earth Democracy: Justice, Sustainability, and Peace*. Berkeley, CA: North Atlantic Books.

Sierra Club. n.d.a. "About Us | Beyond Coal." Retrieved March 2, 2018 (https://content.sierraclub.org/coal/about-the-campaign).

———. n.d.b. "Explore, Enjoy and Protect the Planet."* Sierra Club website, home page. Retrieved February 28, 2018 (https://www.sierraclub.org).

Sturm, Circe. 2011. *Becoming Indian: The Struggle over Cherokee Identity in the Twenty-First Century*. Santa Fe, NM: School for Advanced Research Press.

Takei, Carl. 2018. "How Police Can Stop Being Weaponized by Bias-Motivated 911 Calls." American Civil Liberties Union. Retrieved October 17, 2018 (https://www.aclu.org/blog/racial-justice/race-and-criminal-justice/how-police-can-stop-being-weaponized-bias-motivated).

Tallbear, Kimberly. 2013. *Native American DNA: Tribal Belonging and the False Promise of Genetic Science*. Minneapolis: University of Minnesota Press.

Taylor, Dorceta. 2016. *The Rise of the American Conservation Movement*. Durham, NC: Duke University Press.

Templeton, Amelia. 2016. "Judge Denies Motion by Ammon Bundy's Lawyer for Mistrial." Oregon Public Broadcasting, September 16. Retrieved February 2, 2018 (https://www.opb.org/news/series/burns-oregon-standoff-bundy-militia-news-updates/malheur-national-wildlife-refuge-trial-facebook-evidence/).

Varinsky, Dana. 2017. "Here's Every Piece of Land Obama Has Put under Protection during His Presidency." *Business Insider*, January 16. Retrieved March 21, 2018 (http://www.businessinsider.com/every-piece-of-land-obama-has-protected-2017-1).

Wolfe, Patrick. 2013. "The Settler Complex: An Introduction." *American Indian Culture and Research Journal* 37(2): 1–22.

Wray, Matt. 2006. *Not Quite White: White Trash and the Boundaries of Whiteness*. Durham, NC: Duke University Press.

CHAPTER 8

LOCAL IMMIGRATION ENFORCEMENT

Shaping and Maintaining Policies through White Saviors and Economic Motivations

FELICIA ARRIAGA

THE 2016 PRESIDENTIAL election reopened conversations about immigration enforcement at the border, yet the subsequent executive orders sought to also bolster immigration enforcement practices within the interior of the United States to target approximately 12 million undocumented people. The focus on the border wall also continued a practice of inattention to and forgetting about a fully functioning deportation machine that was used to remove 2.5 million people through immigration orders between 2009 and 2015. Because Immigration and Customs Enforcement (ICE) has limited personnel to "manage" individuals they wish to detain and deport, they must depend on local law enforcement to assist them. Yet we know very little about local law enforcement's practices. Furthermore, this level of collaboration forces us to ask, Who is responsible for local immigration enforcement?

This chapter identifies two justifications (white savior efforts and economic motivations) used in the initiation of one particular local-level partnership—Section 287(g) of the Immigration and Nationality Act—and its persistence within North Carolina, a state known as the testing ground and early adopter of many immigrant enforcement partnerships. Ignoring the racist justifications of these local programs is just one example of what Charles Mills (2007) calls collective amnesia. This amnesia, as it pertains to race, allows for "conflicting judgements about what is important in the past and what is unimportant." Although many legal scholars focus on the racialized history of immigration policy construction at the federal level, little research in sociology ties those federal-level histories to localized racist histories of adoption and implementation, particularly for the 287(g) program implemented in North Carolina. Such programs authorize local law officers to detect, detain, and deport unauthorized immigrants through an agreement with ICE (Nguyen and Gill 2010; Pedroza 2019). The particular partnership between ICE and local North Carolina sheriffs was introduced in the late 1990s and was amended to the 1996 Illegal Immigration Reform and Immigrant Responsibility Act (IIRIRA), although few localities showed interest in 287(g) programs until after 9/11 in 2001.

In this chapter, I seek to answer the following: How do whites frame and justify the persistence of this particular immigration enforcement partnership? Also, what forms of white resistance are occurring in response to questions of transparency and accountability? I begin by briefly reviewing the relevant literature on collective amnesia before problematizing two of the justifications that emerged: namely, the role of white saviors then and now, and how white economic interests complicate this understanding of amnesia.

The present political climate—characterized by the blatant anti-immigrant rhetoric during the 2016 presidential elections that continues today—has also encouraged local-level resistance from Latino community members against immigration enforcement partnerships. An example of this resistance was seen in the 2018 sheriff elections in North Carolina. In some ways, this reflects conditions similar to the 2006 Latino waves of protest, which emerged under conditions of Republican Party control, strong post-9/11 nativist sentiments, and a looming legislative threat in the Sensenbrenner Bill (the Border Protection, Antiterrorism and Illegal Immigration Control Act) of 2005 (Zepeda-Millan 2017). Furthermore, few national efforts prior to the Trump presidential administration had forced the Democratic Party, both locally and nationally, to address these concerns. Although the 2016 elections focused mainly on potential class divisions within the white population, less attention was paid to the economic motivations of more agriculturally dependent locations like North Carolina, where white resistance to harsh immigration rhetoric and proposed policy actually follows a different path. Instead, white resistance/mobilization in the state occurs in two ways: to maintain a mostly Latino immigrant workforce, and in order for sheriffs to maintain their political positions in the 2018 elections.

THEORETICAL BACKGROUND

Nationwide studies of immigration enforcement policies and practices can provide useful information but often fail to account for the blatantly racist rhetoric used to implement local policies in areas receiving less attention, as well as the ways in which whites (beyond law enforcement) maintain those practices while simultaneously embarking in collective amnesia about the initial implementation. Below I briefly outline the term *collective amnesia* and the justifications that emerged to explain the initiation of local immigration enforcement, its persistence, and the new tensions in the Trump era.

Collective Amnesia

Although the local law enforcement partnerships with ICE called 287(g) programs drew public attention in the beginning (between 2006 and 2008 in North Carolina), they became invisible through normalized enforcement practices, subsequent collective amnesia of the program's impetus, and competing priorities, which prevented community members from maintaining a sustained resistance. I suggest that this amnesia is upheld by the frames of white innocence, ignorance, and white savior mentality (Bonilla-Silva 1997; Mills 2007; Vera and Gordon 2003; Moore and Pierce 2007; Ross 1990). Charles Mills writes about collective amnesia,

> But if we need to understand collective memory, we also need to understand collective amnesia. Indeed, they go together insofar as memory is necessary selective—out of the infinite sequence of events, some trivial, some momentous, we extract what we see as the crucial ones and organize them into an overall narrative.... Thus there will be both official and counter-memory, with conflicting judgments about what is important in the past and what is unimportant, what happened and does matter, what happened and does not matter, and what did not happen at all. So applying this to race, there will obviously be an intimate relationship between white identity, white memory, and white amnesia, especially about nonwhite victims. (2007:29)

Although I find white ignorance and white innocence to be two frames of collective amnesia that go hand in hand to maintain immigration enforcement partnerships, I focus more on the role of "saviors" in this chapter to further flesh out how these segments of the population navigate local practices. I label economic saviors to highlight their controversial perspectives of pushing for "positive" changes in immigration laws to maintain their own economic position while simultaneously advocating for a deportable labor force.

White Saviors

Substantial attention has been paid to the surge of white voter participation in the 2016 election (Frey 2016; Morgan and Lee 2018), while white community mobilization in North Carolina was simultaneously occurring at the local level, particularly at 287(g) steering committee meetings. These are yearly meetings to discuss partnerships with ICE adopted by local sheriffs. In 2016, there was what Howard Winant (2004) might call a "politicization of whites," which stems from the racial egalitarianism of the post–civil rights era. Yet that politicization accurately describes white liberal mobilization in the current moment that continues to reify white liberal *individualism* (Lipsitz 1998; Moore and Pierce 2007). Vera and Gordon (2003) also argue against the classification of whites into racists and antiracists so as not to reduce and negate the ways in which *all* whites uphold white supremacy, something that must be interrogated in this moment when the Indivisible movement is mimicking the form of the Tea Party movement (Roth 2018). Extensive research focuses on white saviors in films (Moore and Pierce 2007), in the public school system (Cheryl 2016; Miller and Harris 2018), in international humanitarian aid (Cole 2012; Bex and Craps 2016), and increasingly in social movement organizations (Flaherty 2016), yet much of this research does not focus on how law enforcement may frame themselves in this manner, particularly if they may perceive themselves as an intermediary between a federal agency and their own localized role of implementing "public safety." Moreover, James Baldwin reminds us that historically, there wasn't such a distinction between law enforcement and local white faith leaders,

> These ministers, however, are of no interest in themselves—at least of no more intrinsic interest than any Deep South Sheriff.... Both believe that they are able to define and privileged to impose law and order; and both, historically and actually, know that law and order are meant to keep me in my place.... In many ways, perhaps in the deepest ways, the minister and the sheriff were hired by the Republic to keep the Republic white—to keep it from sin. (2011:199–200)

Furthermore, instead of supporting the wishes of directly affected local communities, these individuals (both law enforcement and community members alike) may demonstrate contradictory positions that ultimately allow them to maintain both economic and political dominance.

Economic "Saviors"

Economic incentives played two roles in maintaining local immigration enforcement. On the one hand, law enforcement agencies could financially gain from taking a "tough on immigration" approach, particularly in the earlier years of implementation when federal and state spending was set aside for operations. On the other, white dominance also relies on surplus labor (Roediger 2007; Stuart 2011), particularly in places like the South where an agricultural system depends on undocumented workers to keep operating costs low. Nowhere else was this more apparent than in the various attempts at the local, state, and federal level to pass legislation that would make it more difficult to hire undocumented workers, and the subsequent responses from local and state agricultural sectors. Elsewhere, Andy Clarno (2017) describes the nature of these types of coercive labor regimes whereby neoliberal racial capitalist systems work to keep a labor force like farmworkers in the economy while ensuring that the gains of such a system remain in the hands of citizens. Abigail Fisher Williamson argues that limited local avenues for revenue generation should force local officials to implement accommodating practices for immigrants because doing so could bolster the economy in three ways: "whether by providing a desirable workforce, enhancing local entrepreneurship, or increasing their city's cultural vibrancy" (2018:126).

RESEARCH DESIGN

I heavily draw on archival resources, which I use to triangulate information from each county (see table 8.1). The documents are described as they appear throughout the chapter, but most of these materials are from newspapers as well as archival data (city and county commissioner documents, including budgets, meeting minutes, and minutes from community forums), particularly from around the time of the adoption of 287(g) partnerships between ICE and local law enforcement (2005–8). Although I use these publicly available documents in this chapter, bolstering some of my claims is possible only through the use of information obtained through public records requests, which are ongoing.

Data collection included sorting through approximately ten years of city- and county-level documentation searching for references to ICE and/or immigrants. In some cases, this included references to the issue of national security, but for the most part it did not. I also sampled available local newspapers for terms related to immigration. Most of the quotes throughout this chapter do not identify speakers by name, unless the information was publicly available. Instead, I have indicated what agency, community organization, or other entity the person is representing (table 8.1). Second, I collected information from newspaper archives, protest flyers, and activist websites. Lastly, I have included relevant interviews and observations from my time as a participant observer. Over the course of three years, I attended relevant community meetings across the state—sometimes alone, sometimes with a crowd like the one that sparked my initial interest.[1] Sometimes people would ask where the sheriff was, sometimes I'd just ask a series of questions. And sometimes the questions would get shut down by ICE officials or local Sheriff Office representatives. In 2015, when community organizers began to revive their fights against local Sheriff Offices, I would observe those efforts while reverting back (by traveling to these locations and by conducting retroactive data analysis and interview collection) to the environment where it all began.

Using a combination of process tracing and modified grounded theory required me to be involved in data collection and analysis simultaneously (Charmaz 2006). Beach and Pedersen describe process tracing as working backward "from the outcome by sifting through the evidence in an attempt

TABLE 8.1. Data collection sources across North Carolina counties

County	Public archival data	Interview data	Public meetings/events
Henderson	Blue Ribbon Committee on Illegal Immigration (2007), County Commissioner meetings (2006–16), MOUs, county budget documents (2006–18)	Blue Ribbon Committee members, county officials, Sheriff's Office personnel	2015 287(g) Steering Committee meeting (only participant), community meeting, Sheriff's Office information session
Gaston	County Commissioner meetings (2006–16), MOUs, county budget documents (2006–18)		2015 and 2016 287(g) Steering Committee meetings (only participant)
Mecklenburg	County Commissioner meetings (2006–16), Mayor's Immigration Study Commission (2006–7), MOUs, county budget documents (2006–18)	Community organization, Immigration Study Commission member	2015 and 2016 287(g) Steering Committee meetings
Wake	County Commissioner meetings (2006–16), MOUs, county budget documents (2006–18)	Community members	2015 and 2016 287(g) Steering Committee meetings
Cabarrus	Visioning meeting of County Commissioners (2007), County Commissioner meetings (2006–16), MOUs, county budget documents (2006–18)		2015 and 2016 287(g) Steering Committee meetings (only participant)

Other: correspondence with 287(g) program managers in North Carolina and with Southern Region communications director (spokesman) for US Immigration and Customs Enforcement.

to uncover" a variety of consequences or processes being studied (2013:19–20). This process allowed me to connect major processes (framing, coalition building, mobilization, etc.) to effects (Zepeda-Millan 2017; George and Bennett 2005; McAdam). Once I completed participant observation field notes, I used a modified grounded-theory approach for coding to identify analytic themes and to organize information.

RESULTS AND DISCUSSIONS

White Saviors

Whites justified their roles in immigration enforcement in three ways: from newly politicized white perspectives, local law enforcement perspectives, and ICE perspectives.

Politicized Whites. According to county commissioner documents, during the initial implementation of local immigration enforcement programs (2006–8), elected officials in a few counties attempted to mitigate some blatant anti-immigrant sentiments by creating opportunities for community dialogues, as showcased in Henderson and Mecklenburg Counties. During that time, coalitions of Latino immigrants and white religious leaders attempted to counter blatantly anti-immigrant sentiments and policies. At times, the goals of these two groups did not align, and once implementation began, few whites continued to pay attention to these practices (until relatively recently). Multiple localities initially created Immigrant Justice Committees or something similar, but they did not continue interrogating the enforcement practices occurring at the local level.

In response to the 2016 presidential election, white people across the country began to organize themselves into Indivisible groups (Roth 2018), foreshadowing the emergence in 2019 of Lights for Liberty. In my experiences in various counties in North Carolina, these individuals also organized themselves without first taking stock of groups that previously organized around immigrant rights. The Indivisible movement proudly points to the effectiveness of the Tea Party's rise and attempts to emulate this strategy, although this should draw some critiques from social scientists who suggest that antiracist organizations are similar in some ways to white supremacist organizations (Indivisible 2018).

Most striking within these predominantly religious groups are the sharp distinctions made between "criminals" who should be deported and law-abiding individuals. In various meetings, I asked whether ICE might be entering into probation and parole settings, and in two different counties, these individuals justified not raising awareness of these instances by suggesting that those on probation and parole "did something wrong." This is in stark contrast to grassroots Latinx groups like one in Asheville, North Carolina, that notifies people on their Facebook page when ICE picks people up from probation appointments (CIMA 2018).[2] Often, white individuals from religious institutions facilitate the idea of members of law enforcement as protectors, echoing law enforcement sentiments about criminals while maintaining an intermediary role between law enforcement and the predominantly Latino immigrant community.

Local Law Enforcement. Overwhelmingly, the law enforcement officers I observed in community meetings reiterated their attempts to "protect" community members from "criminals." Yet this sentiment of desiring to "save" or "protect" (in this current moment) Latino immigrants drastically differs from the blatant anti-immigrant sentiments that their predecessors used when advocating for the protection of white community members (Arriaga 2017). Not only does this contradiction showcase law enforcement's patronizing relationship with community members, but it also does so without evidence that they are solely removing "criminals." Local law enforcement and local elected officials, in 287(g) counties and elsewhere, use the following rhetoric to maintain their stance on local level implementation of federal immigration enforcement:

> That's not how we do business—my ability to do the job has to do with communication with the community.... If anyone calls us for any service, please understand we don't care and don't ask about how you came here, we're here to make you more secure.... We have access to a criminal database to see who is in our community, most of y'all don't want them either. (Sheriff Charles S. McDonald, qtd. in Latino Information Network 2017)

> In that time, [Sheriff Irwin] Carmichael said, the department has discovered it was holding undocumented immigrants who were wanted for felony child abuse, murder and possessing a weapon of mass destruction. As a result of such arrests, Carmichael believes participating in 287(g) makes both his staff and the community safer. (qtd. in Bell 2017)

I think that's what the president is saying and I know that's what I'm saying—if you're a bad guy regardless of who you are—I want you out of Wake County. (Sheriff Donnie Harrison, qtd. in Brown 2017)

ICE Perspectives. Prior to the 2018 sheriff races in North Carolina, only three sheriffs claimed not to honor detainer requests (requests to hold immigrants in local jails while ICE decides whether to pick them up) from ICE, yet ICE did not make direct statements against those policy changes. That is, until July 25, 2018, when ICE officials made comments to the *Herald Sun* about the Orange County Sheriff's Office's decision to release an undocumented man without first notifying ICE. Orange County allegedly ended that policy in 2017. In this instance, ICE focused on the individual's previous offense; an ICE official stated, "What is not in dispute is the sheriff's major failed to contact ICE to let us know he had an egregious criminal offender he was about to return to community" (qtd. in WRAL 2018). ICE painting itself as morally above the decisions of the local sheriff is an attempt to sway public opinion, particularly since this statement was not directed at the sheriff himself but was passed on to media first. Alternatively, ICE also continued to emphasize "saving" community members from collateral arrests, if local-level jail identification and notification did not persist. This ultimatum, whereby ICE may need to conduct more field operations instead of finding immigrants in local jails, is also an attempt to repress community organizing efforts against these localized collaborations.

ECONOMIC "SAVIORS"

The persistent invisibility of 287(g) program operations also protects white economic interests and benefits majority-white communities. In the program's early years, during community input sessions, business representatives expressed concerns about the negative impact of extra immigration enforcement. Yet similar concerns were not raised about additional income resulting from detaining and housing undocumented immigrants. In the initial years of implementation, incentives to detain and house individuals also came from state and national entities.

Business Interests

Although only one of the counties with a 287(g) program—Henderson County—relies heavily on agriculture that employs primarily immigrant labor, the state's other ninety-five immigrant-dependent counties, which were not operating with 287(g) programs, would also face negative consequences from anti-immigrant worker legislation. To the extent that this is expected, the North Carolina Farm Bureau steps in to lobby against any bills that would make it easier to deport immigrant workers.

> The owners of several local agriculture businesses have penned a letter to Meadows, Burr and Tillis asking them to support immigration reform legislation that allows them to keep their workforce. The Town of Mills River's Agricultural Advisory Committee crafted the letter Thursday and addressing it to U.S. Rep. Mark Meadows, U.S. Sen. Richard Burr and U.S. Sen. Thom Tillis.
> "Congress must pass legislation that preserves agriculture's experienced workforce by allowing current farm workers to earn legal status," the letter says.
> "For future needs, legislation must create an agricultural worker visa program that provides access to a legal and reliable workforce moving forward. This visa program needs to be market-based and have the flexibility to meet the needs of producers, including those with year-round labor needs, such as dairy and livestock." (Lacey 2017)

Around the same time, a local community group in the Piedmont Triad (the state's central region) reposted a visit Senator Tillis made to a dairy farm to highlight the contradiction of supporting immigrant labor while not supporting additional areas of integration (Moore and Pierce 2017).

This economic benefit was one of the only areas cited as a "positive" aspect of the increased immigration to these counties. To simplify this argument from a pro-business perspective, in eastern North Carolina, state representatives who also own larger farms passed legislation in the 2017 Farm Bill meant to dissuade any organizing and collective bargaining agreements of farmworkers—particularly those affiliated with the Farm Labor Organizing Committee (Bouloubasis 2017). FLOC president Baldemar Velasquez emphasized this self-serving purpose, stating, "Politicians that are also growers shouldn't pass self-serving laws simply because they don't want their workers to unionize" (SPLC 2017).

Recently, a federal court blocked the North Carolina Farm Act of 2017 after a lawsuit was filed by the Southern Poverty Law Center and other civil rights groups, claiming that the law violates Fourteenth Amendment rights (SPLC 2018). In some ways, farmworkers are "protected" from the same E-Verify employment eligibility verification processes that targeted larger pork and poultry factories like Smithfield in eastern North Carolina back in 2007 (Collins 2007). Unfortunately, this lack of protection also keeps them in a precarious position, as demonstrated when migrant workers called 911 for help during Hurricane Florence. Instead of listening to these individuals, emergency services communicated with their employer, who told them that the workers "had everything they needed as far as food and water" (Hernandez 2018).

Law Enforcement Incentives

Vargas and McHarris (2017) describe the financial relationship between federal aid and racial threat responses, yet they ignore the roles that states and individuals have in advocating for this funding. That relationship is clear in North Carolina, where the state legislature set aside funding for the 2007 Illegal Immigration Project/Sheriffs Immigration Enforcement Agreement (North Carolina Sheriffs' Association 2008). This bill, sponsored by North Carolina House representatives Marion McLawhorn, Harry Warren, and Joe Kiser, moved money from the General Fund to the Governor's Crime Commission of then the Department of Crime Control and Public Policy, allocating $750,000 in Fiscal Year 2007–8. For the 2008–9 fiscal year, it also allocated $1 million to the North Carolina Sheriff's Association to provide technical assistance and advice for the 287(g) program, provide technical assistance to sheriffs seeking to negotiate MOUs with ICE, and enable sheriffs to send personnel to training by reimbursing travel costs and the officer's salary during training.[3]

In 2008, the Burlington *Times-News* reported that Alamance County, at the onset of their 287(g) program, would probably earn a combined $5.5 million to $6 million for housing immigration detainees and detainees of the US Marshals Service. The jail took in about $400,000 in bed rentals for February alone, Sheriff Terry Johnson said (Boyer 2008).

Furthermore, Jim Pendergraph, former Mecklenburg sheriff, "was hired in 2007 to head up ICE's Office of State and Local Coordination in part to oversee the 287(g) process nationally" (Coleman 2012). Pendergraph's influence would then shape the North Carolina Sheriffs Association's stance on local involvement in immigration enforcement. It's clear, however, that he was not the only outspoken anti-immigrant voice of the Sheriff's Association.

Taxpayer Confusion

In 2010, Mai Nguyen and Hannah Gill (2010) were the first to estimate some of these costs of local law enforcement partnerships, namely the 287(g) partnership. They did so by combining the estimated salaries of Sheriff Office

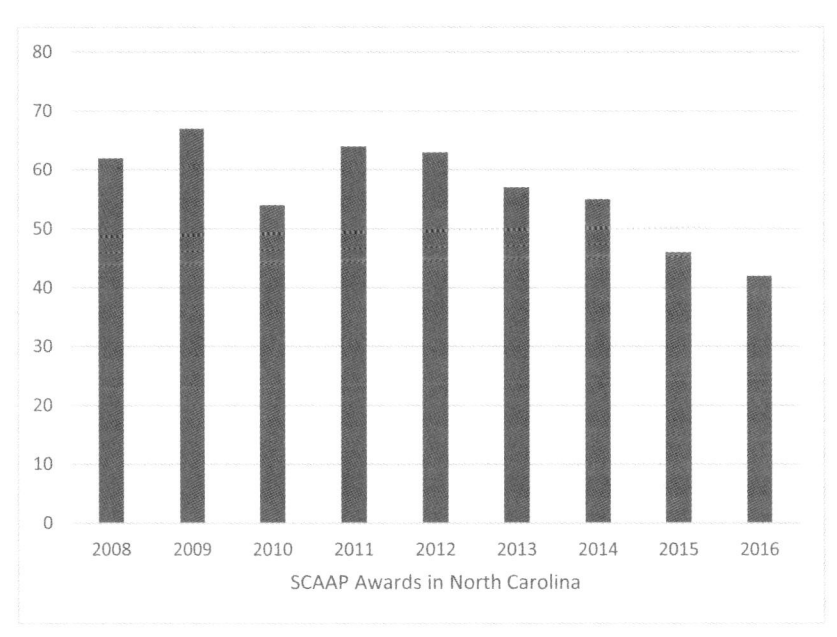

FIGURE 8.1. Counties receiving SCAAP awards in North Carolina, 2008–2016

personnel involved with the program, training costs, and the annual cost of detaining undocumented immigrants. They did this for two counties—Mecklenburg and Alamance—for the initial year of operation. Similar financial concerns surfaced most recently in 287(g) steering committee meetings. Yet it's difficult to construct a clear understanding of the costs of the program and to trace financial exchanges across a variety of local immigration enforcement partnerships. One clear way to track the costs is by highlighting a reimbursement process available to every jail, the State Criminal Alien Assistance Program (figure 8.1)—yet this approach results in conservative estimates (Office of Justice Programs 2018; Arriaga 2018). There are one hundred counties and one hundred sheriffs in North Carolina, and over the past decade, every year forty-plus sheriffs have participated in some way economically by receiving reimbursements from the federal government "due to incarceration of undocumented criminal aliens during a particular 12-month period" (Office of Justice Programs 2015–18).

CONCLUSIONS

When it comes to local immigration enforcement, whites adopted a variety of frames to rationalize concerns about the initial implementation, persistence, and current transparency and accountability. In some counties, the duality of economic incentives (labor force and possible jail revenue) pointed to white mobilization as a response to a perceived economic threat. Moreover, during the 2018 sheriff elections, white sheriffs were interrogated for their immigration enforcement practices, forcing them to resist threats to a political office historically viewed as the epitome of white political power at the local level (Shaffer 2018).

In county-level administrative records, blatantly racist and anti-immigrant sentiments of those in power emerged, setting the direction for the persistence of these practices. We must acknowledge this history and also acknowledge that those on both sides of the aisle allowed "deporters in chief" to persist with the help of local law enforcement. And we can definitely not blame the persistence of these programs on immigrants and Latinos, since they do not have the highest rates of political participation in the forms of voting and being involved with local county meetings. Some of this undoing of a collective amnesia begins by acknowledging that ten years have passed with no continuous efforts to uncover immigration enforcement practices at the local level. This, of course, is not the only arena that deserves more attention, since immigration enforcement practices are just one of many problems of local law enforcement that go unchecked.

Policy Implications

Acknowledgment. After acknowledging how whites and particularly local governing bodies are complicit in immigration enforcement, we can begin to interrogate these practices before moving on to local and state level changes. I suggest these two areas first since the national climate has proven time and time again, under two administrations, to not have the answers for people most directly affected. I also suggest this approach because on a practical level, ICE has limited resources to continue its enforcement without the assumed participation of localities across the country.

Interrogation. We must be critical of the government bureaucracy and not adopt a "rational ignorance" approach when it comes to matters of local law enforcement (Robbins, Simonsen, and Feldman 2008). Not only should we consider prearrest protocols across the board but we should be concerned with draconian state laws like those in 2006 that stripped undocumented immigrants of their driver's licenses. Furthermore, we can do the following:

- Ask local law enforcement about their operating procedures when it comes to those driving without a license.

- Ask whether they collaborate with ICE.
- Request that they stop collaborating with ICE, dependent on community decision-making processes.
- Ask if they pass along information to ICE.
- Get your city and county officials involved.
- Ask if there is deputized staff in the jail to handle immigration matters.
- Ask if the sheriff honors ICE detainers.
- Ask if they receive additional funding for holding immigrants in the jail.
- Ask if they have programs to assist immigrants, like the U-Visa process, which is meant to assist victims of certain crimes.

Accountability, Transparency, and Reform

Across the country, local immigration enforcement practices and local elected officials' stances on immigration are under scrutiny as wedge issues in local elections. Moreover, this level of transparency and accountability is targeting both sides of the aisle. "Flip NC" became a rallying cry for many, mostly newly activated, whites to encourage the restoration of a Democratic-controlled state legislature. Prior to the 2016 elections, the Republican Party had a supermajority in the state, greatly limiting the effectiveness of the Democratic governor.

Two incidents exemplify how being associated with blatantly anti-immigrant stances like those of the Trump administration are not helping Democrats win local races. First, Cathy von Hassel-Davies, a Democratic candidate for the North Carolina State House in an Alamance County district, dropped out of the 2018 race after anti-immigrant comments from an old blog post surfaced. Initially the North Carolina Democratic Party did not make a statement, but eventually they distanced themselves from her (Specht 2018). The local Hispanic-American Caucus had also met with her and asked her to bow out. Second, in the fall of 2014, the Durham People's Alliance had endorsed Sheriff Mike Andrews for re-election (Fall 2014 endorsements), but their goal of holding local elected officials accountable 365 days of the year was not fulfilled during the course of his tenure as sheriff. As a result, the People's Alliance ultimately endorsed the challenger for this position in 2018. Because the local governments in Mecklenburg and Durham Counties are Democrat controlled, many voters assumed that sheriffs in these counties should be more aligned with Democratic values. But two things are generally true about sheriffs: both Republican and Democrat sheriffs participate in immigration enforcement collaborations, and sheriffs typically don't run on enforcement-lite campaigns. If newly politicized whites and white liberals are serious about their progressive ideals, then they will begin to hold local elected officials accountable for both immigration enforcement practices and broader policies of the criminal justice system.

Symbolic resolutions can no longer be the answer to local immigration enforcement practices. Instead, routes such as creating immigration defense funds, like the ones in Denver (Murray 2018; Vera Institute of Justice 2018) and San Diego (Morrissey 2018), can at least help mitigate the consequences for immigrants living in localities that choose to collaborate with ICE. Although researchers have focused on the profits resulting from the private prison industry, which has increasingly taken on ownership of immigration detention, less research has gone into the economics of local immigration enforcement. By starting hyperlocal, we can begin to see our own role in local immigration enforcement, the place where I believe there is currently the most energy to see positive change.

NOTES

1. "Our perception of this program is completely different. Let me tell you that, the 287(g) Program didn't work from the beginning and didn't work from day 1 and HB318 is not going to work. Because we're not safer now. Do you think we are safer than before 9/11? I don't think so. It will not work. Why? Because from the beginning you decided to [doubt] the community, [throw] the Latino community under the bus. You decided not to work for the people's safety. Instead, you decided to work on behalf of the private prison shareholders. Why are so many Latinos deported for nothing? Just for a traffic violation? What is this? How do we take the racial component from this issue? Is it ethnic cleansing? Do you know that 50% of the undocumented people came by plane? We are not safe. We are less confident. We are actually scared. So that is why we are demanding ICE out of North Carolina. We are demanding ICE out of every jail in North Carolina. The system is not working." Gregorio Morales, Comité Popular Somos Raleigh, December 2015, 287(g) Steering Committee meeting, Wake County Sheriff's Office.

    Once Gregorio stood up and made this statement at the annual 287(g) ICE enforcement partnership steering committee meeting, held at the Wake County Detention Center, community members, most of whom proudly wore a black T-shirt that read "ICE out of NC" in white letters on the front and "Stop the Hate" in red letters on the back, began shouting "ICE out of North Carolina" as they left the room. Most left, but four stayed, along with representatives from both Spanish-language and English-language media, to continue participating in the Q&A portion of the meeting, which lasted about 40 minutes longer.

2. This practice can be used to circumvent so-called sanctuary policies, yet this is not typically a local-level decision. Instead, parole and probation is under

the purview of the Department of Public Safety. At this time, interviews are ongoing with this department about their current practices and local-level variation in ICE communication.
3. No news about this proposed legislation appeared in a statewide search of news coverage for the years 2007 to 2008.

REFERENCES

Arriaga, Felicia. 2017. "Relationships between the Public and Local Law Enforcement in North Carolina Counties with 287(g) Programs in North Carolina." *Sociology of Race and Ethnicity* 3(3): 417–31.

Baldwin, James. *The Cross of Redemption: Uncollected Writings*. Edited and with an introduction by Randall Kenan. New York: Pantheon, 2011.

Beach, Derek, and Rasmus Brun Pedersen. 2013. *Process-Tracing Methods: Foundations and Guidelines*. Ann Arbor: University of Michigan Press.

Bell, Adam. 2017. "Meck Sheriff to Community: We Don't Decide Who Gets Deported by ICE." *Charlotte Observer*, March 2. Retrieved May 12, 2020 (http://www.charlotteobserver.com/news/local/article135984403.html).

Bex, Sean, and Stef Craps. 2016. "Humanitarianism, Testimony, and the White Savior Industrial Complex: What Is the What versus Kony 2012." *Cultural Critique* (92): 32–56.

Bonilla-Silva, Eduardo. 1997. *Racism without Racists*. Lanham, MD: Rowman & Littlefield.

Bouloubasis, Victoria. 2017. "The Farm Labor Organizing Committee Sues Governor Cooper on Behalf of Farmworkers, Saying a New State Law Is Discriminatory." *IndyWeek*, November 15. Retrieved May 12, 2020 (https://indyweek.com/food-and-drink/news/farm-labor-organizing-committee-sues-governor-cooper-behalf-farmworkers-saying-new-state-law-discriminatory/).

Brown, Joel. 2017. "Outrage, Fear as ICE Cracks Down in Immigration Raids." ABC11, February 15. Retrieved May 12, 2020 (https://abc11.com/politics/outrage-fear-as-ice-cracks-down-in-immigration-raids/1753441/).

Charmaz, Kathy. 2006 *Constructing Grounded Theory: A Practical Guide through Qualitative Analysis*. Thousand Oaks, CA: Sage.

Clarno, Andy. 2017. *Neoliberal Apartheid: Palestine/Israel and South Africa after 1994*. Chicago: University of Chicago Press.

Cole, Teju. 2012. "The White-Savior Industrial Complex." *Atlantic*, March 21.

Coleman, Mathew. 2012. "The 'Local' Migration State: The Site-Specific Devolution of Immigration Enforcement in the U.S. South." *Law and Policy* 34(2): 159–90.

Collins, Kristin. 2007. "Screening Flags Illegal Workers at N.C. sites." *News and Observer* (Raleigh, NC), February 5, A1.

Flaherty, Jordan. 2016. *No More Heroes: Grassroots Challenges to the Savior Mentality*. Chico, CA: AK Press.

Frey, William. 2016. "The Demographic Blowblack That Elected Donald Trump." Brookings, November 10. Retrieved April 16, 2020 (https://www.brookings.edu/blog/the-avenue/2016/11/10/the-demographic-blowback-that-elected-donald-trump/).

George, Alexander, and Andrew Bennett. 2005. *Case Studies and Theory Development.* Cambridge, MA: MIT Press.

Hernandez, Salvador. 2018. "Hurricane Florence Has Left Farmworkers Stranded without Work, Food, or Aid." *Buzzfeed News*, September 28. Retrieved May 12, 2020 (https://www.buzzfeednews.com/article/salvadorhernandez/farmworkers-hurricane-florence-north-carolina).

Indivisible. 2018. "Summary: Grassroots Advocacy." Retrieved October 19, 2018 (https://www.indivisible.org/guide/summary/).

Lacey, Derek. 2017. "Immigration: Ag Leaders Speak Out as Employees Skip Work." BlueRidgeNow.com, *Times-News* (Burlington, NC) online, February 17. Retrieved May 12, 2020 (https://www.blueridgenow.com/news/20170217/immigration-ag-leaders-speak-out-as-employees-skip-work).

Latino Information Network. Meeting, April 12, 2017.

Matias, Cheryl. 2016. "White Skin, Black Friend: A Fanonian Application to Theorize Racial Fetish in Teacher Education." *Educational Philosophy and Theory* 48(3): 221–36.

Menjivar, Cecilia, and Leisy J. Abrego. 2012. "Legal Violence: Immigration Law and the Lives of Central American Immigrants." *American Journal of Sociology* 117(5): 1380–1421.

Miller, Lisa, and Victor Harris. 2018. "I Can't Be Racist—I Teach in an Urban School, and I'm a Nice White Lady!" *World Journal of Education* 8(3): 1–11.

Mills, Charles. 1997. *The Racial Contract.* Ithaca, NY: Cornell University Press.

———. 2007. "White Ignorance." Pp. 13–28 in *Race and Epistemologies*, edited by Shannon Sullivan and Nancy Tuana. Albany: State University of New York Press.

Moore, Wendy Leo, and Jennifer L. Pierce. 2007. "Still Killing Mockingbirds: Narratives of Race and Innocence in Hollywood's Depiction of the White Messiah Lawyer." *Qualitative Sociology Review* 3(2): 171–87.

Morgan, Stephen, and Jiwon Lee. 2018. "Trump Voters and the White Working Class." *Sociological Science* 5(10): 234–45.

Morrissey, Kate. 2018. "Bond Fund to Help Detained San Diego Immigrants." *San Diego Union-Tribune*, October 5.

Murray, Jon. 2018. "Denver Launches Growing Immigrant Defense Fund to Aid People with Problems Stemming from Their Legal Status." *Denver Post*, March 19.

Nguyen, Mai Thi, and Hannah Gill. 2010. *The 287(g) Program: The Costs and Consequences of Local Immigration Enforcement in North Carolina Communities.* Chapel Hill: University of North Carolina Latino Migration Project.

North Carolina Sheriffs' Association. 2008. "Final Legislative Report 2008." Retrieved January 2016 (http://www.ncsheriffs.org/Weekly%20Legislative%20Report/NCSA.FLR.2008.pdf).

Office of Justice Programs. 2015–18. "State Criminal Alien Assistance Program (SCAAP)." US Department of Justice, Bureau of Justice Assistance. Retrieved from https://bja.ojp.gov/program/state-criminal-alien-assistance-program-scaap/overview.

Pedroza, Juan. 2019. "Where Immigration Enforcement Agreements Stalled: The Location of Local 287(g) Program Applications and Inquiries (2005–2012)." *SocArXiv*, January 4. Retrieved May 12, 2020 (osf.io/preprints/socarxiv/2a8kz).

Robbins, Mark D., Bill Simonsen, and Barry Feldman. 2008. "Citizens and Resource Allocation: Improving Decision Making with Interactive Web-Based Citizen Participation." *Public Administration Review* 68(3): 564–75.

Roediger, David. 2007. *The Wages of Whiteness: Race and the Making of the American Working Class*. Haymarket Series. London: Verso.

Ross, Thomas. 1990. "The Rhetorical Tapestry of Race: White Innocence and Black Abstraction." *William & Mary Law Review* 32(1): 1–40.

Roth, Benita. 2018. "Learning from the Tea Party: The US Indivisible Movement as Countermovement in the Era of Trump." *Sociological Research Online* 23(2): 539–46.

Shaffer, Josh. 2018. "With Focus on Immigration, Voters in NC's Seven Largest Counties Elected Black Sheriffs." *News and Observer* (Raleigh, NC), November 8.

Specht, Paul. 2018. "After Rant Surfaces about 'Mexicans,' NC Democrat Drops out of House Race." *News and Observer* (Raleigh, NC), July 25.

SPLC. 2017. "Union Sues North Carolina over Law Stripping Rights from 100,000 Farmworkers." SPLC: Southern Poverty Law Center, November 15. Retrieved May 12, 2020 (https://www.splcenter.org/news/2017/11/15/union-sues-north-carolina-over-law-stripping-rights-100000-farmworkers).

———. 2018. "Federal Court Blocks North Carolina Law that Stripped Rights from Farmworkers." SPLC: Southern Poverty Law Center, September 21. Retrieved May 12, 2020 (https://www.splcenter.org/news/2018/09/21/federal-court-blocks-north-carolina-law-stripped-rights-farmworkers).

Stuart, Forrest. 2011. "Race, Space, and the Regulation of Surplus Labor: Policing African-Americans in Los Angeles' Skid Row." *Souls: A Critical Journal of Black Politics, Culture, and Society* 13(2): 197–212.

Vargas, Robert, and Philip McHarris. 2017. "Race and State in City Police Spending Growth: 1980 to 2010." *Sociology of Race and Ethnicity* 3(1): 96–112.

Vera, Hernan, and Andrew Gordon. 2003. *Screen Saviors: Hollywood Fictions of Whiteness*. Lanham, MD: Rowman & Littlefield.

Vera Institute of Justice. "Safety and Fairness for Everyone (SAFE) Network." 2018. Retrieved May 12, 2020 (https://www.vera.org/projects/safe-network).

Williamson, Abigail Fisher. 2018. *Welcoming New Americans? Local Governments and Immigrant Incorporation.* Chicago: University of Chicago Press.

Winant, Howard. 2004. *Behind Blue Eyes: Contemporary White Racial Politics.* Minneapolis: University of Minnesota Press.

WRAL. 2018. "Orange Sheriff, ICE Square Off over Release of Inmates in US Illegally." WRAL News, July 25. Retrieved July 25, 2018 (https://www.wral.com/orange-sheriff-ice-square-off-over-release-of-inmates-in-us-illegally/17724377/).

Zepeda-Millan, Chris. 2017. *Latino Mass Mobilization: Immigration, Racialization, and Activism.* New York: Cambridge University Press.

CHAPTER 9

RECRUITING WHITE "VICTIMS"

White Supremacist Flyers on College Campuses

DAVID DIETRICH

Since the election of Donald J. Trump as president in 2016, we have seen a dramatic rise in white supremacist activism in the United States. While most media attention has focused on rallies such as the "Unite the Right" rally in Virginia in 2017, white supremacists have also been engaging in another kind of activism that has gone largely unnoticed nationally: the posting of flyers on college campuses. Since spring 2016, flyers promoting white supremacist ideas and goals have been posted on campus buildings across the nation (SPLC 2017b). While events like rallies and speeches may be more conspicuous and draw large one-time crowds, the flyers have the potential to reach a much greater audience of students, those who would not go to a speech by an avowed white supremacist. Posted in prominent locations across campuses, the flyers communicate a simple message of white supremacy and seek to recruit new adherents by leading them to white supremacist websites.

Through affirmative action and multicultural education, most colleges have made (arguably superficial) attempts to bring both a diverse student body and diverse ideas to their campuses. Given this environment, one would think college students would be unsympathetic to white supremacist arguments. However, Gallagher (1995) argues that the embracing of diversity and multicultural education has created a vicious backlash in academia from both conservative organizations outside the university and white students within it. Whereas whiteness had previously been a background, almost invisible, trait, affirmative action motivated students to begin thinking of themselves in terms of their racial group membership, engendering a sense of group position (Blumer 1958) with regard to whiteness (Gallagher 2004). This led many students to interpret diversity goals as attacks on whiteness and multicultural education as a punishment imposed on them for the crimes of their ancestors. With these points of similarity between white student backlash on college campuses and white supremacist frames, it is not surprising that white supremacists target college campuses.

The purpose of this chapter is to address the following questions: How do white supremacists try to appeal to college students? What kinds of appeals do they hope will resonate within what should be a haven for diversity and multiculturalism? Through a qualitative content analysis of white supremacist flyers reported posted on college campuses, I show how white supremacists tailor their messages to college students. I argue that white supremacists use a master frame of white victimization, portraying diversity as victimizing white students and relying on existing color-blind racist narratives such as those regarding affirmative action.

THE FRAMES OF CONTEMPORARY WHITE SUPREMACIST ACTIVISM

The civil rights movement forced a rearticulation of white supremacy to the point that many adherents no longer identify as "white supremacists." Instead, they are more likely to call themselves "white nationalists" or "white separatists," which allows them to rationalize their message as one of love, not hate (Barkun 1994; Berbrier 1998). However, underlying their argument for racial separatism is the belief that the races are inherently different and unequal and cannot coexist. White nationalists argue that the white race is being destroyed through racial mixing and can be saved only by creating a separate white state (Berbrier 2000).

For both traditional white supremacists and the newer white nationalists/separatists, victimization is central to how they frame their movement. They perceive several sources of victimization from the outside, including not only minority races but also whites who advocate diversity and multiculturalism, so-called race traitors. These sources of victimization include intermarriage, minority population growth, an (allegedly) growing minority crime rate, increasing immigration, and whites losing jobs to minorities (Berlet and Vysotsky 2006; Dobratz and Shanks-Meile 1997; Daniels 1997). Many white supremacists/separatists, if not anticapitalistic, view big business as exploiting or impeding advancement of the white worker (Ferber and

Kimmel 2000). Similarly, government programs such as affirmative action, gun control legislation, and purported permissiveness toward illegal immigration are painted as betrayal of white citizens by a government that no longer represents them (Perry 2000). These two grievances merge into the conspiracy theory of the "New World Order," an international elite group, including major politicians, capitalists, and controllers of mass media, promoting their own interests while reducing the living conditions of white workers to those of the third world (Dobratz and Shanks-Meile 1997; Ferber and Kimmel 2000).

Berbrier (2000) distinguishes five elements in the victim ideology of white supremacists. The first is that whites as oppressed victims of discrimination. White supremacists use the "culturally resonant master frame" (Berbrier 1998) of cultural pluralism to create a new kind of white identity—one in which "whites" must defend their racial identity just as racial minorities defend theirs. The second element is the abrogation of whites' rights. White separatists today increasingly paint themselves as merely another ethnic or minority group that seeks nothing more than to do the same thing as other minority groups: create organizations to promote their own racial interests; in the process, they establish a false equivalence between whites and other minority races (Beck 2000). The third element is stigmatization and shame. White supremacists claim that a double standard exists in today's society: activities that emphasize racial or ethnic pride for nonwhites are defined as unacceptable for whites. The fourth and fifth elements involve short- and long-term harm to whites, from a loss of self-esteem due to an inability to express racial pride to threats to the survival of the "white race." Survival will naturally trump "less important" values such as tolerance and compassion.

The recruitment and mobilization strategy for white supremacist activism boils down to creating and instilling a white identity—that is, developing the consciousness of white people as "Whites," who are defined as a class of victims (Hughey 2014). I contend that this shapes the messages of the white supremacist flyers on college campuses.

White Supremacy on College Campuses

In recent years, hundreds of flyers have been put up on campuses across the nation, but most of them have been produced by just a few national white supremacist organizations (SPLC 2017b). One such group is Identity Evropa, which launched a campaign called "Project Siege" in September 2016 to target college students by distributing flyers at college campuses throughout the US. Another group responsible for many of the flyers is Vanguard

America, known for expressing more explicitly fascist and neo-Nazi views (SPLC 2017b). While Identity Evropa and Vanguard America have been responsible for the vast majority of reported flyer incidents, a number of smaller organizations have engaged in similar tactics. American Renaissance, like Identity Evropa, embarked on an explicit campaign targeting college students with what has been described as primarily "pro-white" propaganda posters. The Right Stuff is an alt-right political blog by Michael "Enoch" Peinovich that uses a "pool party" structure involving local meetups of contributors and podcast pundits, out of which grew their own flyer distribution. Finally, Atomwaffen Division is a small neo-Nazi hate group whose members include Stephen Billingsley, who held a sign saying "God Hates Fags" while protesting a vigil for the Pulse Nightclub shooting (SPLC 2017b). In addition to these national organizations, there are other local organizations, such as the Texas State Vigilantes, the Boise State Nationalists, and the U of L Identitarians (University of Louisville), who are usually responsible for flyers only at their own specific campuses.

Relying on the backlash against and debates about diversity and multiculturalism, white supremacist organizations have targeted colleges and universities to curate a receptive audience of disaffected white students who may be receptive to their message of white superiority and separatism. Add to this the notable shift in the discourse surrounding race and immigration in the past few years as well as the election of Donald Trump, and the timing of the rash of flyers being posted on campuses across the nation becomes apparent. But what kinds of messages do these flyers communicate? Are they the "diplomatic" frames of the white student unions, emphasizing white racial pride and avoiding any negative mention of other racial groups? Do they emphasize the purported victimization of whites and the "stigma" of whiteness? Or do they directly attack minorities, emphasizing supposed threats from immigrants and other minority groups to white interests? These are the questions I address in my examination of white supremacist flyers found on college campuses.

RESEARCH DESIGN

To examine the messages these white supremacist organizations use to attract college students, I conducted a qualitative content analysis of all available flyers, banners, and cards posted on college campuses from March 2016 through the end of December 2017. These flyers were posted at places on campus with high student traffic, such as bulletin boards with other school announcements, doors and windows to major classroom buildings, libraries, and even places like "trash bins, newspaper racks, lampposts, . . . and paper-towel dispensers" (Jones 2017). I chose March 2016 as my starting point for data collection as this was the point in time the Southern Poverty Law Center (SPLC 2017b) identified as the beginning of the most recent surge in flyer activity.[1]

To obtain images or narrative descriptions of the flyers, banners, and cards (heretofore collectively referred to as flyers), I conducted online searches. Starting with listings produced by the Anti-Defamation League and the Southern Poverty Law Center, I searched for specific incidents by date and university to verify each event listed and, where possible, found images of the flyers themselves. In addition, I conducted my own Internet searches for terms including "supremacist," "racist," and "nationalist" in conjunction with "flyers" to obtain any flyers from incidents not listed by the aforementioned organizations. In total, I verified 325 incidents at 209 colleges and universities. From these incidents, I obtained images or descriptions of 120 unique flyers. Because many flyers were produced by only a handful of organizations and were reused in multiple incidents at campuses across the nation, the total number of unique flyers is not commensurate with the total number of incidents reported. From the over 300 incidents, only 20 national-level and 10 local-level groups acknowledged responsibility for the flyers. Over a fifth of the flyers were either posted anonymously or not attributed to a particular group.

To systematically analyze the flyers, I employed techniques of ethnographic content analysis (ECA) (Altheide 1987, 1996; Krippendorff 2004). ECA involves a reflexive research design in which documents are analyzed repeatedly to allow for the discovery of previously unknown patterns and categories of analysis (Bernhard, Futrell, and Harper 2010). While ECA is guided by pre-established categories drawn from previous research and experience, it allows for "constant discovery and constant comparison" of patterns within the data (Altheide 1987:68).

First, I coded for white victimization, both generally and using specific subcodes for Berbrier's (2000) elements of white victim ideology: victims of discrimination, abrogation of whites' rights, stigmatization and shame, and harm to whites. Second, I coded for sources of victimization to whites. This included victimization from minority groups (Dobratz and Shanks-Meile 1997), in which I coded for identification of threats from particular minority groups as well as for expressions of negativity or hatred toward specific minority races (Berlet and Vysotsky 2006). I also coded for victimization by big business or capitalism (Ferber and Kimmel 2000), by government action (Perry 2000), by the educational system—such as that expressed by the concept of "miseducation" (Hughey 2012)—and by the "New World Order" of global elites (Ferber and Kimmel 2000). Additionally, I coded references to "white pride" and framing of opposition to white supremacy as "hate" (Berbrier 1998). Finally, I identified a handful of emergent categories that could have been used to appeal to college students that were not previously identified in the scholarship. These categories included mention of Donald Trump or aspects of the Trump campaign, such as use of the phrase "make America great again," and specific appeals to the youth/college generation.

RESULTS

Victimization

Expressions of white victimization were found in just over half, sixty-four, of the unique flyers, making it by far the most common trait. Virtually all of the flyers that expressed white victimization exhibited multiple elements (Berbrier 2000). For example, one unattributed flyer posted at Clemson University in October 2017 said, "ATTENTION WHITE PEOPLE. ARE YOU TIRED OF BEING BLAMED FOR EVERYTHING? WONDERING WHY ONLY WHITE COUNTRIES NEED MULTICULTURALISM? REALIZING DIVERSITY MEANS 'LESS WHITE'? TIRED OF BEING CALLED RACIST FOR WANTING AN IDENTITY? DO YOU SEE A FUTURE FOR YOU AND YOUR FAMILY? TIRED OF POLITICAL CORRECTNESS? JOIN THE ALT RIGHT."[2] This flyer exhibits three elements of Berbrier's (2000) white victim ideology, expressing feelings of discrimination and stigmatization with references to being "blamed for everything" and "being called racist" as well as long-term threat to whites by implicitly referencing white genocide with a phrase implying that diversity, multiculturalism, and political correctness are threatening the "future for you and your family." Another flyer, attributed to Vanguard America, features several victimization and threat subframes, including victimization by global capitalism and the "Jewish media," as well as stigmatization of whites: "This land is soaked in which European blood, and its heritage and culture is being ripped away for the benefit of global finance. Should your children grow up a tiny, hated minority in their own country? Have you had enough of the lying, Jewish media's indoctrination?"

I identified several purported victimizers of whites. Unsurprisingly, most perceived threats (nineteen out of thirty-four) were from minority groups (Berlet and Vysotsky 2006; Dobratz and Shanks-Meile 1997).[3] Antiblack expressions were the most common, found in twelve flyers. For example, a flyer attributed to AltRight.com and posted at the University of Michigan in September 2016 was titled "Why White Women Shouldn't Date Black Men." It described how black men are supposedly more prone to violence and sexually transmitted diseases. Another unattributed flyer, found at the University of Texas at Austin in May 2017, depicted a racist caricature of a black man holding a knife in a threatening manner with a caption reading "... Around BLACKS NEVER RELAX!"

Anti-Semitism was also common, appearing in nine flyers, with one local group in particular, the Auburn White Student Union, producing two flyers focused solely on anti-Semitic messaging. One of them showed several photographs of Jewish individuals, including one meeting with former president Obama, with a caption reading, "Will YOU Disobey The Anti-Christian, TOP SECRET NOAHIDE LAWS?" This flyer was notably the only one, even among all anti-Semitic flyers, to associate whiteness with Christianity, or even to mention Christianity at all. Another unattributed flyer, found at Princeton University in December 2017, is specifically addressed to a social justice advocate named Linda Oppenheim and reads, "Hey Linda (((Oppenheim))), instead of inciting anti-White animosity with your lines about so called 'White Privilege,' why don't you discuss the real privilege in America? JEWISH PRIVILEGE." This flyer also blames Oppenheim, who is identified as Jewish through the use of three sets of parenthesis to emphasize her family name, for discrimination against whites due to "inciting anti-White animosity" through discussion of white privilege.

Other less common expressions of minority threat targeted Muslims (five flyers). One Vanguard America flyer found at the University of Texas in February 2017 and Bellevue College in April 2017 showed a picture of the World Trade Center's twin towers with text reading, "*Imagine* A MUSLIM FREE AMERICA." This framing again implies long-term harm by referencing the threat of Islamic extremist terrorism happening again in America. Similarly, a flyer by Identity Evropa, posted at Millersville University in Pennsylvania in September 2017, read, "SO RADICAL YOUR PROFESSORS WILL BLUSH" with a photograph of the book cover for *Understanding Islam* by Guillaume Faye (2016). Faye is a far-Right French author who argues that Islam is incompatible with democracy and seeks the destruction of all other civilizations.

Given the prevalence of immigration in mainstream conservative political discourse, it was surprising that anti-Latino expressions were few, with only one flyer containing an explicitly anti-Latino message. The Texas State Vigilantes, a local group at Texas State University, posted a flyer in November

2016 that proposed stocking the Rio Grande with predators such as "gators, snakes, and piranahs [sic]" to create a "gladiator spectacle of illegal messicans [sic]" to be "snatched and eaten by predators" as they try to cross. This was included within a three-page antidiversity screed that concluded with the sentence, "'Multiculturalism' and 'diversity' are code-words for white genocide."

Several flyers communicated a broader anti-immigrant message. In March and April 2017, a flyer attributed to Vanguard America was found on the campuses of George Washington University, Tarleton State University, the University of Texas Arlington, and Adolphus Gustavus University in Minnesota. It stated, "A NOTICE TO ALL WHITE AMERICANS. IT IS YOUR CIVIC DUTY TO REPORT ANY AND ALL ILLEGAL ALIENS TO U.S. IMMIGRATIONS AND CUSTOM ENFORCEMENT. THEY ARE ALL CRIMINALS. AMERICA IS A WHITE NATION." Not only does this flyer reference the criminal threat of "illegal aliens," it explicitly racializes that threat by defining them as nonwhite in contrast to "white Americans."

Expressions of victimization from groups other than minorities were much fewer, though seven flyers specifically mentioned communism, socialism, or Marxism as a source of threat. For instance, a flyer by Vanguard America found at Portland State University in December 2017 showed an image of an eagle carrying the hammer and sickle symbol, with text reading, "NOT HERE, NOT EVER," while another, found at Arizona State in August 2017, warned of "Cultural Marxist professors." A few flyers mentioned other sources of victimization, including threats from big business or capitalism (two flyers), the educational system (three flyers), global elites (one flyer), and the media (two flyers). Interestingly, while victimization by the government was described in the literature as a common theme among white supremacists (Perry 2000), I found no explicitly antigovernment messages in flyers posted on the college campuses during my period of study.

White Pride

Appeals to white identity were prominent and often included references to white victimization, usually in terms of guilt or shame. One flyer attributed to American Renaissance, found at the University of Wisconsin and Bowling Green State in March 2017 and Boston College in October 2017, depicted Uncle Sam with a caption instructing observers: "I WANT YOU TO LOVE WHO YOU ARE. DON'T APOLOGIZE FOR BEING WHITE." Another flyer, produced by a local group called the "U of L Identitarians" at the University of Louisville, referenced "political intimidation," stating, "For those of you who feel alone in caring about the future of European people and the preservation of European culture, you are not alone. At U of L, political intimidation for caring about your own people may seem rampant, but no longer must you stay silent."

A few white identity flyers went further than simply white pride, referencing the concept of "white genocide" (Berbrier 2000). One such flyer from the Right Stuff, found at Ohio State in November 2016 and again at Ball State in March of 2017, read, "LOVE WHO YOU ARE. White people exist. White people have the right to exist. White people have the right to exist as white people. BE WHITE." Another flyer from the Right Stuff, found on the campus of Iowa State University in October 2016, read, "IN 1950 AMERICA WAS 90% WHITE. IT IS NOW ONLY 60% WHITE. WILL YOU BECOME A MINORITY IN YOUR OWN COUNTRY?" Not only does this play upon racial anxieties regarding the percentage of nonwhites in the United States, it implies a sense of racially based proprietary claim to the nation as a whole for whites (Dietrich 2014). And an unattributed flyer found on the campus of Weber State University in Utah explicitly associated diversity with white genocide, saying, "White Countries Flooded With Non White Immigrants. 'DIVERSITY' IS A CODE WORD FOR WHITE GENOCIDE. White Areas Chased Down And Forced To Diversify."

Appeals to Youth/College Experience

A number of flyers, fourteen in total, attempted to address the college situation directly. One unattributed flyer at Arizona State University in August 2017, under the headline "WELCOME TO COLLEGE WHITE BOYS AND GIRLS," stated, "For the next four years your Cultural Marxist professors will beat you over the head with shame and guilt to convince you that you are second-class citizens." Not only does this statement reference the "shame and guilt" supposedly imposed on white students by professors, it attempts to capitalize on anticommunist sentiments by specifically referring to professors as "Cultural Marxists." A flyer attributed to the Right Stuff found at both Drexel University and Rutgers in July 2017 said, "RACE IS REAL. YOUR PROFESSORS ARE LYING TO KEEP THEIR JOBS," while another, found at Iowa State University and Lebanon Valley College in October and December 2016, respectively, read, "ARE YOU SICK OF ANTI-WHITE PROPAGANDA IN YOUR COLLEGE? YOU ARE NOT ALONE." Thus, while universities may be promoting messages of diversity and acceptance of difference, these flyers attempt to reframe those messages as propaganda perpetrated by dishonest professors to serve a nebulous ideological agenda.

Trump

This timing of this surge in white supremacist activism on college campuses is conspicuously correlated with the presidential candidacy and eventual election of Donald J. Trump. Trump announced his candidacy in June 2015, was elected in November 2016, and was inaugurated in January 2017. The Southern Poverty Law Center reported an initial surge in flyer incidents in March 2016, followed by another peak in September of that year, with continued high levels of activity reaching their zenith in February 2017 (SPLC 2017b) but still continuing in 2018. While the racist content of Trump's statements and actions during his candidacy have been debated in the media, a handful of flyers, nine in total, suggest that Trump's candidacy and presidency have encouraged white supremacist activism. For example, the previously discussed flyer by the Texas State Vigilantes actually referred to the president as "our man Trump," saying: "Now that our man TRUMP is elected and republicans own both the senate and the house - - time to organize tar & feather VIGILANTE SQUADS . . ." A number of business-size cards left in the library of Iowa State University in January 2017, attributed to Vanguard American by the SPLC, explicitly connected Trump and his slogan to whiteness in America, reading in part, "MAKE AMERICA GREAT AGAIN. TRUMP IS THE FIRST STEP. WE'RE THE NEXT." While these were the only mentions of Trump by name, additional flyers referenced the Trump campaign in other ways. One flyer attributed to Identity Evropa that was posted at Baylor University, California State University Long Beach, and California State University Stanislaus in February 2017 simply had the message "LET'S BECOME GREAT AGAIN" superimposed on what appears to be an image of the top of Michelangelo's statue of David, presumably symbolizing a pan-European ideal of whiteness as well as ancient "white" civilization.

CONCLUSIONS AND POLICY IMPLICATIONS

The mantra of white victimization was found in over half of the flyers. These flyers described whites as victims of discrimination, suffering shame and stigma due to their status as whites and suffering harm, both individual and collective, including the threat of "white genocide." However, white victimization was not omnipresent. Consistent with Berbrier's (1998) argument that white supremacists have increasingly made efforts to emphasize love and pride in whiteness, about one-quarter of the flyers emphasized a "white pride" message. Such messaging has the potential to add an air of legitimacy to white supremacists by eschewing the overt hatred of traditional white supremacist rhetoric. Nevertheless, a significant number of flyers explicitly expressed hatred toward minorities, particularly blacks and Jews, for being victimizers of whites. Yet even among these clearly racist flyers, the evidence suggests that the overall strategy of these organizations is consistent with Berbrier's (2000) argument that contemporary white separatists/supremacists are engaging in an identity strategy: attempting to create a positive white identity as a class of victimized persons. And even though these flyers were posted to college campuses for the presumed purpose of recruiting students, only fourteen of them made explicit attempts to appeal to or address the college experience or young adult generation, while most simply communicated generic messages of white supremacy. Finally, several flyers made either explicit or implicit reference to Donald Trump, suggesting that his election emboldened these particular groups to engage in these new tactics.

While mentions of Trump were not ubiquitous among the flyers, those instances, combined with the highly conspicuous timing of the Trump presidential campaign and the surge in flyer activity, suggests a connection between the two. Dobratz and Shanks-Meile (1997) have argued that several contributing factors constituted political opportunity (McAdam 1982) for white supremacists in the 1980s and 1990s, including a greater openness of the political system, the presence of elite allies, and a reduction in the state's propensity for repression. I argue that this may be even more true today. First, Trump and similar candidates (for example, Joe Arpaio's campaign for the US Senate) represent a much greater openness to overtly discriminatory and racist dialogue and acts than at any point since the civil rights movement. Second, Trump himself arguably represents an elite ally for white supremacists, as seen through his characterization of people on "both sides" of the Charlottesville rally as "very fine people" (Gray 2017) as well as his other numerous utterances of racial bias. Third, the failure of Trump and the federal government as a whole to take a strong stand against white supremacy even in the face of violence and murder, as in Charlottesville, suggests that, at least at the federal level, the government has little appetite for repressing the white supremacist movement. If true, this would mean that now is an ideal time for white supremacist activism.

While the flyer campaign has certainly been sustained and widespread, whether it actually has an effect of attracting people to the movement remains to be seen. To date, the conspicuous response to these activities has been condemnation from university officials and many students, as well as some criminal investigations into the posting of the flyers. A study of those students who are attracted by these flyers and exactly what appeals to them could be a fruitful means to understanding not only white supremacist activism in a post-Trump world but also the potential for white supremacy to persist and even grow in the coming years.

So what can be done to combat these campaigns? Their nature limits the policy avenues available to colleges and universities to stop white supremacist activism on their campuses. Most of the flyers were posted in secret, often under the cover of darkness, both to avoid confrontation due to their subject matter and because posting flyers outside designated areas is usually a violation of campus policies and could be considered a form of vandalism, opening the perpetrators to criminal liability. Thus, any additional rules or regulations regarding the posting of white supremacist materials are not likely to yield significant results. Moreover, placing restrictions specifically on the posting or dissemination of white supremacist materials opens colleges and universities to potential First Amendment complaints (Strange 2017).

Consequently, I argue that the most fruitful avenue for combating white supremacists on college campuses is to concentrate not on the perpetrators but on the audience: the targeted students. The messages being communicated through these flyers can only resonate if students remain ignorant of the facts about the nature of race and racism, the effects of racial discrimination (both overt and covert), and the power dynamics between majority and minority racial groups. Colleges and universities could include courses on racial inequality in the required curriculum for all students in order to provide an ideological breakwater against white supremacists' arguments, which rely on a systematic and purposeful misapprehension of the very notion of race in America today. While requiring such courses would almost inevitably be framed by white supremacists as yet another imposition on whites, this would not change the fact that every student would be exposed to the facts about race and inequality in the United States, under which most of the arguments of white supremacists could not stand.

Only a few years ago, many politicians and others were proclaiming the end of racism in the US and our entrance into a new era of being a "postracial society," as symbolized largely by the election of the first black president of the United States, Barack Obama. What we are seeing today appears to be a vicious whiplash effect—a regression to older, more overt forms of racial discrimination and hatred. These flyers represent only one vector in the new trajectory of race relations in the United States, alongside minority voter suppression and disenfranchisement, police violence against minorities, and increasing racist dialogue from politicians running for some of the highest offices in the country. It is imperative that we understand how we got to this point after the Obama era, how groups long lingering in the darker corners of our society have taken advantage of this new climate, and ultimately how we may combat these messages of hate that attempt to drag us back to forms of racism believed long gone in our society.

NOTES

1. The SPLC data on flyer incidents began in February 2016.
2. The text in this flyer, and all subsequent quotations from flyers, is reproduced as written on the flyer itself, including any use of bold, capitalization, or other stylistic attributes.
3. It was interesting to note that there appeared to be no significant pattern with regard to which minority groups were singled out as threats in relation to the demographics of the universities in question.

REFERENCES

Altheide, David L. 1987. "Ethnographic Content Analysis." *Qualitative Sociology* 10(1): 65–77.
———. 1996. *Qualitative Media Analysis*. Thousand Oaks, CA: Sage.
Barkun, Michael. 1994. *Religion and the Racist Right: The Origins of the Christian Identity Movement*. Chapel Hill, NC: University of North Carolina.
Beck, E. M. 2000. "Guess Who's Coming to Town: White Supremacy, Ethnic Competition, and Social Change." *Sociological Focus* 33(2): 153–74.
Berbrier, Mitch. 1998. "'Half the Battle': Cultural Resonance, Framing Processes, and Ethnic Affectations in Contemporary White Separatist Rhetoric." *Social Problems* 45(4): 431–50.
———. 2000. "The Victim Ideology of White Supremacists and White Separatists in the United States." *Sociological Focus* 33(2): 175–91.
Berlet, Chip, and Stanislav Vysotsky. 2006. "Overview of U.S. White Supremacist Groups." *Journal of Political and Military Sociology* 34(1): 11–48.
Bernhard, Bo J., Robert Futrell, and Andrew Harper. 2010. "'Shots from the Pulpit': An Ethnographic Content Analysis of United States Anti-Gambling Social Movement Documents." *UNLV Gaming Research and Review Journal* 14(2): 15–32.
Blumer, Herbert. 1958. "Race Prejudice as a Sense of Group Position." *Pacific Sociological Review* 1(1): 3–7.
Daniels, Jessie. 1997. *White Lies*. London: Routledge.
Dietrich, David R. 2014. *Rebellious Conservatives: Social Movements in Defense of Privilege*. New York: Palgrave Macmillan.
Dobratz, Betty A., and Stephanie L. Shanks-Meile. 1997. *"White Power, White Pride!" The White Separatist Movement in the United States*. New York: Twayne.
Faye, Guillaume. 2016. *Understanding Islam*. London: Arktos Media.

Ferber, Abby L., and Michael Kimmel. 2000. "Reading Right: The Western Tradition in White Supremacist Discourse." *Sociological Focus* 33(2): 193–213.

Gallagher, Charles A. 1995. "White Reconstruction in the University." *Socialist Review* 24: 165–87.

———. 2004. "Transforming Racial Identity through Affirmative Action." Pp. 153–70 in *Race and Ethnicity: Across Time, Space, and Discipline*, edited by Rodney D. Coates. Leiden, The Netherlands: Koninklijke Brill NV.

Gray, Rosie. 2017. "Trump Defends White-Nationalist Protesters: 'Some Very Fine People on Both Sides.'" *Atlantic*, August 15.

Hughey, Matthew W. 2012. *White Bound: Nationalists, Antiracists, and the Shared Meanings of Race*. Stanford, CA: Stanford University Press.

———. 2014. "White Backlash in the 'Post-Racial' United States." *Ethnic and Racial Studies* 37(5): 721–30.

Jones, Abigail. 2017. "White Supremacists Blamed for Racist, 'Muslim-Free America' Posters Appearing at University of Houston." *Newsweek*, September 18.

Krippendorff, Klaus. 2004. *Content Analysis: An Introduction to Its Methodology*. 2nd edition. Thousand Oaks, CA: Sage.

McAdam, Doug. 1982. *Political Process and the Development of Black Insurgency, 1930–1970*. Chicago: University of Chicago Press.

Perry, Barbara. 2000. "'Button-Down Terror': The Metamorphosis of the Hate Movement." *Sociological Focus* 33(2): 113–31.

SPLC. 2017a. "The Alt-Right on Campus: What Students Need to Know." SPLC: Southern Poverty Law Center, August 10. Retrieved January 11, 2018 (https://www.splcenter.org/20170810/alt-right-campus-what-students-need-know).

———. 2017b. "White Nationalist Fliering on American College Campuses." SPLC: Southern Poverty Law Center, October 17. Retrieved January 5, 2018 (https://www.splcenter.org/hatewatch/2017/10/17/white-nationalist-fliering-american-college-campuses).

Strange, Deborah. 2017. "UF Denies White Nationalist Richard Spencer a Campus Platform." *Gainesville (Florida) Sun*, August 16. Retrieved January 11, 2018 (http://www.gainesville.com/news/20170816/uf-denies-white-nationalist-richard-spencer-campus-platform).

CHAPTER 10

THE WHITENING OF SOUTH ASIAN WOMEN

BHOOMI K. THAKORE

IN THE SO-CALLED Trump era of the late 2010s, ideologies of pro-Whiteness (and, by default, anti-Blackness) are rooted in an overt resistance to social-justice-oriented solutions for social problems—for example, by responding to increased demographic diversity with strict immigration policies and support of discriminatory practices. Such policies are used as justification for these pro-White ideologies among White Americans. Or perhaps this justification merely reflects deep-rooted racism, and current political events have merely provided the justification for their resurgence.

Nowhere is this buildup to a dominant pro-White rhetoric more obvious than on the screen—defined as the spaces where popular culture is visualized. While the screen was traditionally considered to refer to television and film, it can now be expanded to include various streaming content, such as that displayed on YouTube, Netflix, and other platforms. These nontraditional spaces allow for freedom in content, which can be sometimes rooted in social justice and equality and sometimes rooted specifically in contrast to those ideals. Consumer-created content, produced by individuals or groups with a particular message in mind, is fundamentally different from consumer-oriented content produced by major production companies with the purpose of finding interest in consumers, usually for profit-motivated reason like advertising and platform subscription costs (Lee, Kim, and Kim 2011). However, while they are different in principle, I argue here that they are similar in their ideological motivations.

In this chapter, I focus on consumer-oriented content as the point of entrance for examining the effects of the Trump era. Specifically, I examine television programming to understand how produced, created, and manufactured content reinforces this era's dominant ideologies of homogeneity, divisiveness, and "making America great again." I discuss the historical context of the perceived attractiveness of "White" features; give a brief overview of the history of women of color in visual media; discuss the marketability of diverse media representations; analyze two key examples of South Asian women in twenty-first-century representations; and provide a matrix for understanding which women and which roles are most and least subjected to these dynamics. Within this argument, it is important to note that diverse representations are in fact increasing—in the twenty-first century, we have more examples of nonwhite characters, actors, writers, and producers than in the history of US media. However, as I will argue here, regardless of physical representation, the ideologies remain based on a dominant reliance on White phenotype—one that is further justified in our current political era in which nonwhiteness is seen as both negative and abnormal.

THEORETICAL AND EMPIRICAL BACKGROUND

Attractiveness as Whiteness

In most of the world, perceptions of attractiveness derive from an understanding that White/Caucasian features are the most beautiful and ideal. These attitudes are at the root of colonialism and inform the social and cultural tensions between colonizers and their colonized (Jordan 1974). Perceptions of Black and Brown natives as primitive, savage, and hypersexual were positioned in stark contrast to the refined culture and behaviors of White Christian Europeans (Forth 2012; McClintock 1995). In twenty-first-century US society, race continues to inform social perceptions of beauty and culture.

Skin-tone discrimination exists in many ethnic communities and is applied to women in particular (Collins 2000; Glenn 2008; Hall 1995; Ono and Pham 2009). Skin-lightening creams and soaps are big business in international markets and even in the US (Glenn 2008; Miller 2006). The consumption of these products reinforces Ronald Hall's (1995) psychological "bleaching syndrome," which is the process of internalizing the negative social associations of skin tone. From one perspective, it could be argued that these companies are simply meeting a consumer need. However, this phenomenon maintains dominant ideologies about the *preference* for fair skin and the role of skin tone as a measure of beauty and social capital.

Women of Color in Visual Media

Representations of women of color in visual media have long been subjected to these White beauty ideals—the preference for women with fair skin, straight hair, small noses and lips, and slim figures (Collins 2000). While perceptions of beauty are mostly aligned with White physical characteristics, charactcristics assigned to Black and Brown bodies (big breasts, hips, or butt) are hypersexualized (McClintock 1995; Riggs 1986). Starting in the 1970s, women characters of color were written to reinforce these racialized gendered dichotomies of exotic/erotic. Ultimately, what are considered attractive traits for women of color remain the same traits that idealize White beauty and normalized Whiteness in US society (Collins 2000; Glenn 2008; R. Hall 1995; Ono and Pham 2009).

These beauty ideals also influence the intentional decisions made by male media producers when casting female roles (Mulvey 1975). Contemporary media gatekeepers use pre-existing tropes to inform character sketches and casting decisions. While media representations of nonwhites have increased since the 1970s, these representations reproduce stereotypes that maintain Otherness (S. Hall 1997, 2003; Gray 2004; Vera and Gordon 2003; Yuen 2016). The literal bodies of the actors in these roles contribute to the corporate media's ideological project on race and limit the opportunities for actors of color who do not "look the part."

As in society, these nonwhite representations are no longer overtly racist but are much more covert in their racial essentializing. Media executives do this by intentionally limiting their character development. Those progressive examples of nonstereotypical characters in the media continue to be popular only among niche audiences—mostly nonwhite audiences and those who live in urban areas. However, the media operates on a simple business model: invest in a program if it is marketable.

Marketability of Diverse Programming

The lack of commitment by media corporations toward more inclusive media representation demonstrates their resistance of the reality of the US racial landscape in the twenty-first century. In general, racism among White Americans is rooted in their false assumption that nonwhites will directly affect their financial and professional success (Bonilla-Silva 2017; Omi and Winant 2015). However, there is no evidence to suggest this—in fact, take-home wealth at all levels has been negatively affected due to such economic factors as wage stagnation and concentration of wealth at the highest classes (Desmond 2017; Keister 2005; Shapiro 2004).

Media producers tend to assume that programming with a majority non-white cast will simply not be marketable. In recent years, this assumption has been challenged by the success of television shows like ABC's *Scandal* and *Black-ish* and films like *Black Panther*. However, these examples still tend to be consumed only by certain markets. As a result, these progressive images never reach the most conservative and nationalistic White audiences who need it the most. Ultimately, it is this audience that media producers most covet and support. As a result, the kinds of images made available to a broader audience will still maintain characteristics that privilege a dominant White paradigm.

RESEARCH DESIGN

In this chapter, I use two data sets. First, I use data collected from my previous work on audience perceptions of South Asians in the media (see, for example, Thakore 2014, 2016). Specifically here, I use data from fifty interviews conducted between May 2011 and January 2012. Ninety-five percent of the respondents ranged in age from twenty-two to forty (average age: thirty-one). Fifty percent of the respondents are White and 50 percent are nonwhite; half identified as men/male and half as women/female. In the interviews, respondents were asked a variety of questions about their backgrounds, their social networks, their media consumption, and their perceptions on historical, contemporary, and future media representations. In this analysis, I focus on responses related to perceptions on gender and beauty in the media.

Second, I rely on analyses of exemplar twenty-first-century South Asian women media characters—Kelly Kapoor, played by Mindy Kaling in the NBC series *The Office*, and Alex Parrish, played by Priyanka Chopra in the ABC series *Quantico*. In this analysis, I focus on the actors' unique paths to success as a way to demonstrate the influences of ethnicity and gender on popular media representations. I examine these two actors through the lenses of audience studies and production studies. Audience studies methodologies aim to understand how audiences are reading, consuming, absorbing, and reproducing the overt and covert messages in these popular media texts (Brunsdon 1978; Gillespie 1995; S. Hall 1980, 1997). Production studies is an interdisciplinary field that examines the cultural practices of media production and offers cultural studies of media industries (Banks, Conor, and Mayer 2015; Mayer 2016). Specifically, production studies help us understand the context behind the images that we see on the screen. As Mayer (2016) writes, these two areas can work in tandem to provide unique insights into the creation and resonance of media imagery.

RESULTS

Audience Perceptions of South Asian Women in Media

When I asked respondents in 2011–12 to identify those South Asian characters and actors that they found "attractive," both men and women were most likely to identify a few specific people. These included Padma Lakshmi from *Top Chef*, Freida Pinto from *Slumdog Millionaire* (2008), Bollywood actress Aishwarya Rai, and the character of Asha from *Outsourced* (2010–11), played by Rebecca Hazlewood. When respondents were asked to discuss what *qualified* these characters as attractive, the most common characteristics stated included skin, hair, and facial features. When grouped together, it is obvious that these actors (all women) share particular physical characteristics, including fair skin, long and straight hair, and White facial features, such as long faces and narrow noses, that reflect dominant ideological perceptions of beauty (Collins 2000) and Orientalist perceptions of South Asian women (Said 1979; Durham 2001). In contrast (no pun intended), a darker shade of skin tone (or at least, slightly darker than White) is a well-established characteristic of ethnic and exotic beauty for women (Beltrán 2005; Beltrán and Fojas 2008). Those actresses who have such features are marketable for a variety of reasons, including their perceived beauty and their less offensive skin tone.

The majority of these "attractive" South Asian characters and actors are either models or have model-like features, such as a tall stature, flawless skin, and thin figures. Padma Lakshmi, a model and the host of the reality cooking show *Top Chef*, was identified by many respondents as an example of an attractive South Asian person in US media. For example, one respondent (Claude, male, late twenties, white) found Lakshmi attractive for a variety of reasons, including her physical attractiveness and the real-life seven-inch surgical scar on her right arm. However, his references to her as "graceful" and "float[ing] on things" suggests a foreignness that is both exoticized and Othered (Said 1979). Lakshmi's fair skin and racially ambiguous physical features not only made her more appealing to the majority of US audiences but also allowed her an easier entrée into popular media.

Lakshmi's position as the host of *Top Chef* and her prior experiences on cooking shows are countered with representations of Lakshmi in exotic, erotic, and sexualized ways. As Meenakshi Gigi Durham (2001) wrote, consumption of South Asian culture translates into consumption of the feminine and the Other. In her work, Durham referenced Gayatri Spivak's (1996) discussion of subaltern subjects and their inability to critique the generalizations imposed upon them by their rulers. Women of color tend not to be in positions to change or influence the production of these images. As a result, South Asian women like Lakshmi continue to be represented in the media as exotic sexual beings through the White, heterosexual male gaze (Mulvey 1975).

The Case of Kaling

Such dynamics of beauty are particularly relevant when examining a popular, well-established, and phenotypically more ethnic South Asian American actress—Mindy Kaling from *The Office*. Kaling was born Vera Mindy Chokalingham on June 24, 1979, in Massachusetts. Her parents were both professionals—her mother an ob-gyn and her father an architect—who had met after migrating from India to work in Nigeria. After meeting and marrying, they moved to the United States to continue their careers. Kaling graduated from the elite Buckingham Browne & Nichols School before attending the equally elite Dartmouth College, where she majored in playwriting and stayed involved with comedy and a cappella troupes. After graduating, Kaling interned with various television programs, but her claim to fame was in 2002, when she cowrote and costarred in the Off-Broadway play *Matt & Ben*, based on the friendship between Matt Damon and Ben Affleck. The play was well received at the 2002 New York International Fringe Festival and recognized by *Time* magazine.

In 2004 Kaling was hired by Jeff Daniels to work as a writer and producer for his forthcoming show, *The Office*. For the second episode, Kaling wrote her character, Kelly Kapoor. In that episode, where she makes her first appearance at the Office Diversity training, Kelly was portrayed as a quiet and subdued Indian woman in frumpy clothing who slapped her boss, Michael Scott, for his racist humor. As the seasons progressed, Kelly became more bubbly and dynamic, obsessed with popular culture and her coworker Ryan. It was this latter representation that many of my respondents have discussed.

What is unique about the character of Kelly Kapoor is that Mindy Kaling herself was not subjected to the same sort of audition scrutiny that most nonwhite actors face in the industry (Mulvey 1975). Specifically, any conversations about Kaling's attractiveness and marketability likely did not happen, or did not happen to the extent that they do for other South Asian actresses and characters. Kaling essentially created this character, and her subsequent characters, in a way that was minimally influenced by (White male) producers, thus subverting the traditional influences of media executives (Entman and Rojecki 2000; S. Hall 2003).

However, Kaling's access to that character is due entirely to her executive role on that show. While Kelly Kapoor in *The Office* was one of the most frequently reported and discussed characters, she was less likely to be included in the list of South Asian characters considered attractive. The primary difference between Kaling and the other South Asian actresses is her physical appearance. One respondent reflected on the character of Kelly in ways that invoked her own self-reflection as an Indian woman. When comparing Kelly to other South Asian women, she said,

> Mindy Kaling is darker, her humor is definitely less innocent I think. [. . .] I respect the fact that she doesn't dumb herself down. [. . .] Kaling is definitely curvier than a lot of the other South Asian actresses on other TV shows [. . .] I like seeing someone who's curvier on TV because I am also. (Bijal, mid-twenties, second-generation Indian American woman)

Kaling's physical appearance resonated with Bijal on a personal level. This is similar to the impact of those media representations for Black and Latinx women (Collins 2000; Gauntlett 2008; Littlefield 2008).

Overall, most of my respondents had little to say about Kaling's attractiveness. For example, when asking a respondent if he thought Kelly Kapoor was attractive, he said, "Uh . . . she uh, not, not particularly, not unattractive" (Alan, early forties, White man). Similarly, a respondent who had previously described Bollywood actress and UK television star Shilpa Shetty (a model/actress who is tall and thin with light skin and white facial features) as attractive, said about Kelly, "I don't have a thing for her so I guess in the middle. Not unattractive" (John, mid-thirties, White man). Notably, while John was quick not to identify Kaling as unattractive, he failed to identify those characteristics that made her attractive or at least "in the middle." Specifically, he did not reference any physical features as he did when discussing Shetty. While John did not state that Kelly was "not unattractive," his description of her attractiveness essentially placed her lower on the hierarchy than South Asian women with White physical characteristics.

The Case of Chopra

Fast-forwarding a few years, we see an exponential level of growth in the number of South Asians actors in US media. These characters continue to break out of the traditional stereotypical molds—at least in their characterizations. This was certainly the case in the 2010s with Priyanka Chopra. Chopra was born on July 18, 1982, in northern India. Her parents were employed as physicians in the Indian Army, so Chopra and her family moved around frequently. When she was thirteen, Chopra moved to the United States to live with her aunt and attend school. By eighteen, Chopra had returned to India and won second place in the 2000 Femina Miss India contest and, from that, went on to win the 2000 Miss World contest. In 2003 Chopra appeared as the second female lead in her first Bollywood film, *The Hero: Love Story of a Spy.* While that film made below-average profits, it established Chopra in the Bollywood industry.

Within a few years, Chopra was seen as a prominent Bollywood figure, having appeared in numerous films over the years. In 2008 she was cast in the film *Fashion,* for which she had to gain approximately thirteen pounds and then lose the weight alongside the plot development of her character. For this role, she won several Indian film awards, including the National Film Award for Best Actress and the Producers Guild Film Award for Best Actress in a Leading Role. She later won her second Producers Guild Film Award for Best Actress for the 2009 film *Kaminey.* Chopra was nominated in 2010 for the Screen Best Actress Award for *What's Your Rashee?*, in which she played twelve different women as the potential love interests of the leading man. That same year, Chopra hosted the third season of the Indian series *Fear Factor: Khatron Ke Khiladi.* In 2011 she again received numerous nominations, as well as the Filmfare Critics Award for Best Actress in *7 Khoon Maff.* In 2012 the film *Barfi!* also yielded numerous award nominations and was chosen as India's entry for the year's US Academy Awards.

This trajectory catapulted her into the international media market. In 2011, after years of performing her own songs as a pageant contestant and in her prior films, Chopra signed a record deal with Universal Music Group with the stipulation that Interscope Records would release her first record in North America. In 2012 she recorded this record in the United States and released three singles, including "In My City." In 2012 she signed a contract with the Creative Artists Agency, a major Hollywood talent agency. In 2013 Chopra voiced a leading character in the Disney animated film *Planes.* Later that year, she was the first Indian woman to pose for the fashion line Guess. She continued to act in Bollywood films over the years, again receiving awards and nominations for her roles in the 2014 film *Mary Kom* and 2015 films *Dil Dhadakne Do* and *Bajirao Mastani.*

In 2014 Chopra signed a talent holding deal with ABC Studios—a contractual retainer agreement that she would appear in an ABC-produced series for the upcoming season, without any other performance obligations.

The former executive vice president of Talent and Casting, Keli Lee, flew to Chopra's home in India to formally recruit her. Lee created the ABC Discovers program, described as "a series of landmark initiatives with a globally focused creative talent recruiting program that leverages technology to allow acting, writing and directing talent to submit their original content online. Winners of the program are offered training, mentorship, and capital in order to scale their skills." Other actors who were recruited through this program include Lupita Nyong'o and Gina Rodriguez (K. Lee 2018). Chopra's talent holding deal, estimated at $3.5 million, included the criteria that she choose to star in one of the numerous pilot scripts that were being slated for the fall 2015 ABC season or have a series written and created for her. Of the scripts she read, *Quantico* was her choice.

The ABC series *Quantico* was conceived by writer Josh Safran, who was known in Hollywood for his prior work on the CW's *Gossip Girl* and NBC's *Smash*. When Safran was later interviewed about the casting decisions for the show, he indicated that it was not his intention to cast any one actor but to cast a diverse group of actors. After Chopra agreed to be cast at the lead character of Alex Parrish, the character was rewritten to have a multiracial background—a White mother and a South Asian (Indian) father. The progression of the series came to include detailed background on these characters, such as the fact that Parrish's father was an FBI agent and died under mysterious circumstances (later to be revealed as being shot by Parrish when she was younger, during a domestic dispute between him and his wife/Parrish's mother).

On the one hand, the nature of the dramatic series often calls for such curveballs in the story progression. The dramatic series is structured around a cast of characters who grow as individuals and bond as a group over the course of episodes. There is a process of "setting the stage" in a fictional story that includes establishing the environment for the characters and story lines. These settings are communicated through an inherently *visual* medium full of overt and covert symbols (S. Hall 1997). A character's tumultuous childhood provides the context to explain a tumultuous present. The crescendo leading up to the revelation that Parrish herself was the one who killed her abusive father is the kind of acting on which television awards are founded. However, while it may be assumed that this is merely fiction, the line between fictive representations and reality should not be taken lightly. For example, it is noteworthy that the character is written as multiracial, even though Chopra herself is not. Additionally, even under the guise of drama, the portrayal of the family unit here with tension rooted in the father (of color) reinforces stereotypes of nonwhite men as violent.

As Sreya Mitra (2017) noted, actors like Priyanka Chopra embody the transnational nature of the media industry—blending the dynamics of opportunity and culture. However, what is prioritized above all is the sexual appeal of such actors, appeal that is based primarily in the appeal to mostly White consumers, with a mostly White phenotypic aesthetic. Mitra, connecting to works by Neepa Majumdar (2009), noted that the typical role of the Bollywood star is to represent both the film and the brand. Popular Bollywood stars are cast in numerous roles per year. This demonstrates a capitalistic nature of the industry—and a renegotiation of the celebrity that incorporates attractiveness and marketability.

As a Bollywood actor, Chopra reflects a beauty ideal that is also popular in Indian society—very fair skin, model-like height and body type—but hardly reflects the physical appearance of most Indian people. This creates two dynamics. First, the perpetuation of a particular White beauty aesthetic is obvious. Notably, an actor like Chopra was successful in Hollywood for many reasons. Her success in Bollywood and interest among Western talent agencies allowed her to be exposed to the Hollywood industry. Second, her success and exposure came at a time when Hollywood was under much scrutiny for their lack of diverse representations. Under programs like the one previously described at ABC, women of color were recruited, mentored, and supported in the process from enrollment to stardom. However, I argue that while the White and Black extremes of the color line remain obvious, the tones are much more "brown" for women in the middle, including South Asian women. The external gaze can determine media success unless a woman has the access to build it herself. However, this gaze is rooted in White beauty ideals, both for content producers and among media consumers. This leaves the question, Can people be what they want, when subjugated by the eyes of others, in the age of Trump?

POLICY IMPLICATIONS

The dynamics of nonwhite representation in the media is neither subjective nor tertiary. The media, as an agent of socialization, affects our early social development and represents a window to our world. As Omi and Winant (2015) noted, the resonance of racialized meaning inherent in visual images, representations, and popular culture are simply larger racial projects under the umbrella of racial formations. In the Trump era, the resistance to any truly diverse representations is merely representative of a cultural age in which such representations are not welcome—literally. For example, as my previous work suggests (Thakore 2014, 2016), South Asian representations are perceived as positive when they are assimilated—or, more specifically, when they adhere to a normative White construction.

In this chapter, I highlight representations of women of color in popular media and discuss the interrelated process of production studies and audience studies. I used Kaling and Chopra as ideal types—significant examples of successful women of color who "made it" under very different circumstances. What distinguishes them is the way they rose to fame and their successes at the top. In Kaling's instance, she had the right academic pedigree and was well enough known in the industry for the Hollywood elite to take a chance on her. However, the primary intention was not to cast her but to use her humor to write for the screen. This is noteworthy, as there has been a long history of women comedians in the US since the 1920s who were hardly judged by mainstream beauty standards. However, Kaling found an opportunity to enter the fold, and the rest is "her-story."

Chopra, on the other hand, was well established and successful in Bollywood and appeared on the radars of Hollywood executives around the same time that multicultural audiences were demanding more diversity in the media. As a result, she was able to obtain a lucrative talent-holding contract and have her pick of series in which she could star. Her success is noteworthy—she was critically acclaimed in many of her Bollywood roles, and she later went on to be the first South Asian woman to win two People's Choice Awards for her performance in *Quantico*. The extent to which Chopra was able to rise up through the ranks in the Hollywood industry reflects back to her ability to represent normalized ideologies of White attractiveness.

What clearly distinguishes these actors from each other is not only their rise to fame but also their physical appearances. This comparative analysis has significant policy implications for understanding representations in Hollywood. Here, I have argued that both actors had, have, and will continue to have very distinct experiences in Hollywood from one another. Much of this can be attributed to their experiences making it in Hollywood—Chopra as an Indian Bollywood actress, Kaling as an elite American with a background in playwriting and comedy. However, given our social understandings of the significance of race, phenotype, and gender in the United States, it is evident that all of these dynamics have contributed to that success. Most importantly, these dynamics are representative of the inherent racialized social structures of Hollywood.

MOVING FORWARD: UNDERSTANDING REPRESENTATIONS OF WOMEN OF COLOR

The future of media representations will be directly influenced by the ever-increasing examples of media representations outside of traditional "Big 5" television broadcast networks (CBS, NBC, ABC, FOX, and CW). There have been many programs either rejected by major channels or written directly for relatively new media outlets such as Netflix, Hulu, and Amazon. Critics and fans alike have recognized the innovation and uniqueness of these programs. Outside the control of traditional media networks, producers and writers have much more freedom with character development and scene-setting. In this new media context, it will become increasingly important to for writers and producers to be aware of the writing and casting decisions made for women of color. Inherently, representations of these women through the lenses of exotic attractiveness and erotic sexuality will serve two purposes: maintaining Otherness and reinforcing White beauty ideals.

As all media is created for the purpose of profit, producers will continue to have the bottom line in mind when crafting characters. It is projected that by the year 2045, nonwhites will become the majority in the United States. Due to these changing demographics, it will be highly unwise for popular media to perpetuate the all-White cast of characters, if only for the risk of alienating the majority nonwhite demographic and negatively impacting their bottom line. However, this risk is often for the benefit of target markets, political philosophies, and the influences that the dominant racial ideologies of the Trump era will have for the years to come.

REFERENCES

Banks, Miranda, Bridget Conor, and Vicky Mayer, eds. 2015. *Production Studies, the Sequel! Cultural Studies of Global Media Industries.* New York: Routledge.

Beltrán, Mary. 2005. "The New Hollywood Racelessness: Only the Fast, Furious (and Multiracial) Will Survive." *Cinema Journal* 44(2): 50–67.

Beltrán, Mary C., and Camilla Fojas, eds. 2008. *Mixed Race Hollywood.* New York: NYU Press.

Bonilla-Silva, Eduardo. 2017. *Racism without Racists: Color-Blind Racism and the Persistence of Racial Inequality.* 5th edition. Lanham, MD: Rowman & Littlefield.

Brunsdon, Charlotte. 1978. *Everyday Television—Nationwide.* London: BFI.

Collins, Patricia Hill. 2000. *Black Feminist Thought: Knowledge, Consciousness, and the Politics of Empowerment.* 2nd edition. New York: Routledge.

Desmond, Matthew. 2017. *Evicted: Poverty and Profit in the American City.* New York: Broadway Books.

Durham, Meenakshi Gigi. 2001. "Displaced Persons: Symbols of South Asian Femininity and Returned Gaze in U.S. Media Culture." *Communication Theory* 11(2): 201–17.

Entman, Robert, and Andrew Rojecki. 2000. *The Black Image in the White Mind.* Chicago: University of Chicago Press.

Forth, Christopher. 2012. "Fat, Desire, and Disgust in the Colonial Imagination." *History Workshop Journal* 73(1): 211–39.

Gauntlett, David. 2008. *Media, Culture and Identity: An Introduction.* 2nd edition. New York: Routledge.

Gillespie, Marie. 1995. *Television, Ethnicity and Cultural Change.* London: Taylor and Francis.

Glenn, Evelyn Nakano. 2008. "Yearning for Lightness: Transnational Circuits in the Marketing and Consumption of Skin Lighteners." *Gender and Society* 22(3): 281–302.

Gray, Herman. 2004. *Watching Race: Television and the Struggle for Blackness.* Minneapolis: University of Minnesota Press.

Hall, Ronald. 1995. "The Bleaching Syndrome: African Americans' Response to Cultural Domination vis-à-vis Skincolor." *Journal of Black Studies* 26: 172–83.

Hall, Stuart. 1980. "Encoding/Decoding." Pp. 128–38 in *Culture, Media, Language,* edited by Stuart Hall, Dorothy Hobson, Andrew Lowe, and Paul Willis. London: Hutchinson.

———. 1997. *Representation: Cultural Representations and Signifying Practices.* Thousand Oaks, CA: Sage.

———. 2003. "The Whites of Their Eyes: Racist Ideologies and the Media." Pp. 89–93 in *Gender, Race, and Class in Media: A Text-Reader,* edited by Gail Dines and Jean M. Humez. Thousand Oaks, CA: Sage.

Jordan, Winthrop. 1974. *The White Man's Burden: Historical Origins of Racism in the United States.* New York: Oxford University Press.

Keister, Lisa. 2005. *Wealth in America: Trends in Wealth Inequality.* New York: Cambridge University Press.

Larson, Stephanie Greco. 2006. *Media and Minorities: The Politics of Race in News and Entertainment.* Lanham, MD: Rowman & Littlefield.

Lee, Doohwang, Hyuk Soo Kim, and Jung Kyu Kim. 2011. "The Impact of Online Brand Community Type on Consumer's Community Engagement Behaviors: Consumer-Created vs. Marketer-Created Online Brand Community in Online Social-Networking Web Sites." *CyberPsychology, Behavior and Social Networking* 14 (1/2): 59–63.

Lee, Keli. 2018. User Profile, LinkedIn. Retrieved September 15, 2018 (https://www.linkedin.com/in/kelilee/).

Littlefield, Marci Bounds. 2008. "The Media as a System of Racialization: Exploring Images of African American Women and the New Racism." *American Behavioral Scientist* 51(5): 675–85.

Majumdar, Neepa. 2009. *Wanted Cultured Ladies Only! Female Stardom and Cinema in India, 1930s–1950s.* Urbana: University of Illinois Press, 2009.

Mannur, Anita. 2005. "Model Minorities Can Cook: Fusion Cuisine in Asian America." Pp. 72–94 in *East Main Street: Asian American Popular Culture*, edited by Shilpa Davé, LeiLani Nishime, and Tasha Oren. New York: NYU Press.

Mayer, Vicki. 2016. "The Places Where Audience Studies and Production Studies Meet." *Television and New Media* 17(8): 706–18.

McClintock, Anne. 1995. *Imperial Leather: Race and Gender in the Colonial Contest.* New York: Routledge.

Miller, Laura. 2006. *Beauty Up: Exploring Contemporary Japanese Body Aesthetics.* Berkeley: University of California Press.

Mitra, Sreya. 2017. "From Bollywood Heroine to 'Cross-Continental Glamour Icon': Priyanka Chopra and the Shifting Trajectories of (Global) Bollywood Stardom." Paper presented at the meeting of the Centre for Media & Celebrity Studies, Los Angeles, CA, March 19.

Mulvey, Laura. 1975. "Visual Pleasure and Narrative Cinema." *Screen* 16(3): 6–18.

Nagel, Joane. 2003. *Race, Ethnicity, and Sexuality: Intimate Intersections, Forbidden Frontiers.* New York: Oxford University Press.

Omi, Michael, and Howard Winant. 2015. *Racial Formation in the United States: From the 1960s to the 1990s.* 3rd edition. New York: Routledge.

Ono, Kent A., and Vincent T. Pham. 2009. *Asian Americans and the Media.* Cambridge, UK: Polity.

Riggs, Marlon. 1986. *Ethnic Notions.* Film. Los Angeles: California Newsreel.

Said, Edward. 1979. *Orientalism.* New York: Vintage.

Shapiro, Thomas. 2004. *The Hidden Cost of Being African-American: How Wealth Perpetuates Inequality.* New York: Oxford University Press.

Spivak, Gayatri Chakravorty. 1996. "Can the Subaltern Speak?" Pp. 271–313 in *Marxism and the Interpretation of Culture*, edited by Cary Nelson and Lawrence Grossberg. Urbana: University of Illinois Press.

Thakore, Bhoomi K. 2012. "Rags-to-Riches in the 21st Century: The Reality behind Representations in *Slumdog Millionaire*." *Humanity and Society* 36(1): 93–95.

———. 2014. "Must-See TV: South Asian Characterizations in American Popular Media." *Sociology Compass* 8(2): 149–56.

———. 2016. *South Asians on the U.S. Screen: Just Like Everyone Else?* Lanham, MD: Rowman & Littlefield.

Vera, Hernan, and Andrew Gordon. 2003. *Screen Saviors: Hollywood Fictions of Whiteness.* Lanham, MD: Rowman &Littlefield.

Yuen, Nancy Wang. 2016. *Reel Inequality: Hollywood Actors and Racism.* New Brunswick, NJ: Rutgers University Press.

CHAPTER 11

COLORFUL ART, WHITE SPACES

How an Art Museum Maintains White Spaces

SIMÓN E. WEFFER, DAVID G. EMBRICK, AND SILVIA DOMÍNGUEZ

MERRIAM-WEBSTER'S DICTIONARY DEFINES a museum as "an institution devoted to the procurement, care, study, and display of objects of lasting interest or value." While the goal for some museums is to curate and preserve collections of artifacts and art for scientific study, increasingly museums have shifted their publicly professed goals to include serving the general public. The most compelling description of museums we have found is in a coffee-table book titled *Museum Display Design* (Whittaker 2014). The back cover of this book states: "Museums are the mental park of cities." To us, this is one of the defining characteristics of museums: to promote a particular history, or set of histories, in order to give people a sense of place, purpose, and celebrate cultural achievements.

However, controversies abound concerning what can be thought of as dormant functions of museums: to preserve and highlight *specific* histories *above others*. Some of these controversies can be found in museums' hiring of staff and curators. In early 2018, the Brooklyn Museum came under fire for hiring a white woman as their consulting curator for African art. This was seen by many as a reflection of the Brooklyn Museum's consistent failures to recognize its part in co-opting and misrepresenting artifacts originating from nonwhite groups (Adisa-Farrar 2018; Greenberger 2018). The *New York Times* captured the disconnect between museums' public pronouncements of diversity and their lack of diversity in their board members, noting that the members of many big museum boards are "strikingly" white (Pogrebin 2018). Indeed, a 2017 report indicated that while museum directors and board chairs note the importance of diversity and inclusion to achieving their missions, most museum boards are all white (BoardSource 2017).

Our contributions to this volume are threefold. First, we suggest that interrogating open and overt resurgence of white domination often minimizes or neglects what happens in the private spheres of society (Picca and Feagin 2007) and what takes place at both the individual and institutional levels. Our research highlights how white supremacy operates under the guise of diversity (Berrey 2015; Embrick 2008); diversity ideology facilitates the illusion of inclusion while allowing for racialized mechanisms that favor exclusion (Embrick 2008, 2011, 2018; Embrick and Rice 2010). We outline three specific mechanisms that take place at the Art Institute of Chicago (AIC) that facilitate institutional white spaces (see Moore 2008). Second, we argue that museums should be seen in the context of racialized social systems, as part of a society that allocates differential rewards along socially constructed racial lines. Bonilla-Silva (1997) notes that these rewards can be economic, political, social, or even psychological. Accordingly, we see museums, and in particular *elite* museums, as racialized organizations that maintain the status quo of white supremacy in racialized social systems. Last, we contend that such museums serve to facilitate both whiteness and elitism and are in fact a call to 1950s nostalgia of a specific type of normativity. In this sense, we can see elite museums as racial projects (Omi and Winant 2014 [1994]) for those elements of the White racial backlash seeking to "interpret, represent, and explain" the superiority of Whiteness in the cultural context of "high art." As we discuss below, museums of this caliber and stature can become a refuge and sanctuary because of how they display art, which artists they display, and most fundamentally by defining *what good art is.* In fact, the gravitation of the right and alt-right to medieval studies and comments by Representative Steve King about the importance of whiteness in saving Western civilization during the "Dark Ages" are examples of public racial projects that are in turn reinforced by how a museum (like the AIC) displays Islamic art, African art, or Mesoamerican art in comparison to the armor room or the art of the impressionists. By relegating Islamic art to the basement while displaying medieval European armor and weapons in a brand new gallery, the AIC becomes a sanctuary for those whites who feel besieged by a society filled with individuals embarking on racial projects that emphasize a more just and egalitarian society.

Our chapter specifically adds to the collective theme of this book by highlighting three specific racial mechanisms (see Hughey, Embrick, and Doane 2015) in museum institutions that help maintain white supremacy and comforts white anxieties, fears, and fragilities about their group position in society. These mechanisms help whites preserve their psychological wages of whiteness (Du Bois 2007 [1935]; Marable 2000; Roediger 2007) in safe white spaces (Moore 2008).

THEORETICAL FRAMEWORKS AND WHITE SPACES

Our interest lies in interrogating the connection between white supremacy and racialized organizational, institutional, and structural social spaces. Specifically, we are interested in better understanding precisely how institutions in a racialized social system facilitate white supremacy. What are the specific racial mechanisms within these institutions that reproduce colorblind and other racial ideologies? How do these institutions serve as both physical and mental white sanctuaries? How are these spaces complicated by class or other positionalities in society? In this chapter, we provide some insights on how the AIC serves to preserve and present our collective identities regarding who we are as a city, state, or nation but that additionally serves to tell us who belongs and who is Othered, which groups are inferior and which groups are superior. Much like other racialized institutions (Ray 2017), museums reinforce the existing social and racial order of the society in which they reside. In the following, we outline some of the essential racial theories that help inform our understanding of museums' place in society and pay specific attention to how our research fits into current literature of racism and space.

White Spaces vs. White Sanctuaries

Recently, we have witnessed a growing backlash against the removal of Confederate statues and other symbols of white supremacy. These battles reflect the racial tensions that have always been present in US society. On the one hand, many whites (and even a growing number of minorities) argue that these symbols have nothing to do with racism and white supremacy—that these symbols represent "our history," "our heritage," or even our sense of "national pride." On the other hand, some have argued that the removal of Confederate statues and other symbols of white supremacy are necessary actions if the nation is to ever get past its racist history.

These arguments, and the conversations taking place about deracializing white spaces in society, are centered on that which lies in the public sphere—e.g., the Confederate statues or flags in our parks, at building entrances, and in other public spaces. We argue that the battle over the removal of Confederate statues is minuscule against the broader foundation of white supremacy. That is, we need to pay more attention to the racial mechanisms present in our racialized institutions (Ray 2017) and even larger social structures that serve to perpetuate both overt and covert racial discrimination. While not as blatant as Confederate flags or statues, white sanctuaries provide a haven that not only promotes white supremacy but provides a relatively "safe" space in which whites can reify their racialized understanding of the world in which they live. More so than white institutionalized spaces (Moore 2008), white sanctuaries often exist within the confines of white habitus (Bonilla-Silva 2003; Bonilla-Silva, Goar, and Embrick 2006) but may also exist within nonwhite (Bonilla-Silva and Embrick 2007) or even more seemingly cosmopolitan spaces (Anderson 2011).

The AIC represents a type of white (racialized) institutional space as well as a white sanctuary. This space is raced and classed, and it operates both overtly and more subtly to reaffirm middle-class whites' position in society. We highlight three ways in which it does this: through its location and practices, through its placement of art, and through the policing of *spaces and bodies*.

Place and Space

The vast majority of sociological research on the spatial dynamics of race and inequality have concentrated on the physical geography of living space—in other words, racial residential segregation and the connection between differential resources and racially organized neighborhoods (e.g., see Massey and Denton 1998). While this literature provides insights into the dynamics of race, space, and hierarchy, most of the scholarship does not go far enough to elucidate the power of racialized space to organize and normalize white supremacy. The sociologist Henri Lefebvre, speaking about space in the context of not *just* geography but also organizational and institutional spaces, noted that social spaces are created via political processes and shaped by politics and ideology (1976:31). It is only in the last decade that sociologists have begun to explicitly examine racialized economic and political spaces and the ideological mechanisms (Coates 2007; Ray 2019) of organizational and institutional white spaces, noting that these social spaces are racially organized in ways that both facilitate and camouflage white supremacy.

Since the early years of the twenty-first century, scholarship has emerged identifying the manner in which other social spaces—namely, social organizations and institutions—similarly connect to differential resources along the lines of race. Drawing on what Ture and Hamilton have termed institutional racism—or "the active and pervasive operation of anti-black attitudes and prejudices" embedded within social institutions—sociologists have noted that the central organizations and institutions that make up the US social structure are racialized to facilitate white supremacy and the oppression of people of color (1992: 112).

In *How Racism Takes Place*, George Lipsitz (2011) discusses how seemingly race-neutral social spaces become ideologically embedded with assumptions that facilitate white privilege and power within these spaces. The reproduction of racialized power dynamics takes place spatially, according to Lipsitz (2011), through the "white spatial imaginary." Lipsitz suggests: "The white spatial imaginary idealizes 'pure' and homogeneous spaces, controlled environments, and predictable patterns of design and behavior. It seeks to hide social problems rather than solve them. . . . This imaginary does not emerge simply or directly from the embodied identities of people who are white. It is inscribed in the physical contours of the places where we live, work, and play, and it is bolstered by financial rewards for whiteness" (2011:29).

Likewise, the concept of white institutional space facilitates an explication of how race privilege is produced and reproduced in organizations and institutions by illuminating the interrelated mechanisms of racialized structures and everyday practices and their connection to the ideologies and discourses that fuel the white spatial imaginary within these settings (Moore 2008; Evans and Moore 2016). Wendy Leo Moore, most recently in *Reproducing Racism: White Space, Elite Law Schools, and Racial Inequality*, has produced scholarship illuminating elite law schools as "racialized spaces where whites rarely think about that racialization" (2008: xi). She develops the conception of white institutional space—spaces in which deeply embedded racial structures, racialized everyday practices, and racial ideologies and discursive frames work in conjunction with one another to maintain the status quo or white supremacy. We argue that as racialized organizations (Ray 2019), museums facilitate white supremacy in similar fashion to Moore's law schools, through decisions regarding selection and placement of art, through access to the museum, and through a number of racial mechanisms that embrace white normativity and maintain the status quo.

Researchers in museum studies have tackled racism by attempts to influence museum education (Teslow 2007; Maleuvre 2012). These studies point to a historically troubled legacy with race and argue that museums are crucial agents in the construction of race through scientific practices and public exhibitions (Teslow 2007:13). Museums have tended to misrepresent minority groups, sometimes to injurious effect (Karp et al. 2006). According to these works, "Racism thrives in all corners of museums—from curatorial decisions that often exclude artists of color and information about the racial context of objects to workplace cultures that prioritize White cultural modes of communication" (Dewhurst and Hendrick 2018:451). Museums in the US have long promoted a view of the dominant culture that supports and encourages the subordination of nonwhite populations (Lavine and Karp 1991). Museums, devoted to the canon of masterpieces by "dead white men," are challenged to open their doors to artwork by women, people of color, and other creative artists. In an era of increased globalization, real cultures are diverging, and, therefore, museum "visitors of today are recognizably diverse." Museum studies have also called for the decolonization of the field of museum education. But the field is slow to address the intersections of institutional racism and its impact on visitors of color (Karp et al. 2006). Given the demographic changes, there is a need to shift a focus on assimilation toward a more progressive and inclusive practice (Hein 2012). Despite the examination of race by museum studies, our research study here goes deeper, being empirically driven by authors who are critical sociologists.

RESEARCH DESIGN

We selected the Art Institute of Chicago as our site of study because it is considered one of the premier art museums in the world. In 2014 the AIC received the coveted distinction of being rated the number one museum in the world by TripAdvisor, a popular website for frequent travelers (Chicago Tribune 2014), beating out the National Museum of Anthropology in Mexico City; the State Hermitage Museum and Winter Palace in St. Petersburg, Russia; the Louvre in Paris; and the Metropolitan Museum of Art in New York City. It has since been ranked in the top four categories of best museums in the world by TripAdvisor. In 2016 the AIC reported a 15 percent attendance growth, bringing a record 1.79 million visitors to its doors (Johnson 2017), largely a result of its tribute exhibition to Vincent Van Gogh, titled *Van Gogh's Bedrooms*.

The AIC was founded in 1879 and continues to reside in its original building, constructed for the 1893 World's Columbian Exposition. It is the second largest museum in the United States, spacewise, after the Metropolitan Museum of Art in New York City. While widely recognized nationally and internationally, the AIC is also often touted as "Chicago's museum." It represents a type of white institutional space—a space that attracts and facilitates the needs of a specific clientele: the white middle and upper classes.

In 2015 the lead and second author of this chapter partnered to do a collaborative ethnography project at the AIC. This project would last three years as we tackled the complexities of working together in a way that would allow us to witness sociological patterns while at the same time allowing for us to negotiate the discrepancies in what we saw or interpreted differently. Collaborative ethnography is not a common methodological practice, as many ethnographers tend to prefer collecting data solo. Collaborative ethnography comes with particular challenges that require trust between colleagues, as well as lots of conversations to make sure both perspectives are included. While this process is challenging, many positives outweigh any shortcomings. According to May and Pattillo-McCoy, "collaborative ethnography can be useful for providing a richer description, highlighting perceptual inconsistencies, and recognizing the influence of ethnographers' personal and intellectual backgrounds on the collection and recording of data" (2000:65). For us, collaborative ethnography allowed us to engage in cointerpretive findings and cocritical assessments of how to link our findings to theories of racism and white supremacy (Lassiter 2005).

Our data comes from several hundred written pages of observation field notes, discussions, and photos of everyday life at the AIC, recorded by the first and second authors. These field notes include collaborative visits to the AIC, representing a significant time at the museum together. We took individual notes but frequently checked in with one another about what we witnessed concerning interactions between museum patrons (paid visitors of a museum) and museum floor staff, whose job is to maintain the security and safety of their assigned exhibits and the patrons who visit those exhibits. We logged many hours of discussions about the architecture of the building; how patrons navigated spaces in the museum; the placement and location of works of art; the specific lighting in each of the rooms, with attention to natural versus artificial lighting; and the traffic flow of patrons. Once we were satisfied that we were in sync with one another, we divided the weekly visits: the first author would go to the museum on Tuesdays, Thursdays, and Saturdays, and the second author was responsible for Mondays, Wednesdays, and Saturdays. This arrangement worked out well, as it allowed us to note differences and similarities that were present during different days of the week but also presented variations in how we were treated during our observations. For example, while the second author often went by himself to the AIC, the first author often went with his four ambiguously ethnic daughters. This alone led to some interesting observations about how we were treated by museum patrons or the floor staff.

FINDINGS

Three specific racial mechanisms speak to how white spaces are created, recreated, and maintained within elite museums: spatiality, the policing of space, and the management of access.

Spatiality

When examining the issue of space in the museum, the first two authors noticed three distinct methods in which space came into play. The first issue is centrality. On the AIC's main floor, in the middle of everything, is the art of antiquity. These are pieces from the classical Greek and Roman periods. These eras are deemed the "genesis of Western civilization" and are seen as superior in both the academy and popular culture. The art itself has often been used as examples of race and aesthetics, overlooking the fact that these pieces were often painted and only appear white as function of time and weathering, not that these pieces were meant to be racially white. From this main floor and entrance, to be able to see either the modern wing, American Art (i.e., art of the US); the Chagall America Windows; or the museum café and members' lounge, any visitor *must* walk through at least one of the hallways with the pieces of antiquity. These exhibits of ancient Greek and ancient Roman pieces are quite literally the physical center of the museum, reifying their *literal* centrality to art and art history.

The second spatial issue we observed was the treatment of Islamic art, in both the size and the placement of its gallery. The Islamic art galleries are on the lower level of the museum and are incredibly isolated. This level is accessible only from one stairway that is difficult to find. As a result, it had the least foot traffic of any gallery in the permanent exhibition that we experienced. There were always very few visitors. The majority of the foot traffic we observed were from museum staff, who used it as a passageway to the "backstage" portions of the museum—where staff offices and storage are located. Being on the lower level, it had poor lighting, certainly in contrast to the airy and open feel of the impressionist galleries on the second floor. While it was not exactly "dark and dank," both natural and electric lighting in the galleries were noticeably less than in the rest of the museum, especially in contrast to the areas with ancient Greek and Roman art. What's interesting is that many of the Islamic art pieces are from the same time period as the Greek and Roman pieces, but the differences in location and lighting indicate the primacy of the "white art" of Greece and Rome in contrast to that of the Islamic world.

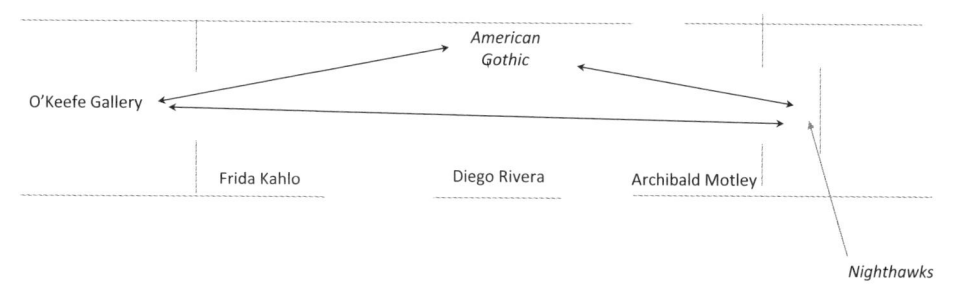

FIGURE 11.1. Map of rooms with flow, highlighting the flow of whiteness

A third spatial dynamic we observed was an unexpected movement pattern. On the second level on the south side of the building resides the Modern American Art wing, which includes artists such as Georgia O'Keeffe, Frida Kahlo, Diego Rivera, Archibald Motley, and Edward Hopper. One afternoon, early in the data collection, the first two authors noticed an interesting pattern: visitors would look at Hopper's *Nighthawks*, then move to Grant Wood's *American Gothic*, and then go to the Georgia O'Keeffe gallery (figure 11.1). In the process, visitors would entirely skip the works of Kahlo, Rivera, and Motley—all artists of color. We have dubbed this pattern "the Bermuda Triangle of Whiteness." Visitors would seemingly disappear into white artists, oblivious to the Latinx and African American masters around them. Over and over we observed this movement pattern, irrespective of time of day, the day of the week, or the season. While predominantly a movement pattern of white visitors, it was a phenomenon we did observe with other groups. While we do not have a definitive answer for why this pattern occurred, we have begun to explore the idea that there are individual artists one expects to see in an internationally recognized museum. This is a function of what is learned vis-à-vis art history, where a primacy is put on white artists. So as a white sanctuary, galleries can serve as safe racial spaces if one ignores those artists not expected in a museum the caliber of the AIC. Work by Hopper, Wood, O'Keeffe, and other white artists can be the safe harbor when in a room surrounded by work of artists of color, as is the case for Wood's *American Gothic*.

Policing of Space

The second racial mechanism we observed in the AIC was the policing of the space itself. The uptick in the policing of spaces by whites comes at a cost for black and brown bodies. While no one called 911 on the authors, we did see how the museum security acted quite differently with us, as two men of color, compared to white visitors, and how the difference existed regarding children of color as well. For example, on the very first day of the joint ethnography data collection, the first two authors entered the first gallery of the impressionist collection, where George Seurat's *A Sunday on La Grande Jatte—1884* is displayed, and captured the experience of this difference in the following field notes:

> As we entered the room, a middle-aged white woman was looking at the painting. She kept getting progressively closer. A short burgundy velvet rope barrier was about 5 feet from the painting to act as a deterrent from visitors touching the masterpiece. The woman then decided that she was not close enough to the painting and leaned out over the rope, to the point where she was perhaps 6 inches away from the painting. We were so startled by how close she was to the painting we took a picture of it. We then wandered around the rest of the gallery, eventually ending up in front of Seurat's painting the woman had just closely inspected. We had been standing a few feet behind the rope for a minute or two when we heard a security guard state "Excuse me, sir. Sir. EXCUSE ME, SIR." We both looked around trying to see to whom she was referring. It turned out she was speaking to us. Despite being at least two feet from the rope (and 7–8 [feet] from the painting), we were singled out, identified as being too close to the painting, and essentially publicly humiliated for the implicit reason that "we did not know how to be in a museum."

Meanwhile, just a few minutes earlier a white woman had been close enough to smell and taste the oil-based paint from 1886 with no reprimand and an absence of humiliation. The researchers were imbued with the not-so-subtle notion of needing to "know their place" in the museum, which is, apparently, not as close to art as white visitors.

There were other examples of policing. For instance, often in the Alsdorf South East Asian galleries, a large seated Buddha would attract a crowd, usually white, and often the "Art Bro" or "Hipster Art Connoisseur" (as we dubbed them) would take it upon himself to touch the statue of Buddha, rub his belly, touch his legs, or otherwise make it an "interactive" exhibit. However, multiple times when the first author was at the museum, he would see young, early elementary aged children of color scolded for getting too close to the sculpture, as if these children could move or damage a five-foot-high, four-foot-wide, multiton statue. However, if the hipster wanted to rub Buddha's belly, that was permitted.

Management of Access

The third racial mechanism is about regulating who has access to the museum. The very location of the AIC, off Michigan Avenue—one of the most expensive retail areas in Chicago—sets the stage for who can visit the museum and who cannot. Those wanting to park in the area should expect to pay upwards of $50 per day depending on the time of day and location. General admission for Chicago residents ranges from $14 to $29, with additional costs to leave items at the coat check or to rent an electronic information guide. A typical family of four can expect to pay over $100 for a day at the museum. To be fair, there are free days to entice locals to enjoy "their" museum. However, what was once free admittance with merely a "suggested donation" has been whittled down over time. At one point the AIC was free; then it offered multiple free days during the week; and now there are merely "free hours," on Thursday evenings from 5 p.m. to 8 p.m. Free hours, however, are not for everyone. An ID is required (or if you do not have an ID the museum asks you to "please bring a lease, bill, or piece of mail that shows your name and Illinois address") to enter during those three hours. These documents ensure the exclusion of some groups, such as the homeless, who are not welcome to what is often touted by the mayor of Chicago as an institution "for the people."

A second manifestation of regulating who has access is the reaction of the paying visitors when free hours begin. We have observed a mass exodus of the paying visitors as if they feared the great unwashed masses ruining their experience. In general, we found no real difference in the behavior of those attending during the "free hours" and the paid patrons of the AIC, though they seemed on average a bit younger—skewing toward those in their early to mid-twenties—and a modest increase of nonwhites. Along with the mass exodus, we observed that the members' lounge also changed during the free hours. The lounge itself was a sanctuary within a sanctuary, with only members of the Art Institute of Chicago (each allowed one guest) allowed entrance. At first, the lounge was closed during free hours. However, for the past year, the lounge has transformed into a small jazz club, with live music playing. It is still only for members and their guests, and it seems that the creation of the jazz lounge is an effort to keep members in the building and purchasing beer or coffees while listening to jazz. Recently, a new attempt to keep members from leaving and to attract a younger demographic emerged on Thursday nights. The modern wing was turned into a dance club, complete with DJs, a light show, and glow sticks. While it did not last for long, it was a transparent attempt to bring in a "different demographic" on Thursday nights.

CONCLUSIONS

These are just a few of our findings that we believe highlight how the AIC helps inform us not only of who we collectively are but also of who is (and is not) included in that collective. The racialized mechanisms in place allow certain groups to feel safe and to celebrate white art achievements in an institution that seemingly legitimizes their beliefs about their place in society. As a sanctuary, it serves as an institution that makes it safe to engage in white resistance. By displaying only those works of art that are canonical and predominantly white, it serves as a shelter from the onslaught of diversity in the rest of the fine arts world and works as a type of racial project for those who perpetuate the whitelash. The need for white resistance in the arts can be seen through the popularity of works like Lin Manuel-Miranda's *Hamilton*, which diversified theater *and* history, or individual efforts of artists such as Misty Copeland, the first African American woman to be the female principal dancer for the American Ballet Theatre, and Venezuelan conductor Gustavo Dudamel. By being an institution where by one can simply avoid artists of color by navigating our Bermuda Triangle of Whiteness, the Art Institute of Chicago reaffirms to the dominant group what they already know in regard to the racial and social order of society. In this sense, they fit Gallagher's arguments about how institutions promote racism through color blindness (see chapter 5).

Studying museums is important because they are institutions that seem harmless, that seem to be producers or purveyors of knowledge for the greater good. Exposing the often-hidden racial mechanisms and inadvertent racial projects that promote white supremacy within these white institutional spaces allows us to rethink who is included and who is not and to challenge the status quo.

REFERENCES

Adisa-Farrar, Teju. 2018. "Why Are White Curators Still Running African Art Collections?" *Guardian*, April 3.

Anderson, Elijah. 2011. *The Cosmopolitan Canopy: Race and Civility in Everyday Life*. New York: W. W. Norton.

Berrey, Ellen. 2015. *The Enigma of Diversity: The Language of Race and the Limits of Social Justice.* Chicago: University of Chicago Press.

BoardSource. 2017. *Museum Board Leadership 2017: A National Report.* Washington, DC: BoardSource, 2017.

Bonilla-Silva, Eduardo. 1997. "Rethinking Racism: Toward a Structural Interpretation." *American Sociological Review* 62(3): 465.

———. 2003. *Racism without Racists: Color-Blind Racism and the Persistence of Racial Inequality in America.* Lanham, MD: Rowman & Littlefield.

Bonilla-Silva, Eduardo, and David G. Embrick. 2006. "The (White) Color of Color Blindness in Twenty-First-Century Amerika." Pp. 3–24 in *Race, Ethnicity, and Education*, volume 4: *Colorblind Racism: Racism/Anti-racist Action*, edited by E. Wayne Ross and Valerie Ooka Pang. New York: Praeger.

———. 2007. "'Every Place Has a Ghetto . . .': The Significance of Whites' Social and Residential Segregation." *Symbolic Interaction* 30 (3): 323–46.

Bonilla-Silva, Eduardo, Carla Goar, and David G. Embrick. 2006. "When Whites Flock Together: The Social Psychology of White Habitus." *Critical Sociology* 32(2–3): 229–53.

Chicago Tribune. 2014. "Art Institute Is the World's Best Museum." *Chicago Tribune*, September 19.

Coates, Rodney. 2007. *Covert Racism.* New York: Roxbury.

Dewhurst, Marit, and Keonna Hendrick. 2016. "Dismantling Racism in Museum Education." *Journal of Folklore and Education* 3: 25–30.

———. 2018. "Decentering Whiteness and Undoing Racism in Art Museum Education." Pp. 451–67 in *The Palgrave Handbook of Race and the Arts in Education*, edited by Amelia M. Kraehe, Rubén Gaztambide-Fernández, and B. Stephen Carpenter II. Cham, Switzerland: Palgrave Macmillan, 2018.

Du Bois, W. E. B. 2007 [1935]. *Black Reconstruction in America: An Essay toward a History of the Part Which Black Folk Played in the Attempt to Reconstruct Democracy in America, 1860–1880.* New York: Oxford University Press.

Embrick, David G. 2008. "The Diversity Ideology: Keeping Major Transnational Corporations White and Male in an Era of Globalization." In *Globalization and America: Race, Human Rights and Inequality*, edited by Angela Hattery, David G. Embrick, and Earl Smith. Lanham, MD: Rowman & Littlefield.

———. 2011. "Diversity Ideology in the Business World: A New Oppression for a New Age." *Critical Sociology* 37(5): 541–56.

———. 2018. "Diversity: Good for Maintaining the Status Quo, Not So Much for Real Progressive Change." Pp. 3–9 in *Challenging the Status Quo: Diversity, Democracy, and Equality in the Twenty-First Century*, edited by David G. Embrick, Sharon M. Collins, and Michelle S. Dodson. London: Brill Press/Haymarket Books.

Embrick, David G., and Mitchell F. Rice. 2010. "Understanding Diversity Ideology in the United States: Historical and Contemporary Perspectives." In *Diversity*

  and Public Administration: Theory, Issues, and Perspectives, 2nd edition, edited by Mitchell F. Rice. Armonk, NY: M. E. Sharpe.
Evans, Louwanda, and Wendy L. Moore. 2016. "Impossible Burdens: White Institutions, Emotional Labor, and Micro-Resistance." *Social Problems* 62(3): 439–54.
Feagin, Joe R. 2006. *Systemic Racism: A Theory of Oppression.* New York: Routledge.
Glenn, Evelyn Nakano. 2015. "Settler Colonialism as Structure: A Framework for Comparative Studies of U.S. Race and Gender Formation." *Sociology of Race and Ethnicity* 1(1): 54–74.
Greenberger, Alex. 2018. "'Simply Not a Good Look': Activist Group Criticizes Brooklyn Museum's Hiring of White Curator for African Art Department—Museum Responds: 'Unanimously Selected an Extraordinary Candidate' [Updated]." *ARTnews*, April 6. Retrieved October 19, 2018 (http://www.artnews.com/2018/04/06/simply-not-good-look-activist-group-criticizes-brooklyn-museums-hiring-white-curator-african-art-department-open-letter/).
Hein, George E. 2012. "'The Museum as a Social Instrument': A Democratic Conception of Museum Education." Pp. 25–37 in *Museum Gallery Interpretation and Material Culture*, edited by Juliette Fritsch. New York: Routledge.
Hughey, Matthew W., David G. Embrick, and Ashley "Woody" Doane. 2015. "Paving the Way for Future Race Research: Exploring the Racial Mechanisms within a Color-Blind, Racialized Social System." *American Behavioral Scientist* 59(11): 1347–57.
Johnson, Steve. 2017. "Chicago Museums Set Attendance Records in 2016." *Chicago Tribune*, January 25.
Karp, Ivan, Corinne A. Kratz, Lynn Szwaja, and Tomás Ybarra-Frausto, eds. 2006. *Museum Frictions: Public Cultures/Global Transformations.* Durham, NC: Duke University Press.
Lassiter, Luke Eric. 2005. "Collaborative Ethnography and Public Anthropology." *Current Anthropology* 46(1): 83–106.
Lavine, Steven D., and Ivan Karp. 1991. "Introduction: Museums and multiculturalism." Pp. 1–9 in *Exhibiting Cultures: The Poetics and Politics of Museum Display*, edited by Ivan Karp and Steven D. Lavine. Washington, DC: Smithsonian Books.
Lefebvre, Henri. 1976. "Reflections on the Politics of Space." *Antipode* 8(2): 30–37.
Lipsitz, George. 2011. *How Racism Takes Place.* Philadelphia, PA: Temple University Press.
Maleuvre, Didier. 2012. "Must Museums Be Inclusive?" *Journal of Educational Media, Memory, and Society* 4(2): 112–25.
Marable, Manning. 2000. *How Capitalism Underdeveloped Black America: Problems in Race, Political Economy, and Society.* Cambridge, MA: South End Press.
Massey, Douglas S., and Nancy A. Denton. 1998. *American Apartheid: Segregation and the Making of the Underclass.* Cambridge, MA: Harvard University Press.

May, Reuben A. Buford, and Mary Pattillo-McCoy. 2000. "Do You See What I See? Examining a Collaborative Ethnography." *Qualitative Inquiry* 6(1): 65–87.

Moore, Wendy L. 2008. *Reproducing Racism: White Space, Elite Law Schools, and Racial Inequality.* Lanham, MD: Rowman & Littlefield.

Omi, Michael, and Howard Winant. 2014 [1994]. *Racial Formation in the United States.* New York: Routledge.

Picca, Leslie Houts, and Joe R. Feagin. 2007. *Two-Faced Racism: Whites in the Frontstage and Backstage.* New York: Routledge.

Pogrebin, Robin. 2018. "It's a Diverse City, but Most Big Museum Boards Are Strikingly White." *New York Times*, January 20.

Ragbir, Lise. 2018. "What Black Panther Gets Right about the Politics of Museums." *Hyperallergic*, March 20. Retrieved October 19, 2018 (https://hyperallergic.com/433650/black-panther-museum-politics/).

Ray, Victor. 2017. "A Theory of Racialized Organizations." *SocArXIV*, April 15. Retrieved May 11, 2020 (http://osf.io/preprints/socarxiv/u75gr).

———. 2019. "A Theory of Racialized Organizations." *American Sociological Review* 84(1): 1–28.

Roediger, David R. 2007. *The Wages of Whiteness: Race and the Making of the American Working Class.* London, UK: Verso.

Teslow, Tracy. 2007. "A Troubled Legacy: Making and Unmaking Race in the Museum." *Museums and Social Issues* 2(1): 11–44.

Ture, Kwame, and Charles V. Hamilton. 1992. *Black Power: The Politics of Liberation.* New York: Vintage Books.

Whittaker, Scott. 2014. *Museum Display Design.* London, UK: Design Media Publishing.

PART III

WHITE EMOTIONS, EXPRESSIONS, AND MOVEMENTS

CHAPTER 12

WHITE NOISE

How White Nationalist Content Creators Reproduce Narratives of White Power and Victimhood on YouTube

C. DOUG CHARLES

DONALD TRUMP'S ARRIVAL on the political scene has been accompanied by a rise in hate crimes (Edwards and Rushin 2018) and violent nationalist demonstrations, including the 2017 Unite the Right rally in Charlottesville. While at the event, avowed white nationalists Richard Spencer and James Allsup streamed and uploaded video accounts of the event to the online video platform YouTube. Earlier that year, investigators found subscriptions to various white nationalist channels on James Jackson's YouTube account after he murdered Timothy Caughman in an effort to stop black men from dating white women (Weill, LaPorta, and Zavadski 2017).

The roots of contemporary white supremacy run deep through the internet's early history (Michael 2016), and its utility as an international, unmoderated space for extremism has been compounded by the meteoric rise of social media and other user-generated content in the past fifteen years. Invigorated by recent political developments, white nationalists have embedded themselves into the center of a smorgasbord of various online far-right groups calling themselves the "alt-right." Using platforms such as YouTube, these groups are able to organize, recruit new members, disseminate media, and fund their political activities (O'Callaghan et al. 2015; Rash 2017).

This chapter focuses on YouTube and seeks to answer the following questions: Why is YouTube an effective platform for white supremacist groups? What themes, frames, and narratives are present in white supremacist

YouTube content? How do these reproduce both hegemony and white resistance to equality?

THEORETICAL BACKGROUND

There is a legacy of research on how online spaces facilitate extremist views (Suler 2004; O'Callaghan et al. 2015). They allow white supremacist groups to easily network with distant users (Michael 2016), anonymously discuss their extremist beliefs unchallenged (Hill and Hughes 1997), raise money (Gerstenfeld, Grant, and Chiang 2003; Conway 2005), and access or build repositories of white supremacist media (Adams and Roscigno 2005). YouTube as a platform excels at each of these—a fact that has not been ignored by the resurgence of white supremacist groups leading up to, and following, the 2016 US election (Valasik and Reid, 2018; King and Leonard 2016:166). YouTube's role as an online recruitment tool lies in its ubiquity, ease of use, and features that facilitate user-to-channel networking (Dogtiev 2018). In their study on YouTube's recommender algorithm, O'Callaghan et al. determined that users who encounter extreme right-wing political content on YouTube can find themselves "[immersed] in an ideological bubble in just a few clicks" (2015:459). YouTube functions as part of what Albrecht, Fielitz, and Thurston call a "digitally driven ecosystem," leveraged by white supremacists for the purposes of "mainstreaming" extremist ideas to the public (2018:13).

In this sense, the "alt-right" can be understood as a newer rebranding of white supremacism, with members committing considerable energy toward rhetorically distancing themselves from white supremacism to recruit more members and avoid the social ramifications of hate-group status (Futrell and Simi 2017). Many opt for more euphemistic labels, such as *identitarian*, *American nationalist*, and *race realist*. However, the ideas are merely repackaged hate of yesteryear, and smokescreens of "irony" or "trolling" allow users to still spread openly racist memes or content while gaslighting their accusers (Topinka 2018). Online extremists exploit the veneer of authenticity offered by user-generated content to attract new followers, while embedding dog whistles in their content to still appeal to existing "hardcore" members (May and Feldman 2018:27).

Today, the libertine Wild West atmosphere of online social spaces may seem like the new playground for online hate, but this is hardly a recent development. As far back as 1985, Tom Metzger, leader of the White Aryan Resistance, used electronic bulletin boards to network with other white supremacists (Michael 2016). Stormfront.org, one of the largest white nationalist websites, was founded as early as 1995. Functioning entirely off a single phone line, it served as a message board for up to four hundred daily visitors to discuss beliefs, coordinate meetings, and recruit new members. Before its recent decline, the website held over three hundred thousand registered members and remained a central hub for white nationalist activity. Stormfront's success demonstrated that going online meant global reach while brick-and-mortar white supremacist communities were limited to local recruitment. Additionally, online anonymity conceals extremist identities and radicalizes discourse through disinhibition and deindividualization (Suler 2004; Hill and Hughes 1997).

White supremacist groups have historically used online platforms to sell apparel, bumper stickers, and other merchandise (Gerstenfeld, Grant, and Chiang 2003). Donations can cover website costs and can be incentivized by platform-based privileges such as premium access or status (Conway 2005). When considering why white nationalism has found a home on YouTube specifically, the sheer monetizing power the platform possesses cannot be understated. In fact, many large companies pulled ads from the website, fearing they were funding extremist groups (Lomas 2017). YouTube's demonetization efforts placated advertisers, but content creators had workarounds. For example, far-right political vlogger Lauren Southern used Patreon to collect $5000 a month from patrons who view her content on YouTube (Broderick 2017). Today, content creators link their bitcoin wallets to video descriptions, enabling users to donate via cryptocurrency.

Like all social movements, white supremacist groups use frames to promote social efficacy (Goffman 1974). Frames are "persuasive devices" (Snow and Benford 1988) that interpret problems faced by a group, assert that they can be solved, and mobilize group members to take action rather than give up. The most effective frames resonate with their audience through the use of narratives—stories, myths, allegories, and tales that organize events into meaningful episodes, supporting a larger moral message. Adams and Roscigno (2005) found that white supremacist leaders are able to create a sense of "allies and adversaries" using symbolic construction of categories that delineate the superior "us" versus the inferior "them." This is very similar to Blumer's (1958) theory of group position as racial prejudice, a theory later expanded by Bobo and Hutchings (1996), which frames prejudice in a group-oriented construction of difference and superiority.

In addition to notions of "us" and "them," group conflict along racial lines, and defensiveness, white supremacist groups employ other frames, such as conspiracism, dualism, and victimhood (Daniels 1997; Lombard 1999; Berbrier 2000; Berlet and Vysotsky 2006). White victimhood has remained a core component of white supremacist messaging since the 1970s. Daniels (1997) argues that this was an effort to "rebrand" the movement following the civil rights era. With overt forms of racism being condemned, these groups had to retreat from the sunlight, so to speak, to reevaluate their approach.

David Duke, former Grand Dragon of the Ku Klux Klan, founded the National Association for the Advancement of White People (NAAWP) as a public response to the National Association for the Advancement of Colored People (NAACP), who, he claimed, supported antiwhite discrimination with its calls for affirmative action (Holstein and Miller 1990). Duke reframed minority groups as ungrateful beneficiaries of hardworking whites, who are the true victims of systemic racism. Similar attempts at equivocality would be found in subsequent calls for white pride months and white pride parades (Dobratz and Shanks-Meile 2006).

Applying Berbrier's (2000) work on the social construction of victimhood to white supremacist rhetoric reveals why whites can so easily leverage their privilege, performing a dizzying reversal of who *really* is the victim here (Lombard 1999). Their appropriation of victimhood serves as an effective silencing tool against oppressed minorities by shifting the conversation and commandeering their platform (Schwalbe et al. 2000). Additionally, it exploits the latent innocence of victimhood to absolve whites' history of systemically oppressing minorities. Finally, building an identity of victimhood allows these movements to spin violence in a more palatable way, motivating embittered whites to take extreme political action (Poletta 1998).

Overall, scholars have demonstrated a multitude of reasons for white supremacist groups' apparent affinity for online platforms. However, despite attention by news outlets (Solon 2018; Broderick 2017), advertisers (Lomas 2017), and platform decision makers (Hogan 2017), the recent surge in white supremacist activity has yielded only a few in-depth forays into specific platforms (King and Leonard 2016; Rash 2017; Lewis 2018). This study aims to break new ground, unpacking current frames and themes used by contemporary white nationalist groups to exploit the digital terrain of YouTube. Through in-depth analysis of white nationalist video content, the latest rhetorical mechanisms used to mainstream extremist ideas and recruit new followers will be laid bare.

RESEARCH DESIGN

While white supremacist groups occupy a variety of social media platforms, I have chosen YouTube for this study because of its ubiquity, its use by far-right content creators, and its effectiveness as a tool for creating, distributing, and monetizing media content. Due to the mammoth amount of content being uploaded daily—as well as how difficult organizing and indexing content can be—scholars who study YouTube communities tend to opt for small, purposive samples (Lange 2007; Rotman and Preece 2010). This study focuses on the YouTube channel Red Ice TV.

Red Ice is a media group dedicated to covering "politics, the culture war, entertainment and current issues from a pro-European perspective" (Red Ice TV n.d.). It prides itself as "the only media outlet bold enough to tell the truth," and its slogan is "The Future is the Past." They produce self-described "alt-right" online radio pieces, videos, and news stories. At the time of writing this, Red Ice TV has uploaded over one thousand videos and currently has over 220,000 subscribers.

After sorting the channel's video list by date uploaded and number of views, I selected thirty videos for sampling: the top ten most viewed, the top ten most recently uploaded, and ten randomly selected videos from the past one hundred most recent uploads. Popularity was chosen as a means of video priority because it can be reasonably correlated with influence and the likelihood that the video will be recommended to other viewers by YouTube's algorithm (Bishop 2018). To ensure relevance of content, videos from older than three years ago were excluded from analysis and replaced with the next video on the sorted list. Recency was determined to be a significant factor given the dramatic shift in white supremacist discourse and tactics leading up to, and following, the 2016 US election (Gusterson 2017; Edwards and Rushin 2018). The thirty videos sampled consisted of two speeches, a cartoon, six radio news segments, a book review, and an assortment of video essays about current events, race, immigration, and politics. They ranged from three minutes to an hour in length.

I transcribed videos using YouTube's automated closed captioning system. Captions were checked for mistakes, and when a video did not have a transcription, sound was rerouted to allow the computer to "listen to itself," and voice recognition was copied down in real time. Through multiple read-throughs, I coded and broke down transcriptions using thematic data analysis. Marshall and Rossman's (1999) six stages of thematic data analysis were applied, and coding involved initial, focused, and thematic stages. One of the strategies during initial and focused coding was the breaking down of these videos into narrative parts to delve into framing techniques.

Following focused coding, themes emerged, representing recurring ideas within the text. This conceptualization was done in multiple parts—first by identifying ways data within those categories converge, noting which concepts contain "recurring regularities" (Patton 2002: 466). Afterward, alternative interpretations of the data were tested, attempting to understand the themes in data through varying levels of extremism. The possibility for different interpretations allows content creators to send dog whistles to fellow white supremacists while appealing to wider audiences. Lastly, the inclusion of top comments under these videos helps identify various interpretations of media and reconcile them with those of the researcher.

RESULTS

Following analysis, five major themes emerged. Videos framed news stories, current events, history, and a variety of other topics into recurring narratives about (1) group warfare and white victimhood, (2) guilt management, (3) race, place, and entitlement, (4) censorship and truth, and (5) impending doom and the question of resistance.

Videos consistently conveyed a strong sense of racialized group conflict. Words like *us* interchangeably switched between *whites* and *Europeans*—even when talking about American whites. Race was the most pertinent measure of difference between people, transcending culture, language, and national boundaries. Also, race and ethnicity were semiotically fused together. Words like *Swedes* or *Germans* were accompanied by images of whites, while words like *immigrant* and *refugee* were accompanied by images of nonwhites. This combination of language and imagery combined the idea of nationality and race, presenting "us" and "them" in a simple, color-coded way. Mixing populations is portrayed as unnatural and therefore undesirable. The animated clip *"Diversity" Is a Weapon against Whites* uses the visual metaphor of how melting various crayons of different colors in a pot will produce a "blah, yucky color" while keeping the crayons separate means that they stay "vibrant and unique."

The appropriation of victim status was common, and whites were portrayed as besieged and beleaguered. Terms like *protect, preserve, defend, liberate, standing up for themselves*, and *fighting for what is theirs* were all used to describe white nationalists. In contrast, immigrants and nonwhites were said to be *invading, attacking, shouting, infecting, encroaching, stealing*, and *committing more crime*. Essentially, the "other" acts, and the "us" reacts. The stakes justify any degree of action, as indicated by videos like *Forced Multiculturalism Makes Nazis*—a cartoon where a white man returns from a world trip to "Evropa" and discovers, to his horror, that people of color are now riding the bus, at his job, and walking around in public. The video ends with him furiously becoming a radical extremist who dons a swastika.

"It's okay to be white. It's okay to love being white. It's okay to want to be around people who look like you. It okay to prefer your own people—everyone else does." This opening line from the video *White DNA Is an Abomination* addresses a common theme across the sample: guilt. Guilt is consistently presented as an emotional burden whites must shed for their own sake. Furthermore, it is insidiously planted into the minds of whites by those with ulterior motives. Whites are not privileged because they suffer guilt from being called racist.

Many videos present a revised, guiltless, version of history. In *Why I Don't Want to Become a Minority,* whites feel guilty and morally obligated to help other races because of slavery and conquest. This is unjust, the viewer is told, because all other races have engaged in that behavior, but only whites get "charged" because they were "the best at it." Any notion of nonwhites facing oppression is summarily dismissed by continuously pointing to all of the "free stuff" nonwhites receive, "courtesy" of whites. "If you're a minority in a white country, you can cash in on affirmative action, special loans, grants, scholarships, jobs, casting calls, diversity programs, all because you are not white." This framing adds a white nationalist twist to the more mainstream "playing the black card" trope—using one's minority status for special treatment.

The sampled videos rely heavily on blending whiteness, nationality, place, and entitlement in order to convey a message of white nationalism. In terms of geographical space, race was most often linked through historical narrative. *White DNA Is an Abomination* lists "white things" other races should be "thankful for." These include "human rights . . . cars, planes, trains, electricity, internet, toilets, medical advancements, photography, printing press, eyeglasses, space travel . . . Having a clean, safe neighborhood, speaking English, table manners, and having a mom *and* dad." Even colonialism is described as whites "cleaning" the land and building "great" things. Thus, imperialism is framed not only as justified but as a "courtesy"—a benevolent gift to the dominated.

The second function is that these narratives link racial identity with geographic place. For instance, whites and nonwhites are said to have their own countries, or "lands," they should be majority in. When justifying this sovereignty, the videos drew on selectively applied logic of historical squatting rights. Consider the following excerpt from *Go Back to Europe*: "We are Nordics, Slavs, Celts, Romans, Germanics, and Europe is ours, and so is America, Australia, Canada, and New Zealand." Here, whites are also entitled to colonized countries, such as North America, Australia, and New Zealand. While this seems contradictory to the notion that place and race are linked through ancient history, whites are the exception because skulls from the earliest American Indians allegedly have a head shape more similar to Eastern Europeans than to East Asians. Race apparently takes the form of hidden genetic indicators when it is convenient to do so.

The very essence of a country itself is symbolically tied to race, as well. A loss in demographic majority is always depicted as the loss of culture and place itself. *"Diversity" Is a Weapon against Whites* shows a cartoon with white stick figures running from a larger group of brown, black, and yellow stick figures. As the whites vacate the various buildings and flee, the schools, churches, and landmarks are changed into shanty towns, mosques, and chain supermarkets. Videos often cited racial demographics of various capital cities from around the world to convey that the white population is shrinking at an alarming rate. "New Europeans" are a lie, and immigrants "can never be us."

In the videos, nationalism, identitarianism, racialism, and separatism are all framed as natural, true components of how the world actually is. As the videos explain, "Reality is racist" and there is a malicious, concerted effort to "hide reality from the natives of the Western world." When hosts discuss events like the media's condemnation of far-right politicians and the deplatforming of white supremacist content creators, they frame them as evidence that truth is being obfuscated. YouTube vlogger Millennial Woes appeared in a Red Ice interview, talking about being banned from Twitter for stating the "well-known," "statistical, criminological fact" that blacks are more prone to violence than other races. When discussing censorship on Facebook, the host describes it as "Orwellian" and laments how the Holocaust cannot be questioned. This thematic thread frames white supremacist talking points like Holocaust denial, white separatism, and nonwhite criminality as good-faith attempts to fight dogma and have healthy discussions in an open marketplace of ideas.

Videos also contained elements of conspiracism, including overt mentions of a Masonic-Jewish conspiracy and prophecies about a Jewish-run New World Order (NWO). More indirect allusions to anti-Semitic conspiracies were present, including a video about blood transfusions possibly being used by the world's elite to live forever. Commenters saw this as evidence for cabals of Jewish vampires and tied the video to conspiracies about pedophilia and globalist human trafficking rings.

Conspiracism served the dual purpose of not only scapegoating Jews but also encouraging viewers not to trust other media sources. "All social media is controlled by a single, hidden hand," and its control extends into universities, which brainwash white youth and publish phony studies to advance an agenda. In a segment on climate change reports, the host encourages viewers to reject the idea of human-caused climate change and see it for what it really is: an insidious plot to get the West to regress back to the preindustrial era and allow nonwhite countries to get ahead.

Apocalypticism is a common theme among many white supremacist groups (Berlet and Vysotsky 2006; Barkun 2013:179), but Red Ice framed conflict in a secular way that tended to eschew any religious, world-ending prophecies. Instead, the white "West" is teetering on the edge of extinction. Perhaps the most distilled demonstration of this is in *The War on Whites Is Real*. Unlike the rest of the videos sampled, its format was more akin to a movie trailer than a video essay. To describe the tone of this video as dire would be an understatement. Its pixelated filter adds to the grittiness, and its dramatic instrumentation rises and falls over four minutes of news clips, interviews, and assorted video footage—all strung together in a tapestry of anxiety, powerlessness, and impending doom. Here, the "war on whites" takes the form of endless waves of unruly immigrants and surges in crime and terrorism. Between these segments are clips of politicians all over the world welcoming and encouraging it. At the end of the video, a voiceover in the style of a film trailer boldly announces, "White genocide is real. Tune in to the only media outlet bold enough to tell the truth."

Notably, videos are vague about ways to fix these alleged issues. They are rife with conversational counterpoints for viewers to use in arguments but conspicuously lack strategies concerning policy or organization. Instead, their messaging resembles patterns in outrage media, where activism and consumerism are indistinguishably blended together (Sobieraj and Berry 2011). When sampled videos *were* specific about what the viewer should do, it was to watch more content, become a member, donate money, and like, comment, and subscribe to the channel. In more recent videos, the emphasis was more on fighting demonetization and deplatforming, but the calls to action remained the same.

CONCLUSIONS

Results from this initial foray into white nationalist YouTube communities revealed notable similarities with framing discussed in the literature. Appropriation of victimhood, conspiracism, emphasis on group conflict, and construction of white power narratives all played central roles in many of the videos. However, where the content differed most was in the particulars of the medium, activism, and community interaction.

Outside of a brief segment showing Twitter users suggesting future content for videos, there were no examples of the content creator responding to or interacting with the viewership in any deliberate way. None of the top comments were from the channel, nor did they acknowledge feedback from viewers. Similarly, they did not resolve disputes between commenters, and in many cases they appeared to direct the viewership away from YouTube to their own website. There, one can pay to become a member, gain access to more content, and have opportunities to interact with the content creators. What this likely indicates is that because of YouTube's monetary restrictions on channels with explicit content, it serves as an entry point for potential members. In future studies, the role of YouTube in white nationalist communities could be examined as a potential pipeline for extremism or as harboring a very specific "band" of extremism on the spectrum of far-right political views.

Recent developments in politics have stoked long-burning coals of racial hatred and white resistance to equality. The same white supremacist groups that fought against racial equality as far back as the Reconstruction period now build new generations of followers from carefully cultivated social media empires (O'Callaghan et al. 2015). If activists, politicians, and scholars alike seek to combat the rising tide of these groups, they must look critically at the ways current online spaces facilitate them. In the sample there were numerous times Red Ice hosts told viewers that videos (or even the entire channel) could be taken down from YouTube. They also reminded viewers that due to retaliation by the platform, the "pro-white" movement depended on their donations and membership subscriptions "now more than ever." Messages like these should be considered when weighing the ethics of social media platforms and the government regulations they operate under. After all, platforms like these not only lend hate groups a megaphone to shout from but fund them with advertisement revenue, bring in a crowd, and help pass the collection plate around.

REFERENCES

Adams, Josh, and Vincent J. Roscigno. 2005. "White Supremacists, Oppositional Culture and the World Wide Web." *Social Forces* 84(2): 759–78.

Albrecht, Stephen, Maik Fielitz, and Nick Thurston. 2018. "Introduction." In *Post-Digital Cultures of the Far Right: Online Actions and Offline Consequences in Europe and the US*, edited by Maik Fielitz and Nick Thurston. Political Science, Vol. 71. Bielefeld, Germany: Transcript.

Barkun, Michael. 2013. *A Culture of Conspiracy: Apocalyptic Visions in Contemporary America*. 2nd edition. Comparative Studies in Religion and Society. Berkeley: University of California Press.

Berbrier, Mitch. 2000. "The Victim Ideology of White Supremacists and White Separatists in the United States." *Sociological Focus* 33(2): 175–91.

Berlet, Chip, and Stanislov Vysotsky. 2006. "Overview of US White Supremacist Groups." *Journal of Political and Military Sociology* 34(1): 11.

Bishop, Sophie. 2018. "Anxiety, Panic, and Self-Optimization: Inequalities and the YouTube Algorithm." *Convergence* 24(1): 69–84

Blumer, Herbert. 1958. "Race Prejudice as a Sense of Group Position." *Pacific Sociological Review* 1(1): 3–7.

Bobo, Lawrence, and Vincent L. Hutchings. 1996. "Perceptions of Racial Group Competition: Extending Blumer's Theory of Group Position to a Multiracial Social Context." *American Sociological Review* 61:951–72.

Broderick, Ryan. 2017. "Far-Right Activists Are Stealing Tricks from YouTubers and It's Going to Get People Hurt." Buzzfeed, June 22. Retrieved August 1, 2019 (https://www.buzzfeednews.com/article/ryanhatesthis/the-far-right-influencer-playbook).

Conway, Maura. 2005. "Terrorist 'Use' of the Internet and Fighting Back." Paper prepared for presentation at the conference Cybersafety: Safety and Security in a Networked World: Balancing Cyber-Rights and Responsibilities, Oxford University, Oxford, UK, September.

Daniels, Jessie. 1997. *White Lies: Race, Class, Gender, and Sexuality in White Supremacist Discourse*. New York: Routledge.

Dobratz, Betty A., and Stephanie L. Shanks-Meile. 2006. "The Strategy of White Separatism." *Journal of Political and Military Sociology* 34(1): 49.

Dogtiev, Artyom. 2018. "YouTube Revenue and Usage Statistics." Business of Apps. Retrieved July 31, 2018 (https://www.businessofapps.com/data/youtube-statistics/).

Edwards, Griffin Sims, and Stephen Rushin. 2018. "The Effect of President Trump's Election on Hate Crimes." *Social Science Research Network (SSRN)*, January 18. Retrieved May 12, 2020 (http://dx.doi.org/10.2139/3102652).

Futrell, Robert, and Pete Simi. 2017. "The [Un]Surprising Alt-Right." *Contexts* 16(2): 76.

Gerstenfeld, Phyllis B., Diana R. Grant, and Chau-Pu Chiang. 2003. "Hate Online: A Content Analysis of Extremist Internet Sites." *Analyses of Social Issues and Public Policy* 3(1): 29–44.

Goffman, Erving. 1974. *Frame Analysis: An Essay on the Organization of Experience*. Cambridge, MA: Harvard University Press.

Gusterson, Hugh. 2017. "From Brexit to Trump: Anthropology and the Rise of Nationalist Populism." *American Ethnologist* 44(2): 209–14.

Hill, Kevin A., and John E. Hughes 1997. "Computer-Mediated Political Communication: The USENET and Political Communities." *Political Communication* 14(1): 3–27.

Hogan, Marc. 2017. "Is White Power Music Finally Getting Booted from the Internet?" *Pitchfork*, August 17. Retrieved August 1, 2019 (https://pitchfork.com/thepitch/is-white-power-music-finally-getting-booted-from-the-internet/).

Holstein, James A., and Gale Miller. 1990. "Rethinking Victimization: An Interactional Approach to Victimology." *Symbolic Interaction* 13(1): 103–22.

King, C. Richard, and David J. Leonard. 2016. *Beyond Hate: White Power and Popular Culture*. New York: Routledge.

Lange, Patricia G. 2007. "Commenting on Comments: Investigating Responses to Antagonism on YouTube." Paper presented at the 61st annual meeting of the Society for Applied Anthropology, March 28–31, Tampa, FL.

Lewis, Rebecca. 2018. *Alternative Influence: Broadcasting the Reactionary Right on YouTube* (Report). *Data and Society*. Retrieved August 1, 2019 (https://datasociety.net/wp-content/uploads/2018/09/DS_Alternative_Influence.pdf).

Lomas, Natasha 2017. "After YouTube Boycott, Google Pulls Ads from More Types of Offensive Content." *TechCrunch*, March 21.

Lombard, Deborah-Eve. 1999. "Racism's Tangible Lifeline: 20th Century Material Culture and the Continuity of the White Supremacy Myth." MA thesis, University of Iowa. https://ir.uiowa.edu/etd/194/.

Marshall, Catherine, and Gretchen B. Rossman. 1999. "The 'What' of the Study: Building the Conceptual Framework." *Designing Qualitative Research* 3: 21–54.

May, Rob, and Matthew Feldman. 2018. "Ideologues, 'Lulz' and Hiding in Plain Sight." In *Post-Digital Cultures of the Far Right: Online Actions and Offline Consequences in Europe and the US*, edited by Maik Fielitz and Nick Thurston. Political Science, Vol. 71. Bielefeld, Germany: Transcript.

Michael, George. 2016. "This Is War! Tom Metzger, White Aryan Resistance, and the Lone Wolf Legacy." *Focus on Terrorism* 14: 29–62.

O'Callaghan, Derek, Derek Greene, Maura Conway, Joe Carthy, and Padraig Cunningham. 2015. "Down the (White) Rabbit Hole: The Extreme Right and Online Recommender Systems." *Social Science Computer Review* 33(4): 459–78.

Patton, Michael Q. 2002. "Two Decades of Developments in Qualitative Inquiry: A Personal, Experiential Perspective." *Qualitative Social Work* 1(3): 261–83.

Poletta, Francesca. 1998. "Contending Stories: Narrative in Social Movements." *Qualitative Sociology* 21: 419–46.

Rash, Sabreen. 2017. "Bringing the Fight to# Cyberspace: Measuring the Effectiveness of Social Media in Building Social Capital for Extremist Organizations." Senior thesis, University of Lynchburg, Lynchburg, VA.

Red Ice TV. n.d. "Home [YouTube Channel]." Retrieved August 1, 2019 (http://youtube.com/RedIceRadio).

Rotman, Dana, and Jennifer Preece. 2010. "The 'WeTube' in YouTube: Creating an Online Community through Video Sharing." *International Journal of Web Based Communities* 6(3): 317–33.

Schwalbe, Michael, Daphne Holden, Douglas Schrock, Sandra Godwin, Shealy Thompson, and Michele Wolkomir. 2000. "Generic Processes in the Reproduction of Inequality: An Interactionist Analysis." *Social Forces* 79(2): 419–52.

Snow, David A., and Robert D. Benford. 1988. "Ideology, Frame Resonance, and Participant Mobilization." *International Social Movement Research* 1(1): 197–217.

Sobieraj, Sarah, and Jeffrey M. Berry. 2011. "From Incivility to Outrage: Political Discourse in Blogs, Talk Radio, and Cable News." *Political Communication*, 28(1): 19–41.

Solon, Olivia. 2018. "YouTube's 'Alternative Influence Network' Breeds Rightwing Radicalisation, Report Finds." *Guardian*, September 18.

Suler, John. 2004. "The Online Disinhibition Effect." *Cyberpsychology and Behavior* 7(3): 321–26.

Topinka, Robert J. 2018. "Politically Incorrect Participatory Media: Racist Nationalism on r/ImGoingToHellForThis." *New Media and Society* 20(5): 2050–69.

Valasik, Matthew, and Shannon E. Reid. 2018. "Alt-Right Gangs and White Power Youth Groups." *Oxford Bibliographies Online: Criminology*. Retrieved August 1, 2019 (https://www.oxfordbibliographies.com/view/document/obo-9780195396607/obo-9780195396607-0243.xml).

Weill, Kelly, James LaPorta, and Katie Zavadski. 2017. "James Jackson Liked Alt-Right Videos, Claimed He Was a Genius in Army Intelligence." *Daily Beast*, April 10.

CHAPTER 13

BLUE LIVES MATTER

Police Protection or Countermovement

MARETTA MCDONALD

HASHTAGS HAVE BECOME more than a label or tag people use to group social media posts about the same topic. From #ManCrushMonday to #ThrowbackThursday, hashtags are part of popular culture, linking posts and people. The development of #BlackLivesMatter from a hashtag to a global movement is an example of people using social media to quickly transform ideas into action (Freelon, McIlwain, and Clark 2016). The #BlackLivesMatter hashtag ignited the oppositional consciousness of people around the world, leading to collective action in the form of protests, mobilizing in order to take steps to reform policing (Bailey and Leonard 2015; Dalton 2015; Morris and Braine 2001). Tensions between the criminal legal system and Black people have long existed, leading to collective consciousness and collective action by members of subjugated communities with the support of their allies. Much of this tension was created by law enforcement's historical involvement in the continued oppression of Black people, from slave patrols, refusal to enforce antilynching legislation, surveillance of Black activists, and facilitation of mass incarceration to the high-profile shootings of unarmed Black men (Alexander 2012; Earl 2003; Holden-Smith 1996; Levin 2002; Rousey 1996).

Conversely, the Blue Lives Matter movement also started as a hashtag. #BlueLivesMatter appeared on Twitter at the end of November 2014 around the time of Darren Wilson's indictment for Michael Brown's murder in Ferguson, Missouri (Anderson and Hitlin 2016). The hashtag gained popularity and widespread use after the ambush-style killing of Officers Ramos and Lui in late December 2014 in Brooklyn (Anderson and Hitlin 2016). Thereafter, the public and politicians began to rally around Blue Lives Matter as a source of social mobilization, associating it with public support for police. Despite no formal organizational structure (e.g., local chapters, leadership), rallies were held, and businesses sponsored advertising dedicated to Blue Lives Matter in many cities (TheGrio 2015).

While research on #BlackLivesMatter provides us with a general understanding of social media's ability to influence collective consciousness and action (Bailey and Leonard 2015; Leopold and Bell 2017; Obasogie and Newman 2016), less is understood about hashtags and countermovements that develop in response to demands for justice. The hashtag #BlueLivesMatter emerged on social media as a rebuttal to #BlackLivesMatter's claims of police misconduct (Bock and Figueroa 2017). The collective action behind Blue Lives Matter spawned legislation in fifteen states increasing penalties for acts of violence against police (Craven 2017). An analysis of Blue Lives Matter provides an excellent example of a countermovement with theoretical, political, and methodological implications.

This chapter seeks a deeper understanding of the nature of Blue Lives Matter ideology, which has garnered widespread support from the public, politicians, and corporations. Drawing on sociological literature on colorblind racism, racial formation, and social movements, I argue that Blue Lives Matter is best understood as a countermovement that emerged from within the neoconservative white racial project (Winant 2001), designed to preserve white supremacy through its use of color-blind rhetoric. As a countermovement, Blue Lives Matter presents itself as the ideological opposite of Black Lives Matter by its branding as a racialized symbol of support for police in a time when Black people are demanding police reform.

LITERATURE REVIEW

Adversarial Movements

Social movements and their countermovement partners develop institutionally (Zald and Ussem 1987; Lo 1982). Scholars argue that oppositional movements have a temporal order, where a social movement must precede a countermovement (Zald and Ussem 1987). Scholars have defined social movements as collective action to "bring about social change" (Wilson 1973, qtd. in Mottl 1980:620) and conceptualized them as "the mobilized sentiments in which people take actions to achieve change in the social structure and allocation of value" (Zald and Ussem 1987:249). Social movements are driven by a collective desire for structural change and a challenge to power by citizens within the population. In contrast, countermovements develop from collective opposition to the foregoing movement. Countermovement supporters have an interest in maintaining the status quo or rolling back or preventing social change. (Lo 1982; Meyer and Staggenborg 1996).

Ideological differences and temporal order are not the only dissimilarities separating social movements and countermovements. Countermovements are often composed of groups located in higher positions in the social hierarchy than participants of the initial social movement (Zald 1979). They often have access to resources not available to social movements, allowing them to be more influential (Mottl 1980). Countermovements can also be reactionary and tend to concentrate their collective efforts on government and society instead of the movement they precede (Meyer and Staggenborg 1996).

The interplay between social movements and countermobilizations is another important component in understanding adversarial movements (Andrews 2002; Meyer and Staggenborg 1996; Mottl 1980; Wilson 1973; Zald and Ussem 1987). A dialectical relationship exists between oppositional movements. The battle between movements is fought in a public arena (the media, courts, or the legislative body) until a winner is declared. If the social movement is victorious, the countermovement takes the battle to a different arena. This strategy limits substantial change (Meyer and Staggenborg 1996; Zald and Ussem 1987). For example, in their discussion of the political debate surrounding abortion, Zald and Ussem (1987) provide evidence of the interplay between adversarial movements. After the abortion rights advocates' victory of *Roe v. Wade*, antiabortion supporters moved their collective attention from the site of their defeat, the judicial branch, to the legislative branch. They used social status and resources to make a successful play in Congress to restrict states' use of federal funds for abortions.

Social movements often organize to demand societal-level change, as seen during the civil rights movement. However, other movements target specific entities or organizations, like the construction of corporate farming industries (Pichardo 1995; Waldinger and Bailey 1991). Countermovements, in cases like this, are often responses of organizations threatened by mobilization (Jasper and Poulsen 1993). When a social movement specifically names its target, countermovement organizations (like trade and professional associations) spring into action to defend their positions and protect their interests.

As social movements change, countermovements adapt. Contemporary countermovements take on a subtler approach, particularly in regard to issues surrounding race. In the era of color-blind racism (Bonilla-Silva 2018) and covert systemic racism (Feagin 2014), Doane (2006:270) argues that "code words and catchphrases" are used as weapons in battles over power and resources. Racism is reimagined by ignoring its existence (claims of a postracial society), making it universal (anyone can be racist), and eliminating the need for structural change (racism is individualistic). This recasting of racism has become an effective tool to derail progress toward social change by those who benefit from the status quo (Doane 2006). For example, the #AllLivesMatter hashtag was created on social media as a response to claims by #BlackLivesMatter (Anderson and Hitlin 2016). Without directly addressing race, the "all lives matter" catchphrase diminishes the impact of the Black Lives Matter movement's use of social media, thereby attempting to retain power over policing in the way Doane (2006) describes.

Theoretical Framework: Color-Blind Racism

After legal racial oppression ended in the 1960s, scholars argue, racism was not legislated away; it still exists in a veiled form called color-blind racism (Bonilla-Silva 2018). Color-blind racism, as theorized by Eduardo Bonilla-Silva (2018), has five elements: use of covert racial language and policies, avoidance of racialized terms and claims of reverse racism, blaming culture for structural issues (including victim blaming), use of covert racist mechanisms, and redesign of Jim Crow–like racial practices. In its analysis of Blue Lives Matter, this chapter focuses on the elements of using language to obscure racialized meanings, covert racist mechanisms, and victim blaming.

Omi and Winant's racial formation theory defines racial formation as "the sociohistorical process by which racial identities are created, lived out, transformed, destroyed" (2014:109). Interactions between structure and ideology are the process by which conceptualizations of race and racism are formed. State agencies, institutions, and organizations throughout society participate in showing that racial difference is significant by supporting or opposing certain racial policies, as well as by mobilizing along racial lines (Alexander 2012; Lipsitz 1995; Winant 2001).

Racial projects are cogs in the machine of racial formation. Racial dynamics are interpreted, represented, and explained through racial projects. Both a side effect and an impetus of the interplay of various racial projects is white anxiety. White anxiety, defined as uncertainty about whiteness (Winant

2001), occurs when white identity's meaning and continued significance is called into question. Historical white anxiety has been rooted in the aspiration to continue white supremacy by using assumed biological difference to defend racial hierarchy and inequality. Winant and others argue that the white supremacist racial project was used to reify racist ideology through racially oppressive laws and policies like slavery and Jim Crow (Winant 2001; Alexander 2012).

As a result of antiracist social movements and the subsequent racial reform policies of the 1960s, Winant argues, whiteness required reconceptualization. Its reimagining, prompted by uncertainty about whiteness, encouraged new racial projects to develop. There are three post–civil rights era white racial projects that can be characterized as neoconservative, liberal, and new abolitionist (Winant 2001). It is important to note that the white supremacist racial project still exists alongside these newer ones and in some ways is stronger than before. In this chapter, I focus on the neoconservative racial project.

The neoconservative racial project reimagines race by denying racial difference, promoting meritocracy, and highlighting cultural differences. Winant (2001) explains that neoconservative racial projects are rooted in a color-blind ideological stance based on the conservative and individualist forms of equality championed by whites. This white racial project combats white anxiety by asserting that inequality is the result of individual failings rather than racial discrimination. Proclaiming that there should be no racial preference of any kind, white neoconservatives consider any proposals for antiracist policies to be reverse racism, race thinking, and race baiting. The neoconservative white racial project uses the same devices black movements used, like lawsuits and protests, as mechanisms for re-embedding white supremacy in the system in a covert, color-blind way.

My study expands the understanding of Blue Lives Matter through in-depth analysis of major newspaper coverage of Blue Lives Matter as a countermovement to Black Lives Matter and consideration of its implications. I integrate theoretical tenets from color-blind racism (Bonilla-Silva 2018), racial formation theory (Omi and Winant 2014), and the neoconservative racial project (Winant 2001) to interrogate how Blue Lives Matter is used as a rhetorical device within American society. Drawing on this integrated theoretical toolkit, I also explore the absence of discourse on Blue Lives Matter found in the media (i.e., online newspaper articles). My findings reveal how Blue Lives Matter is used to reify racial ideology within social structures, such as the creation and implementation of new laws.

RESEARCH DESIGN

I conducted a Nexis Uni newspaper search for news articles using the search terms Blue Lives Matter and #bluelivesmatter from January 1, 2014, to April 30, 2018. This search retrieved 1687 results categorized as news. Restricting the search to newspapers in North America reduced the sample to 479 articles. Following precedent set by previous content analysis research on Black Lives Matter, I further delimited the data to newspapers with larger circulations: the *New York Times, USA Today,* and the *New York Post*. I also included the *St. Louis Post-Dispatch* from Missouri because of its valuable work on Black Lives Matter, especially involving deceased local youth Michael Brown (Leopold and Bell 2017). I used the 74 remaining articles as the population from which to draw a proportional, stratified random sample by publication using a random number generator. The resulting sample contains 30 news articles, including opinion pieces and editorials.

I used a constructivist grounded theory methodological approach for analysis (Charmaz 2014). I read each news article multiple times to identify patterns and wrote memos containing emergent thoughts and revelations about those patterns. I created codes to describe the data's relationship with the research question (Hesse-Biber 2017). From a preliminary analysis of one-third of the news articles emerged approximately fifty codes, which I then used as guides for analyzing the remaining two-thirds. Overall, roughly seventy descriptive codes emerged. I then conducted more focused coding, resulting in seven different categories. More abstract themes relevant to this analysis include juxtaposing Black Lives Matter and Blue Lives Matter, rallying white voter support, pro-police advocacy, and choosing sides.

RESULTS: POLICE PROTECTION—WHITE PRETENSION

"If I Say Black Lives, You Say Blue Lives"

The most common theme that emerged from the data is the juxtaposition of Black Lives Matter and Blue Lives Matter. Across articles and publications, Blue Lives Matter was rarely mentioned without Black Lives Matter. The movement and countermovement are presented as moral and ideological opposites with equal ethical and moral value. *USA Today* admonished the public for supporting either side: "In the absence of facts, shouting slogans, clinging to false narratives or arguing over the merits of 'Black Lives Matter' vs. 'Blue Lives Matter' will only get in the way of addressing a crisis that diminishes all lives" (USA Today Editorial Board 2016). The *New York Post* discussion about the deaths of Alton Sterling and Philando Castile, as well as the killing of Dallas and Baton Rouge police officers suggests that the events divided the country, asking, "Whose side were you on? Which victims did you mourn?" (Healy and Hannah-Jones 2016). By providing what journalists call balanced coverage, they imply that both sides of the debate around police reform have equally valid claims.

The strategy of presenting Black Lives Matter and Blue Lives Matter as equally valid is best explained through racial formation theory. Dismissing racial inequality is a color-blind-racism rhetorical tool of the neoconservative white racial project. By positioning these two perspectives as equal, the injustice of police brutality is minimized and conflated with antipolice bias. As a countermovement, Blue Lives Matter blurs the overarching issue of state-sanctioned violence against Black bodies into a quagmire of confrontation and deflection. Such discourse obscures the marginalization of Black people within American society by suggesting dropping both sides, thus preserving white supremacy and maintaining white advantage.

United We Stand

The data also revealed that "Blue Lives Matter" was used as a rallying cry. It emerged as a racialized symbol of solidarity in majority white spaces. Several articles provide evidence of its figurative use during the Republican National Convention (RNC). A reference to the term in the *New York Post* reads, "Milwaukee Sheriff David Clarke wasted no time getting to his point, starting his passionate remarks with 'Blue Lives Matter,' a line that earned a rousing ovation" (Goodwin 2016). *USA Today* also highlights Clarke's remarks: "And Sheriff David Clarke of Milwaukee, one of several African-American speakers to draw prestigious speaking slots, received one of the biggest cheers of the night when he said, 'Blue lives matter in America'—a reference to his colleagues in law enforcement" (Bacon and Wolf 2016). Throughout the data, an exclamation of "Blue Lives Matter" led to a powerful affective response from majority white audiences.

The news articles data reflect how Clarke and other nonwhite Republicans provide legitimacy to Blue Lives Matter while delegitimizing Black Lives Matter. First, one article specifically highlights that Clarke is a Black man. Second, they emphasized that he was not the only Black Trump supporter. Similar to the way people use their alleged friendship with a Black person as a common form of color-blind rhetoric (Bonilla-Silva 2018), the RNC presented black bodies to temper the racialized tone of Blue Lives

Matter. Additionally, countermovement literature points out that embedding representatives from the opposing community into the countermovement is used as a strategy to delegitimize their opposition (Mottl 1980). A Black man promoting "Blue Lives" supports the neoconservative white racial project's objective to reduce the legitimacy of social equality. Additionally, Clarke supporting Blue Lives Matter bolsters the ideology of individualism, neoliberalism, and conservativism. The underlying assumption is that if all Black people would just work hard and get an education like Clarke, there would be no inequality. Through the lens of color-blind racism (Bonilla-Silva 2018), this is a covert racist mechanism used to diminish how historical and contemporary structural barriers limit Black upward mobility.

Blue Lives Matter and Criminality

An important subtheme that emerges within the category of Blue Lives Matter as a rallying cry is using law-and-order rhetoric to band white voters together based on shared anti-Blackness. Connections between Blackness and crime have long been a part of the political landscape (Alexander 2012). In an article about the 2016 presidential election, a Trump supporter uses Blue Lives Matter when discussing the state of crime in the United States, "Anybody who watches the news knows we need to have law and order reinstalled and we need to have more support for Blue Lives Matter" (Alcindor 2016). In an article that discussed condemnation of police, the journalists wrote that "David Clarke Jr., the sheriff of Milwaukee County, declared that 'blue lives matter' and argued that the Black Lives Matter movement was contributing to 'a collapse of social order'" (Healy, Alcindor, and Peters 2016). This racialized rhetoric of associating social protest with criminality while linking Blue Lives Matter to a return to a "Great America" has historical and theoretical significance.

Civil rights era protests organized to express outrage over police brutality and to demand racial equality in education, public accommodations, and employment were framed as "criminal rather than political" by state officials and law enforcement (Alexander 2012:41). Politicians asserted that "If [Blacks] conduct themselves in an orderly way, they will not have to worry about police brutality" (Alexander 2012:42). After the passing of the Civil Rights Act of 1964, conservatives began the "get tough on crime" countermovement to calm white anxiety (Mauer 2009). Through this lens, we see how Blue Lives Matter is situated within a history of dominant group resistance to challenging the status quo. By equating the return to law and order with support of Blue Lives Matter, the neoconservative white racial project denies racial difference in the way Black people experience policing. Masking racial inequality, in the form of police brutality, behind color-blind narratives of individual immoral behavior—such as selling pirated DVDs, resisting arrest, or selling loose cigarettes—protects white supremacy (Obasogie and Newman 2016).

Police Need Love Too

Interestingly, there was a lack of discussion connecting Blue Lives Matter with support for police in mainstream news media. The concepts were only associated with one another in one article in the sample. The article, written about the police murders in New York City, reads, "After the killings on Saturday, the protest motto of 'Black Lives Matter' was joined by a chorus of 'Blue Lives Matter' on social media, in support of officers" (Robbins and Stewart 2014). The absence of explicit reference to Blue Lives Matter as a form of support for police speaks to mainstream media influences on public perception about salient topics within society (Bonilla-Silva and Ashe 2014). The lack of discourse of Blue Lives Matter as a form of police support elevates the racialized aspects of the narratives. Additionally, missing discourse forces people to choose an ideological side based on their preexisting cognitive frames (Kinder and Sanders 1996).

CONCLUSIONS

The goal of this chapter was to gain a deeper understanding of Blue Lives Matter on- and offline by examining the news media conceptualization. My study found that media framed Blue Lives Matter as the antithesis of Black Lives Matter morally, politically, and racially and only understood Blue Lives Matter as it related to Black Lives Matter. My examination of Blue Lives Matter uncovered its countermovement characteristics, showing that "Blue Lives Matter" is a rhetorical device used to reify neoconservative white racial projects. Relevant to all emerging themes was the juxtaposition of the Black Lives Matter movement to Blue Lives Matter. By remaining adjacent to its social movement counterpart, Blue Lives Matter's position on the ideological spectrum made counterclaims, invalidated the initial movement's concerns, and challenged Black Lives Matter's validity in order to maintain white supremacy. The integration of aspects from Bonilla-Silva's and Omi and Winant's theoretical frameworks helps us explore and understand how Blue Lives Matter is a contemporary example of White resistance in response to Black Lives Matter's push for social change.

Policy Implications

My findings show that Blue Lives Matter comes to life as a tool of conservatives to maintain the status quo by positioning itself as the moral alternative to Black Lives Matter. As a countermovement, Blue Lives Matter depends on Black Lives Matter to be understood (Mottl 1980). There is a lack of evidence suggesting that Blue Lives Matter centers police protection. When Blue Lives Matter began, violence against police was at an all-time low, especially ambush-style killings (Maguire, Nix, and Campbell 2016). The false narrative that danger to law enforcement professionals had increased was the impetus for creating new laws in fifteen states (Olson 2017). My analysis contradicts this narrative and prompts new questions about the justification for Blue Lives Matter laws, a category of laws that enhance penalties for violence against police or add crimes against police to existing hate crime laws.

Blue Lives Matter laws are problematic for a number of reasons. Laws are not only pieces of legislation; they are texts about society and its values in which the ideology of those in power can be traced (Foucault 1972). Hate crime laws protect groups who have a legacy of oppression in this country (Levin 2002). Extending hate crime protections to police sends a message to the powerless that they no longer deserve protection, which historically included protection from law enforcement. This analysis shows that a pervasive fear for the safety of police is not the motivation behind the Blue Lives Matter movement; therefore, Blue Lives Matter laws can be viewed as a reification of the neoconservative white project's efforts to maintain white supremacy.

My analysis reveals that Blue Lives Matter is a neoconservative white racial project that helps maintain white supremacy. It acts as a color-blind mechanism to trivialize racial inequality as a result of personal failings. Because of deep investment in the status quo, Republicans used Blue Lives Matter as a racialized device to rally people who oppose progressive social change. Conservatives built a strong majority-white contingent to help elect the new Republican president using these rhetorical devices. As the data reflects, Blue Lives Matter exists in majority-white contexts, bound together by anti-Blackness. This level of racialized groupthink has historically led to more oppression for people of color, even though the mechanisms used have changed (Alexander 2012; Du Bois 2001).

My findings show that the same neoconservative devices developed in the post–civil rights era are being deployed to maintain racial stratification. In addition, my study expands research on countermovements by illuminating the similarities between Blue Lives Matter and historical countermovements. The similarities are revealed in the racialized tone, the use of Black bodies, and the transition from rhetoric to legislation of Blue Lives Matter. As demonstrated with mass incarceration (Alexander 2012), the laws that resulted from these countermovements have the potential to negatively and disproportionately affect Black citizens.

My findings are an important starting point from which to expand sociological research on countermovements in the digital age. Nonetheless, these findings should be read in light of some limitations. My textual analysis included national newspapers to provide an overview of how Blue Lives Matter is represented in textual discourse. However, most of the debate surrounding Blue Lives Matter occurs at the state and local levels. For a more sophisticated analysis, future research should examine local newspapers as well as social media sites such as Facebook and Twitter. By conducting a digital ethnography on these social media sites, we can explore the dialectical relationship between Blue Lives Matter and Black Lives Matter (Bonilla and Rosa 2015). My study's contribution expands countermovement research, bringing it into the digital age as online communities cross the threshold from virtual reality to everyday life.

REFERENCES

Alcindor, Yamiche. 2016. "Minorities Worry What a 'Law and Order' Trump Presidency Will Mean." *New York Times*, November 12.

Alexander, Michelle. 2012. *The New Jim Crow: Mass Incarceration in the Age of Colorblindness*. New York: The New Press.

Anderson, Monica, and Paul Hitlin. 2016. "Social Media Conversations about Race." Pew Research Center: Internet and Technology (Washington, DC), August 15. Retrieved April 25, 2018 (https://www.pewresearch.org/internet/2016/08/15/social-media-conversations-about-race/).

Andrews, Kenneth T. 2002. "Movement-Countermovement Dynamics and the Emergence of New Institutions: The Case of 'White Flight' Schools in Mississippi." *Social Forces* 80(3): 911–36. doi: 10.1353/sof.2002.0001.

Bacon, John, and Richard Wolf. 2016. "Anti-Trump Action Signals Chaotic Start; Campaign Quells Rules Rebellion by Several Delegates." *USA Today*, July 19.

Bailey, Julius, and David J. Leonard. 2015. "Black Lives Matter: Post-Nihilistic Freedom Dreams." *Journal of Contemporary Rhetoric* 5(1/2): 67–77.

Bock, Mary Angela, and Ever Josue Figueroa. 2017. "Faith and Reason: An Analysis of the Homologies of Black and Blue Lives Facebook Pages." *New Media and Society*. doi: 10.1177/1461444817740822.

Bonilla, Yarimar, and Jonathan Rosa. 2015. "# Ferguson: Digital Protest, Hashtag Ethnography, and the Racial Politics of Social Media in the United States." *American Ethnologist* 42(1): 4–17.

Bonilla-Silva, Eduardo. 2018. *Racism without Racists: Color-Blind Racism and the Persistence of Racial Inequality in America*. Lanham, MD: Rowman & Littlefield.

Bonilla-Silva, Eduardo, and Austin Ashe. 2014. "The End of Racism? Colorblind Racism and Popular Media." Pp. 57–83 in *The Colorblind Screen: Television in Post-Racial America*, edited by Sarah Nilsen and Sarah E. Turner. New York: NYU Press.

Charmaz, Kathy. 2014. *Constructing Grounded Theory*. Thousand Oaks, CA: Sage.

Craven, Julia. 2017. "32 Blue Lives Matter Bills Have Been Introduced across 14 States This Year." *Huffington Post*, March 1. Retrieved May 4, 2017 (http://www.huffingtonpost.com/entry/blue-black-lives-matter-police-bills-states_us_58b61488e4b0780bac2e31b8).

Dalton, Deron. 2015. "The Three Women behind the Black Lives Matter Movement." *Madame Noire*, May 4. Retrieved June 27, 2018 (http://madamenoire.com/528287/the-three-women-behind-the-black-lives-matter-movement/).

Doane, Ashley W. 2006. "What Is Racism? Racial Discourse and Racial Politics." *Critical Sociology* 32(2–3): 255–74.

Du Bois, W. E. B. 2001. *Black Reconstruction in America, 1860–1880*. New York: Atheneum.

Earl, Jennifer. 2003. "Tanks, Tear Gas, and Taxes: Toward a Theory of Movement Repression." *Sociological Theory* 21(1): 44–68. doi: 10.1111/1467-9558.00175.

Feagin, Joe R. 2014. *Racist America: Roots, Current Realities, and Future Reparations*. New York: Routledge.

Foucault, Michel. 1972. *The Archaeology of Knowledge*. London: Routledge.

Freelon, Deen, Charlton D. McIlwain, and Meredith D. Clark. 2016. "Beyond the Hashtags: #Ferguson, #Blacklivesmatter, and the Online Struggle for Offline Justice." Center for Media and Social Impact (Washington, DC), February 29. Retrieved May 12, 2020 (https://cmsimpact.org/resource/beyond-hashtags-ferguson-blacklivesmatter-online-struggle-offline-justice/).

Goodwin, Michael. 2016. "The GOP Is Playing Politics—and Giving Voters a Clear Choice." *New York Post*, July 19.

Healy, Jack, and Nikole Hannah-Jones. 2016. "Seeking Unity, Nation Debates Racial Chasm." *New York Times*, July 10, A1.

Healy, Patrick, Yamiche Alcindor, and Jeremy W. Peters. 2016. "Convention Speeches Unsettle Blacks in G.O.P." *New York Times*, July 20, A1.

Hesse-Biber, Sharlene Nagy. 2017. *The Practice of Qualitative Research: Engaging Students in the Research Process*. Thousand Oaks, CA: Sage.

Holden-Smith, Barbara. 1996. "Lynching, Federalism, and the Intersection of Race and Gender in the Progressive Era." *Yale Journal of Law and Feminism* 8: 31–78.

Jasper, James M., and Jane Poulsen. 1993. "Fighting Back: Vulnerabilities, Blunders, and Countermobilization by the Targets in Three Animal Rights Campaigns." *Sociological Forum* 8(4): 639–57.

Kinder, Donald R., and Lynn M. Sanders. 1996. *Divided by Color: Racial Politics and Democratic Ideals.* Chicago: University of Chicago Press.

Leopold, Joy, and Myrtle P. Bell. 2017. "News Media and the Racialization of Protest: An Analysis of Black Lives Matter Articles." *Equality, Diversity, and Inclusion: An International Journal* 36(8): 720–35. doi: 10.1108/EDI-01-2017-0010.

Levin, Brian. 2002. "From Slavery to Hate Crime Laws: The Emergence of Race and Status-Based Protection in American Criminal Law." *Journal of Social Issues* 58(2): 227–45. doi: 10.1111/1540-4560.00258.

Lipsitz, George. 1995. "The Possessive Investment in Whiteness: Racialized Social Democracy and the 'White' Problem in American Studies." *American Quarterly* 47(3): 369–87. doi: 10.2307/2713291.

Lo, Clarence Y. 1982. "Countermovements and Conservative Movements in the Contemporary U.S." *Annual Review of Sociology* 8: 107–34. doi: 10.1146/annurev.so.08.080182.000543.

Maguire, Edward R., Justin Nix, and Bradley A. Campbell. 2016. "A War on Cops? The Effects of Ferguson on the Number of U.S. Police Officers Murdered in the Line of Duty." *Justice Quarterly* 34(5): 1–20. doi: 10.1080/07418825.2016.1236205.

Mastro, Dana. 2015. "Why the Media's Role in Issues of Race and Ethnicity Should Be in the Spotlight." *Journal of Social Issues* 71(1): 1–16.

Mauer, Marc. 2009. "Two-Tiered Justice: Race, Class, and Crime Policy." Pp. 169–84 in *The Integration Debate: Competing Futures for American Cities*, edited by C. Hartman and G. Squires. New York: Routledge.

Meyer, David S., and Suzanne Staggenborg. 1996. "Movements, Countermovements, and the Structure of Political Opportunity." *American Journal of Sociology* 101(6): 1628–60.

Morris, Aldon D., and Naomi Braine. 2001. "Social Movements and Oppositional Consciousness." Pp. 20–37 in *Oppositional Consciousness: The Subjective Roots of Social Protest*, edited by J. J. Mansbridge and A. Morris. Chicago: University of Chicago Press.

Mottl, Tahi L. 1980. "The Analysis of Countermovements." *Social Problems* 27(5): 620–35. doi: 10.2307/800200.

Obasogie, Osagie K., and Zachary Newman. 2016. "Black Lives Matter and Respectability Politics in Local News Accounts of Officer-Involved Civilian Deaths: An Early Empirical Assessment Symposium Issue: Critical Race Theory and Empirical Methods." *Wisconsin Law Review* 2016: 541–74.

Olson, Lisa M. 2017. "Blue Lives Have Always Mattered: The Usurping of Hate Crime Laws for an Unintended and Unnecessary Purpose." *Scholar* 20: 13–56.

Omi, Michael, and Howard Winant. 2014. *Racial Formation in the United States.* New York: Routledge. Retrieved April 25, 2018 (https://bookshelf.vitalsource.com/#/books/9781135127503/).

Pichardo, Nelson A. 1995. "The Power Elite and Elite-Driven Countermovements: The Associated Farmers of California during the 1930s." *Sociological Forum* 10(1): 21–49. doi: 10.1007/bf02098563.

Robbins, Liz, and Nikita Stewart. 2014. "At Demonstrations, a Change." *New York Times*, December 22, A22.

Rousey, Dennis Charles. 1996. *Policing the Southern City: New Orleans, 1805–1889*. Baton Rouge: Louisiana State University Press.

TheGrio. 2015. "Blue Lives Matter Billboards Don't Honor Fallen Officers, They Discredit Black Humanity." TheGrio (website), October 8. Retrieved April 23, 2018 (https://thegrio.com/2015/10/08/blue-lives-matter-billboards-erase-black-humanity/).

USA Today Editorial Board. 2016. "Policing Debate Needs More Facts, Fewer Slogans." *USA Today*, July 21.

Waldinger, Roger, and Thomas Bailey. 1991. "The Continuing Significance of Race: Racial Conflict and Racial Discrimination in Construction." *Politics and Society* 19(3): 291–323.

Wilson, John Melbourne Ogilvy. 1973. *Introduction to Social Movements*. New York: Basic Books.

Winant, Howard. 2001. "White Racial Projects." Pp. 97–112 in *The Making and Unmaking of Whiteness*, edited by Birgit Brander Rasmussen, Eric Klinenberg, Irene J. Nexica, and Matt Wray. Durham, NC: Duke University Press.

Zald, Mayer N. 1979. "Macro Issues in the Theory of Social Movements." CRSO Working Paper No. 204. Princeton, NJ: Center for Research on Social Organization, Princeton University.

Zald, Mayer N., and Burt Ussem. 1987. "Movement and Countermovement Interaction: Mobilization, Tactics, and State Involvement." Pp. 247–72 in *Social Movements in an Organizational Society: Collected Essays*, by Mayer N. Zald and John D. McCarthy. New Brunswick, NJ: Transaction Books.

CHAPTER 14

ECHOING DERRICK A. BELL

Black Women's Resistance to White Supremacy in the Age of Trump

MARLESE DURR

WHITE SUPREMACY IS omnipresent within the American social structure despite the civil rights–era legislation proposed, ratified, and signed into law in the mid-1960s. One of the most relevant products from this epoch is affirmative action, which seeks to improve the employment and educational opportunities of racial and ethnic minorities and women. Since its implementation, black women on average have moved from domestic work to better-paying employment (Blau and Beller 1992; Goldin 1990). Pettit and Ewert (2009) suggest that several scholars in the early 1980s proclaimed near equity in salary between young, highly skilled black and white women. However, after these pronouncements, black women's occupational mobility, employment, and earnings slowed through the 1980s and 1990s. Black women hoped to see a return to progressive lawmaking, employment opportunities, and social change ending white supremacy's slow rise. Many felt that the last two Republican administrations were slowly erasing the gains of the 1960s and 1970s. Along with white women, other women of color, and immigrants, they rallied to ensure the election of William J. Clinton as the forty-second president of the United States. He won.

During Clinton's second term in office (1996–2000), Derrick Bell's (1996) novella "The Electric Slide Protest" appeared in *Essence* magazine. In the novella, Bell emblematically swipes at Clinton's withdrawal of support for Lani Guinier as Assistant Attorney General for Civil Rights, ignores two hundred or more church bombings between 1995 and 1998, supports conservative legislation on welfare reform (1997), and endorses affirmative action while ignoring an increasing schism between black and white citizens' assessments of racial issues (Kim 2002; Minchin 2008). White citizens were still silently unsettled about the passage of civil rights legislation, and African Americans were disappointed with how the current and previous Clinton administrations had handled race and employment issues. Darity and Mason (1998) and Grodsky and Pager (2001) have argued that affirmative action and antidiscrimination laws promoted black wage gains in government and professional occupations, weakening explicit wage discrimination. Additionally, through affirmative action, black men and women working in the public sector earned state and federal cabinet-level appointments. Yet affirmative hiring seemed to exclude black women from prestigious law schools (see Butterfield 1990) and government appointments. For example, no African American woman had received an assignment to a federal cabinet-level post since President Gerald Ford appointed Patricia Harris in 1977. Despite black women's occupational mobility within the public sector, Bell's assessment of the administrations' pledges to these women resembled a dance—sidestep to the right and sidestep to the left, crisscross. So the Electric Slide, a popular African American line dance, became his tale's metaphor to recount black women's resistance in front of the US Capitol to save the mythical Freedom of Employment Act ending affirmative action. But it was also Bell's way of expressing black women's frustration with promises never coming to pass. As the story progresses, women of all colors begin to "slide" to reverse the impending vote. Moving gracefully in concert, all in tune with the same melody, they danced to compel legislators to heed their requests, implying a promise of return if needed. In the novella, women succeeded that day—the vote was put off.

Twenty-one years after Bell's fictional dance-off, a sizeable number of white citizens still oppose affirmative action, are unmoved by church bombings, and *are* indifferent about products of the civil rights movement—mythical or real. Several *actual* social movements (i.e., the alt-right, Right to Life, and the Tea Party) sprang up to oppose women, especially black women and women of color, and immigrants, both naturalized and American-born. Clothed in calls for governmental reform, a confrontation between these publics was inevitable as nativist white citizens raised their voices against those deemed to be "others." Their hidden grievances, spanning over five decades, became clear-throated calls to dismantle laws and regulations that are perceived as protecting immigrants and giving "handouts" to racial and ethnic minorities and women while undermining their (white) economic privileges and values. Assertions of whiteness and class were no longer made in the form of susurration and dog whistles but were amplified roars tied to long-held beliefs that *their* America, *white* America, was under siege.

Through rallies and marches, they made demands for domestic reforms in the name of the "American people," "working people," and "The Heartland" and removed politicians who would not accede to their demands—an approach often labeled as populism (Muddle and Kaltwasser 2017). Solidifying their pleas was J. D. Vance's *Hillbilly Elegy* (2016), elucidating the plight of working-class whites as a population in crisis. Nativist whites served as sentinels for birthright citizenship and demanded control of southern borderlands, urban streets, voting booths, sexual and reproductive decisions, and employment lines. Just as the fictional "slide" victory radiated across the nation, shots heard in the Nevada ranchlands, the National Mall, the Kansas City Jewish Community Center, the Sikh Temple of Wisconsin, and Charleston AME Church became sites of their violent retaliation (Durr 2016). Bell had issued a wordless presage that was now full bore. White supremacy was calling for like-minded supporters.

In 2016, presidential candidate Donald J. Trump responded, making their agency part of his electoral challenge to "Make America Great Again." His campaign did not disappoint—labeling Mexicans as criminals, murders, and rapists; calling for the surveillance of Muslim mosques and neighborhoods; denigrating a Gold Star family of color; demeaning a federal justice of Mexican descent; mocking the disabled; and harassing women, journalists, and politicians. Consequently, white citizen discontent, once manifested as a veiled wink and nod, became unrestrained fury directed toward women (especially women of color) and immigrants as they clamored to restore "their" America. Why? Countless white working-class citizens believed that Barack H. Obama's election foretold a weighty change in the nation's governance, altering cliché-ridden but sustained timeworn issues of race, class, and gender hierarchy (Bonilla-Silva 2010).

Upon becoming the forty-fifth president of the United States in 2017, President Trump issued a Muslim travel ban, implemented seven days later; by May, he fired James Comey; and in October of the same year, he defamed the widow of Sgt. La David Johnson, a black soldier. As Trump egged on his supporters' aggression, Susan Rice's security clearance was revoked and Chief of Staff John Kelly rebuked Congresswoman Frederica Wilson for listening to a presidential phone call. By summer 2018, Trump referred to Congresswoman Maxine Waters as "Low IQ Maxine" while White House press secretaries Sean Spicer and Sarah Huckabee Sanders disrespectfully spoke or gave condescending ripostes to African American journalists April Ryan and Kristen Welker. Trump had kept his pledge of agency to his supporters. In keeping his promise, his supporters' fear, that "whiteness" in America was being replaced, was assuaged.

Still, these same citizens silently queried why the pre-1964 social structure had changed. Women generally, especially women of color, were out of place and became "red meat." Race and gender stereotypes describing cosmetic appearance and intellect, such as "horse-faced" and "low IQ"—preludes to racial to hierarchy—were back. Omi and Winant (2014) argue that the Right's revisiting of racial politics passed through stages using politically coded concepts such as "reverse racism" in the 1970s and "color blindness" in the 1980s. These concepts and beliefs, coupled with the conservative principle of individual economic responsibility, were visually experienced and verbally expressed during and at the end of the Obama administration. Now that white nativists had a president who shared their views and interests, the act of voting became linked to white supremacy. With little notice, many once financially conservative and socially liberal white voters moved to the Republican Party.

Zingher (2018) reasons that this constituent shift began with government passage of the Civil Rights Act of 1964, the Voting Rights Act of 1965, and implementation of affirmative action in 1961 and 1965. He and others (Carmines and Stimson 1989; Layman 2001; Brewer and Stonecash 2001) argue that as the Republican Party increased in "racial conservatism," opposing civil rights and placing emphasis on cultural and moral traditionalism, the masses followed. Still, other scientists suggest that changes in philosophy may have triggered a "sorting" of the electorate. Individuals identified and voted with the political party matching their beliefs (Green, Palmquist, and Schickler 2002; Levendusky 2010; Smidt 2017; Zingher and Flynn 2018). Demographic transformation decreased the proportion of whites to nonwhites in the electorate (from 11 percent nonwhite in 1976 to 19 percent in 2000 and 29 percent in 2016).

Yet working-class whites still make up a sizable share of voters in the South and Upper Midwest swing states that flipped from blue to red (Zingher 2018). In 2018, the Pew Research Center reported that women had become more Democratic leaning, estimating that 54 percent of women registered voters leaned Democratic in 2016 and 56 percent in 2017—up from 2010–15 levels of 51–52 percent. More importantly, whites identifying as Democrats or Democratic leaning rose from 40 percent to 43 percent between 2009 and 2016. As women voters and nonwhite voters increased, the greater part of white voters were now right of center on economic issues and left of center on social issues (Zingher 2018). Social discontent and financial fears from as far back as 1964, coupled with changing demographics trends, were converted into predictors of voting behavior in the federal 2014 midterm and 2016 presidential elections. The Right was deploying politics of resentment (Omi and Winant 2014) after fifty-plus years of progressive social policies. Language became a potent weapon, as epithets by speech, tweet, and political commentary once again made their way into the social fabric.

In the third presidential debate of the 2016 race, Trump supporters chanted "lock her up" and "Make America Great Again" and Trump referred to Senator Hillary Clinton as a "nasty woman." Senator Elizabeth Warren called for "Nasty Women" to organize and fight what appeared to be on the horizon: regressive administration policies. In 2017, Congresswoman Maxine Waters called the White House the "White Supremacist House" after President Trump's defense of the white supremacist and neo-Nazi rally in Charlottesville, Virginia. Then, in 2018 Congresswoman Waters labeled the president as racist for his behavior toward persons of color. These women joined with others globally to challenge what appeared to be an end to their and others' treatment as citizens. They were "women to the rescue" against white supremacy, parading collectively around the world in the Women's March on January 21, 2017. They "strolled" to save immigration rights and protections, health-care reform and reproductive rights, the environment, LGBTQ rights, racial and gender equality, religious freedom, and workers' rights against President Trump's "human carnage." Black women joined in resisting white supremacy in the age of Trump.

POPULISM: A RECURRING THEME IN US HISTORY

Populism is a recurring theme within American culture, in which there are periodic calls by citizens to be represented by a party or movement that serves their interests. In today's America, such requests tend to take the form of exhortations to "drain the swamp" or dismissals of "fake news." Depending on where the citizenry sits, these calls can be racist, discriminatory attacks. Bonilla-Silva (1997, 2001) argues that racism is materialist in custom and action but that it also constructs a racial hierarchy within the social structure. This hierarchy is informed by social and economic philosophies that contour racial and ethnic minority citizens' life chances. Such a structure, he contends, accounts for the construction and reproduction of racial advantage for some but not for others. To that end, our social structure is constructed to place citizens of color in shared social locations that nurture and sustain an "us" versus "them" continuum of identity and fellowship. Race and racism are established social categories reified and enacted in day-to-day encounters within our social spaces. Bonilla-Silva (2001) argues that migration makes racism an ongoing societal element as new arrivals are racialized and added to our racial hierarchy. Indeed, European immigrants of various nationalities and ethnicities became white (Jacobson 1999; Painter 2010), displaying the flexibility of racial hierarchy. From these observations, racial formation theory was born.

Omi and Winant (2014) describe racial formation as a sociohistorical process fused to our social structure by definitions of race and racial categorization. They identify particular sets of sociocultural and economic dynamics that construct and deploy the changing aspects of race projects historically over time. Such above-the-surface attitudes arise from unfounded beliefs, accompanied by media images that justify race as the reason some have less wealth and others have more. Omi and Winant characterize racial hierarchy as consistently enduring, affecting citizens' societal experiences culturally and economically, and now also politically. Thus, race announces culturally and financially to white right-wing populists that a bidirectional relationship exists between racial projects and our social structure—denoting that change too far in one direction necessitates a change in the other.

Still, Omi and Winant's discussion points to a representation of racial others as "less than" or "deviant," leading to exclusion from employment, educational advances, and political offices but subjecting them to higher rates of poverty, disenfranchisement, conviction, and incarceration. Within the hierarchy, whites' differences in wealth and income are of no consequence. They are white, and their class and skin color are the determining factors of citizenship. Omi and Winant suggest that lingering parts of a process embedded with our society determine behavioral expectations, beliefs, worldviews, and judgments about intelligence. Implied within Omi and Winant's scholarship is that this process is ongoing, societally present across hundreds of years. As Bonilla-Silva and Omi and Winant remind us, as race custom and race projects remain tautological, black women are put to the test again.

NEOLIBERAL FEMINISM'S LINK TO POPULISM

As President Trump continues his tirades against women generally and of color to display his displeasure with them to supporters, black women are additionally troubled by neoliberal feminism's link to populism. Many black women feel that this latest form of feminism connects with populist attacks on women's gains and maintains male hegemony. Other women think that neoliberal feminist theories appear to be overtaking second-wave feminists' focus on supporting equality and fighting discrimination to one of accepting the free market system's emphasis on economic freedom, choice, and agency for women, which will not challenge patriarchal and sexist norms (Cudd 2014). Some advocates of neoliberal feminism (Prügl 2015; Rampton 2008; Eisenstein 2009) submit that it embodies the second wave's historical development in capitalist economies, while other supporters, such as McRobbie (2015), suggest that the neoliberalism of the 1970s overlapped with second-wave feminism when state-managed capitalism limited women's autonomy. Yet McRobbie also asserts that understanding women's independence as an individualist effort erects a competitive environment where success is determined by the elite and is not reachable for all women.

Critics, including Americans and Europeans, regard this brand of feminism as "dangerous" because of its advance through the political and social spheres to a greater extent than liberalism (Kendall 2003). For example, Rottenberg (2014) advises that the US is witnessing the introduction of neoliberal feminism through Sheryl Sandberg's bestselling book *Lean In: Women, Work, and the Will to Lead* (2013). She notes that Sandberg attributes women's limited professional achievements and limited advancement into corporate leadership to their own reticence to commit to their careers enthusiastically. Rottenberg also draws attention to Sandberg's references to companies' eagerness to employ women because diversity is good business but affirmative action is not. Emphasizing that women should "internalize the revolution," be responsible for their own success, and embrace their insecurities as obstacles to success, Sandberg, according to Rottenberg, neglects to discuss the power dynamics of personal responsibility and the unseen social pressures that are holding women back. But also missing from the book is a cost-benefit itemization to fashion a suitable work/family balance, paying attention to well-being and self-care (Rottenberg 2014). For African American women, who are paid less and get fewer promotions, are to be seen not heard, and have to deal with skin-tone bias, a cost-benefit analysis becomes a significant obstacle in the workplace, where whiteness and elitism are tied together. So black women must choose where their priorities are with and without collegial support in the workplace.

Williams (2014), in a review of *Lean In* titled "The Happy Marriage of Capitalism and Feminism," notes the book's popularity and discusses its bent toward neoliberal feminism while emphasizing its class bias. She notes that unlike liberal feminism, which looks to the state to rectify unequal opportunities and underrepresentation, neoliberal feminism promotes individual choice and accountability in the context of limited government and market-driven solutions to social problems—strong elements of conservative populism (see Hochschild 2003). By focusing on occupational success, Sandberg deems being at the table or in a position of power a way to dispel sexist stereotypes, leading to more power opportunities for women since women sometimes hold themselves back (internalized sexism). Still, Williams suggests that Sandberg's emphasis on occupational success denies other meaningful goals that women might pursue. In assessing *Lean In*'s implications for feminism, Williams notes that the author absolves capitalism of playing a role in women's oppression.

Sandberg contends, in fact, that the capitalist free market is the solution to gender inequality and that corporations would hire and promote more women if it were not for governmental interference (e.g., antidiscrimination laws, laws making it illegal to ask about future family plans or to mention gender in the workplace, affirmative action). Finally, but most compelling, Williams criticizes Sandberg's use of sociological scholarship by feminist scholars such as Gloria Steinem, Betty Friedan, and Alice Walker as studiously bipartisan. She is trying to speak to many groups of women, that it is vital for them to pay close attention to her message. In issuing a wakeup call for feminist scholars and nonacademics, Williams proposes that women find distinct ways of thinking about the structural basis of social and economic justice and the necessity for the state to rectify women's unequal opportunities and underrepresentation.

Where Williams left off, Uwujaren and Utt (2015) take up the mantle to argue that neoliberal feminism does not address low-income or marginalized women's struggles. Nor does it consider the interface between women's experiences and sexism or contribute to the reality of intersectionality—the linked intersecting of race, class, and gender as symbiotic systems of discrimination or disadvantage. However, today a feminist identity has been popularized through Sandberg's redefinition of the concept, without the benefit of liberal feminism's critique of social structure. A womanist perspective, examining social theory based on the everyday experiences of black women and other women of color (Eaton 2007; James 2001; Phillips 2006), is never considered. For black women, tensions between these competing feminist approaches affect their workplaces and society at large in a time of white supremacy's return. But black women's resistance to white supremacy comes from their belief in womanist feminists. Their resistance is seen when they battle white supremacists (populists) and neoliberal feminists who attacked Michelle Obama in 2013.

Sisters Dancing: Feminist Critiques of Michelle Obama

Family/work balance is part of black women's cultural belief system and ideas of feminism. For instance, black women understand womanism as addressing race- and class-based oppression. Accordingly, we understood Michelle Obama making her family a priority. So when *Politico* columnist Michelle Cottle's (2013) article "Leaning Out," subtitled "How Michelle Obama Became a Feminist Nightmare," questioned the First Lady's national initiatives (i.e., aerobic exercise, healthy food, reading to children, working with veterans), but most crucially her choice to act in the role of "mom-in-chief," black women began pulling on and lacing up their dancing shoes. Cottle's vitriolic commentary linked neoliberal feminism and populism concretely and sharpened white supremacist hostile responses toward black women. Black women began the "slide."

In an open letter, Harris-Perry queries the seriousness of Cottle's remarks that the First Lady was not feminist because her most important job was being "mom-in-chief," which Cottle critiqued as "safely and soothingly domestic" or fluff. Harris-Perry educates her by highlighting that although Cottle thinks Michele Obama is steering clear of the "Angry Black woman" stereotype, she is rejecting the role of "Mammy." Essentially, according to Harris-Perry, she is saying, "You, Miss Ann [a term used for white women since slavery], will have to clean your own house." Michelle was burying "Mammy" and embracing motherhood—something black women historically have been unable to do. Then, Harris-Perry stridently informs Cottle that if she thinks there's no political risk for Michelle Obama, she hasn't been paying attention to her role as the first African American First Lady during a period of political, social, and electoral acrimony (Elder and Frederick 2019). As she ends her boogie with a pirouette to start the slide line, Harris-Perry offers to send Cottle a syllabus on Black feminism.

A second feminist columnist, Linda Hirshman (who writes for the *New York Times*, the *Washington Post*, *Slate*, *Salon*, and the *Daily Beast*), charges Michelle Obama with antifeminist offenses like "gardening," "tending to wounded soldiers," and "reading to children." Michelle Obama, the author argues, should be a politically involved activist, not a "mom-in-chief." She has an obligation to the "women of America" (meaning white women), and she should represent all that feminism has achieved. Hirshman's assessment, validated by Lilith Dornhuber, is that Michele Obama's speeches indicated that feminism was dead to the Democratic Party. This comment was followed by Leslie Morgan Steiner's "Are fashion and body-toning tips all we can expect from one of the most highly educated First Ladies in history?"

She continues, "I, for one, have seen enough of her upper appendages and her designer clothes and read enough bland dogma on home-grown vegetables and aerobic exercise to last me several lifetimes." Keli Goff (2013), a columnist for the *Root*, became the second line dancer as she invited Michelle to do a "no holds barred" First Lady "sermon," discussing everything from Supreme Court nominees to racism and issues of reproductive and sexual health. Goff was actively joining Harris-Perry in the "slide" and pirouetting. Said differently, but more plainly, they were beginning the rescue call to black women to assist a "sister" under attack.

But it was Brittney Cooper's "Lay Off Michelle Obama: Why White Feminists Need to Lean Back" that lay bare the historical, social location of African American women—First Lady or not. In her petition to "Lean Back, Way Back" and take their hands off Michelle, Cooper charges Cottle with backhandedly cosigning white supremacist attacks on black women. Her use of the methodological concept of "holding constant" brings race to the fore as an ever-present variable for black women and pointedly emphasizes that black women were never seen as "unthreatening and bucolic" or nonthreatening genteel ladies of the manor—this was the province of white women. Nor were their apparel and appearance seen as salient, just their service to whites. bell hooks's 2013 essay "Sisterhood: Political Solidarity between Women" critiques feminism for its alienation of Blacks and women of color due to their perception that aspects of their (our) culture are counter to feminist causes, both liberal and neoliberal. For example, Black women refuse to self-victimize, which excludes them from feminism. hooks also argues that different groups face distinctive oppressions, which feminism struggles to realize, limiting its philosophical appeal to various groups.

For these reasons, akin to the novella's dance-off, Black women "came to the rescue," poetically dancing with pen and paper to dispel disparaging suppositions that are regrettably still in existence. To them, it was clear that white feminists and white supremacists questioned Black women's activism and use of their intellect while also reproachfully questioning their decision making. The expositions from Harris-Perry, hooks, Goff, and Cooper were a rebuke to feminist and populist stereotypical images of derelict uneducated Black women and mothers. Such images are still part of contemporary media commentary and talk radio as jezebels and welfare queens who are domineering, unintelligent, and drug-addicted. So despite these feminists' not so subtle critique of Michelle Obama, Black women had done another dance, the "shout and twist" on white feminists' lack of knowledge about Black women. But as this dance-off ended, populism still loomed.

Populism is tightly stitched into the body politic; neoliberal feminism unwittingly or wittingly becomes its confederate and a concern for Black women. For example, neoliberal feminists' statements held a set of shrewdly disguised expectations for Black women to accede and adhere to. Neoliberal feminists, like dissatisfied white citizens, were calling for agency assistance. Black women began to ask themselves questions: Are we still viewed as soldiers shaped to *their* purpose? Do white women still feel we need to be shepherded according to *their* dictates and perceptions? Is this emerging form of disquieting "feminist populism" requiring Black women to meet *their* expectations at home and work? Still more unsettling, what does white women's evolving philosophy convey to younger generations of Black women whose hair and style of dress represent the use of their bodies to fight white supremacy?

Sandberg, Cottle, Steiner, Dornhuber, and Hirshman heightened Black women's awareness that after fifty-four years of working together, including adopting and embracing feminist principles, white feminists still accommodated gender over and against race. White society as a whole did as well. Black women, who had fully integrated into societal governance and feminist causes, now faced populist and feminist interrogation. Like their sister Fannie Lou Hamer, Black women "were sick and tired of being sick and tired" and faced off against liberals, neoliberal feminists, and white supremacy disguised as populism in the age of Trump. Our dancing, parading, and pirouetting had come to an end. Guided by second- and third-wave scholarship of women of color feminists, Black women raised their voices, ran for public office, and used rap, hip-hop lyrics, and spoken word to battle these foes (Beal 1969; Mohanty 1994; Purkayastha 2005; Desai 2009; Walker 1983; King 1988; Collins 2000).

Black feminist scholars (e.g., Lipsitz 1998; Kitwana 2002, 2004; Bynoe 2004; Cole and Guy-Sheftall 2003) suggest that hip-hop culture and rap music cultures operate on a progressive political plane to examine racist, sexist, economic, police, and community violence. Morgan (1999) and others (e.g., Davis 1995; Pough 2002) argue that this music holds radical and liberating potential, while Breines (2000) emphasizes that identity politics has its place for Black women. Still, like many womanists, they find racial equality and family to be more critical than rejecting patriarchy. It is here that Black feminists diverge from White feminists by being politically progressive and acknowledging identity politics. It provides the strength to thwart the backlash of white supremacists and feminists. They are today's dancers coming to rescue Black women. These women act without hurling insults. They are unafraid of identity politics because it serves as part of their resistance to right-wing populism and neoliberal feminism. Simply stated, they voted for

Hillary Clinton in the 2016 election in plain sight (94 percent of Black women voted for Hillary). Young women Patrisse Khan-Cullors, Alicia Garza, and Opal Tometi were cofounders of Black Lives Matter. They researched and understood the lessons of Black women freedom fighters of the 1960s. Bree Newsome removed South Carolina's Confederate flag in a fashion similar to Rosa Parks. Therese Patricia Okoumou climbed the Statue of Liberty on July 4, 2019, to protest Trump's immigration policies. They acted!

CONCLUSION

Omi and Winant (2014) suggest that as members of society, we have the power to change our racialized social structure. The newest class, women of color elected to Congress, are resisting. They are not being quiet or "going lightly"; they address their dissatisfaction with populism neoliberal feminism alongside social, cultural, environmental, and economic romanticism concerns. They are also dancing. It is not just dance-off but a, sure enough, throw-down (dance contest) as they fight for sustained social transformation. They must continue to practice since populists and some feminists believe themselves to be today's agents of social, political, and governmental change. Black women and women of color, alongside immigrants, do not and must not consent to supremacists' wishes for the days of John Wayne sung about in Gil Scott-Heron's "B-Movie" in the 1980s. They must resist white supremacy in the age of Trump.

Both Trumpian and feminist populism appear to be woven into the societal moment as society-wide policy prescriptions. Despite Obama's electoral victory in 2008, signifying a supposedly postracial America, his win muted a comprehensive citizen philosophy. Omi and Winant (2014) and Bonilla-Silva (2001) are correct in their descriptions of racism and racial hierarchy. However, as projects form a continual loop and the racial hierarchy remains intact, racism is structural and does not need to rely on blatantly racist individuals. More critically, policy prescriptions for social change appear to be fleeting. But once again, women are coming to the rescue. Our society is more than echoing Derrick Bell. We are playing out his fictional battle with women of color leading. Bell foretold a future conflict, with women of color and immigrants now fighting to save the day by continuing the electric slide.

REFERENCES

Beal, Frances M. 1969. *Black Women's Manifesto; Double Jeopardy: To Be Black and Female.* New York: Third World Women's Alliance; Random House.

Bell, Derrick. 1996. "The Electric Slide Protest." *Essence* 27(3): 78–81.
Blau, Francine, and Andrea Beller. 1992. "Black-White Earnings over the 1970s and 1980s: Gender Differences in Trends." *Review of Economics and Statistics* 74: 276–86.
Bonilla-Silva, Eduardo. 1997. "Rethinking Racism: Toward a Structural Interpretation." *American Sociological Review* 62(3): 465–80.
———. 1999. "The Essential Social Fact of Race." *American Sociological Review* 64(8): 899–906.
———. 2001. *White Supremacy and Racism in the Post–Civil Rights Era.* Boulder, CO: Lynne Rienner.
———. 2003. "Racial Attitudes or Racial Ideology? An Alternative Paradigm for Examining Actors' Racial Views." *Journal of Political Ideologies* 8(1): 63–82.
———. 2010. Review of *Racial Justice in the Age of Obama*, by Roy L. Brooks. *Ethnic and Racial Studies* 33(9): 1669–70.
———. 2015. "The Structure of Racism in Color-Blind, 'Post-Racial' America." *American Behavioral Scientist* 59(11): 1358–76.
Breines, Winifred. 2000. *The Trouble between Us: An Uneasy History of White and Black Women in the Feminist Movement.* New York: Oxford University Press.
Brewer, Mark D., and Jeffrey M. Stonecash. 2001. "Class, Race Issues, and Declining White Support for the Democratic Party in the South." *Political Behavior* 23(2): 131–55.
Brewer, Rose M. 1993. "Theorizing Race, Class and Gender: The New Scholarship of Black Feminist Intellectuals and Black Women's Labor." Pp. 13–30 in *Theorizing Black Feminisms: The Visionary Pragmatism of Black Women*, edited by Stanlie M. James and Abena P. A. Busia. New York: Routledge.
Butterfield, Fox. 1990. "Harvard Law Professor Quits until Black Woman Is Named." *New York Times*, April 24.
Bynoe, Yvonne. 2004. *Stand and Deliver: Political Activism, Leadership, and Hip-Hop Culture.* New York: Soft Skull Press.
Carmines, Edward, and James Stimson. 1989. *Issue Evolution: Race and the Transformation of American Politics.* Princeton, NJ: Princeton University Press.
Cole, Johnetta B., and Beverly Guy-Sheftall. 2003. *Gender Talk: The Struggle for Women's Equality in African American Communities.* New York: Ballantine Books.
Collins, Patricia Hill. 2000. *Black Feminist Thought: Knowledge, Consciousness, and the Politics of Empowerment.* 2nd edition. New York: Routledge.
Cooper, Brittney. 2013. "Lay Off Michelle Obama: Why White Feminists Need to Lean Back." *Salon Magazine*, November 29.
Cottle, Michelle. 2013. "Leaning Out." *Politico Magazine*, November 21.
Cudd, Ann E. 2014. "Is Capitalism Good for Women?" *Journal of Business Ethics* 127(4): 761–70.

Darity, William A., and Patrick L. Mason. 1998. "Evidence on Discrimination in Employment: Codes of Color, Codes of Gender." *Journal of Economic Perspectives* 12: 63–90.

Davis, Elisa. 1995. "Sexism and the Art of Feminist Hip-Hop Maintenance." Pp. 127–41 in *To Be Real: Telling the Truth and Changing the Face of Feminism*, edited by Rebecca Walker. New York: Anchor Books.

Desai, Manisha. 2009. *Gender and the Politics of Possibilities: Rethinking Globalization*. New York: Rowman & Littlefield.

Durr, Marlese. 2016. "Removing the Mask, Lifting the Veil: Race, Class, and Gender." *Social Problems* 63(2): 151–60.

Eaton, Kalenda C. 2007. *Womanism, Literature, and the Transformation of the Black Community, 1965–1980*. New York: Routledge

Eisenstein, Hester. 2009. *Feminism Seduced: How Global Elites Use Women's Labor and Ideas to Exploit the World*. Boulder, CO: Paradigm.

Elder, Laurel, and Brian Frederick. 2019. "Why We Love Michelle: Understanding Public Support for First Lady Michelle Obama." *Gender and Politics* 15(3): 403–30.

Friedan, Betty. 1963. *The Feminine Mystique*. New York: W. W. Norton.

Goff, Keli. 2013. "Preach, Michelle: Five Things We Want to Hear from the First Lady." *The Root*, November 5.

Goldin, Claudia. 1990. *Understanding the Gender Gap*. New York: Oxford University Press.

Green, Donald, Bradley Palmquist, and Eric Schickler. 2002. *Partisan Hearts and Minds: Political Parties and the Social Identities of Voters*. New Haven, CT: Yale University Press.

Grodsky, Eric, and Devah Pager. 2001. "The Structure of Disadvantage: Individual and Occupational Determinants of the Black-White Wage Gap." *American Sociological Review* 66: 542–67.

Harris-Perry, Melissa. 2013. "Michelle Obama a 'Feminist Nightmare'? Please." MSNBC Blog, November 23.

Hochschild, Arlie. 2003. *The Commercialization of Intimate Life*. Berkeley: University of California Press.

hooks, bell. 2013. "Sisterhood: Political Solidarity between Women." *Feminist Review* 23: 125–38.

Jacobson, Matthew Frye. 1999. *Whiteness of a Different Color: European Immigrants and the Alchemy of Race*. Cambridge, MA: Harvard University Press.

James, Joy, ed. 2001. *The Black Feminist Reader*. Reprint edition. Malden, MA: Blackwell.

Jamilla, Shani. 2002. "Can I Get a Witness? Testimony from a Hip-Hop Feminist." Pp. 382–94 in *Colonize This! Young Women of Color on Today's Feminism*, edited by Daisy Hernandez and Bushra Rehman. New York: Seal Press.

Kendall, Gavin. 2003. "From Liberalism to Neoliberalism." Pp. 1–14 in *Social Change in the 21st Century 2003 Conference Refereed Proceedings*, edited by Laurie Buys, Jeff Lyddon, and Rebecca Bradley. Queensland, Australia: Centre for Social Change Research, School of Humanities and Human Services, Queensland University of Technology.

Kim, Claire Jean. 2002. "Managing the Racial Breach: Clinton, Black-White Polarization, and the Race Initiative." *Political Science Quarterly* 117(1): 55–79.

King, Deborah K. 1988. "Multiple Jeopardy, Multiple Consciousness: The Context of Black Feminist Ideology." *Signs* 14(11): 42–72.

Kitwana, Bakari. 2002. *The Hip-Hop Generation: Young Blacks and the Crisis in American Culture.* New York: Basic Civitas.

———. 2004. "The State of the Hip-Hop Generation: How Hip-Hop's Cultural Movement Is Evolving into Political Power." *Diogenes* 51(3): 115–20.

Layman, Geoffrey. 2001. *The Great Divide: Religious and Culture Conflict in American Party Politics.* New York: Columbia University Press.

Levendusky, Matthew S. 2010. "Clearer Cues, More Consistent Voters: A Benefit of Elite Polarization." *Political Behavior* 32(1): 111–31.

Lipsitz, George. 1998. "The Hip-Hop Hearings: Censorship, Social Memory, and Intergenerational Tensions among African Americans." Pp. 395–411 in *Generations of Youth: Youth Cultures and History in Twentieth-Century America*, edited by Joe Austin and Michael N. Willard. New York: New York University Press.

McRobbie, Angela. 2015. "Notes on the Perfect." *Australian Feminist Studies* 30: 3–20

Minchin, Timothy J. 2008. "One America? Church Burnings and Perceptions of Race Relations in the Clinton Years." *Australasian Journal of American Studies* 27(2): 1–28.

Mohanty, Chandra. 1994. "Maiden Voyages through Virgin Lands: Mapping Feminism in the World." *Contemporary Literature* 35(2): 391–94.

Morgan, Joan. 1999. *When Chickenheads Come Home to Roost: My Life as a Hip-Hop Feminist.* New York: Simon and Schuster.

Muddle, Cass, and Cristobal Rovira Kaltwasser. 2017. *Populism: A Very Short Introduction.* New York: Oxford University Press.

Omi, Michael, and Howard Winant. 2014. *Racial Formation in the United States.* 3rd edition. New York: Routledge.

Painter, Nell Irvin. 2010. *The History of White People.* New York: W. W. Norton.

Pettit, Becky, and Stephanie Ewert. 2009. "Employment Gains and Wage Declines: The Erosion of Black Women's Relative Wages since 1980." *Demography* 46(3): 469–92.

Phillips, Layli. 2006. *The Womanist Reader.* New York: Routledge.

Pough, Gwendolyn. 2002. "Love Feminism but Where's My Hip-Hop? Shaping a Black Feminist Identity." Pp. 85–95 in *Colonize This! Young Women of Color on*

Today's Feminism, edited by Daisy Hernandez and Bushra Rehman. New York: Seal Press.

Prügl, Elisabeth. 2015. "Neoliberalising Feminism." *New Political Economy* 20(4): 614–31.

Purkayastha, Bandana. 2005. *Negotiating Ethnicity: Second-Generation South Asian Americans Traverse a Transnational World*. New Brunswick, NJ: Rutgers University Press.

Rampton, Martha. 2008. "Four Waves of Feminism." *Pacific: The Magazine of Pacific University*. Retrieved May 12, 2020 (https://www.pacificu.edu/magazine/four-waves-feminism).

Rottenberg, Catherine. 2014. "The Rise of Neoliberal Feminism." *Cultural Studies* 28(3): 418–37.

Sandberg, Sheryl. 2013. *Lean In: Women, Work, and the Will to Lead*. New York: Alfred A. Knopf.

Smidt, Corwin. 2017. "Polarization and the Decline of the American Floating Voter." *American Journal of Political Science* 61(2): 365–81.

Smith, Barbara. 1983. *Homegirls: A Black Feminist Anthology*. New York: Kitchen Table: Women of Color Press.

Tomaskovic-Devey, Donald, and Kevin Stainback. 2012. *Documenting Desegregation: Racial and Gender Segregation in Private Sector Employment since the Civil Rights Act*. New York: Russell Sage Foundation

Uwujaren, Jarune, and Jamie Utt. 2015. "Why Our Feminism Must Be Intersectional (And 3 Ways to Practice It)." *everyday feminism* magazine, January 11.

Vance, J. D. 2016. *Hillbilly Elegy: A Memoir of a Family and Culture in Crisis*. New York: Harper.

Walker, Alice. 1983. *In Search of Our Mothers' Gardens: Womanist Prose*. New York: Harcourt Brace.

Williams, Christine. 2014. "The Happy Marriage of Capitalism and Feminism." *Contemporary Sociology* 43(1): 58–61.

Zingher, Joshua. 2018. "Whites Have Fled the Democratic Party. Here's How the Nation Got There." *Washington Post*, May 22.

Zingher, Joshua N., and Michael E. Flynn. 2018. "From On High: The Effect of Elite Polarization and Mass Attitudes and Behaviors." *British Journal of Political Science* 48(1): 23–45.

Zooks, Kristal Brent. 1995. "A Manifesto of Sorts for a Black Feminist Movement." *New York Times Magazine*, December 3.

CHAPTER 15

SOLIDARITY AND STRUGGLE

White Antiracist Activism in the Time of Trump

MARY K. RYAN AND DAVID L. BRUNSMA

EVEN AS THE United States established its statehood upon fundamentally racist institutions, practices, and, indeed, epistemological, ontological, and moral projects (Mills 1997), antiracist action on the part of those who have been socially, politically, and somatically constructed (by, of, and for whites) has been ever present in the social fabric of the United States since its inception (Aptheker 1992). Throughout this history, antiracist activism has been mobilized around numerous issues, including abolitionism, Quaker-inspired back-to-Africa movements, and opposition to structural and systemic racism, individual racist speech acts, individual racist acts, institutional racism, racial ideology, implicit bias, and inequitable distribution of land, wealth, and power (Olson 2004; Feagin 2013; Kendi 2017). At every stage along the way, white antiracist action has taken varying shapes, been birthed from varied locations in the intersectional social structure, narrated its motivations in various ways, etched itself into individual and organization identities, taken aim at particular manifestations of racial domination, and had differential (re)productive impacts. At every step along the way, these manifestations have been affected by the racialized social structure (Bonilla-Silva 2018) and dominant racial ideologies (Omi and Winant 2015) used to justify such a structure at each historical turn as it interfaced with social, cultural, political, and economic realities.

As a result of such realities, it is important to analytically acknowledge that the white antiracist organization, as it constructs the discursive contours of its mission and outreach, and the white antiracist activist individual, as she narrates her motivations, actions, and moral compass, are locked in the racialized grammar (Bonilla-Silva 2012), discourse (Doane 2006), and affective racial terrain (Thomas 2014) of the period. Though white antiracist action has been a part of the larger fabric of antiracist mobilization throughout US history, as well as antiracist activism led by people from within communities of color (Aptheker 1992), the vast majority of scholarship engaging with it has, interestingly enough, largely been conducted in the post–civil rights era and with samples largely coming of age within its discursive milieu (e.g., O'Brien 2001; Thompson 2001), with several prominent antiracist public intellectuals and their publications (e.g., Ignatiev and Garvey 1996; McIntosh 1988; Wise 2011) reaching some widespread attention, and with some attention to global developments (e.g., Bonnett 1999). While there is no clear indication of the contours of the third century of white antiracist organizing, mobilization, and action, the scholarship indicates that most origin stories point to antiracist activism taking place in the mid-1980s (e.g., The People's Institute for Survival and Beyond, or PISAB), with more and varied growth paralleling the rise of the internet (1990s) and social media (the early years of the twenty-first century). From color blindness through Obama-era postracialism and now, in the post-Obama era, antiracism has changed and continues to change its shape. The Trump era will be no exception.

For some, the beginning of the Trump era, when business mogul Donald Trump declared his intention to run for US president on June 16, 2015, marks a new phase of antiracist activism. We now find ourselves in a historic moment with an overtly bigoted, xenophobic, and racist president who has been declared by the United Nations to be a human rights violator. On the one hand, Trump's election has been seen as emboldening, energizing, and giving permission for white fascists, neo-Nazis, white supremacists, Ku Klux Klan members, and other white bigots, nativists, nationalists, and members of the alt-right to fight to preserve their perceived heritage, express their opinions, and publicly torment those who do not look or think like they do. As has always been the case, however, alongside these newly motivated defenders of white supremacy, there is potentially renewed hope for a new wave of antiracist activism to overcome this surge of hatred and push the United States closer to its democratic ideals of equality and justice for all.

In this chapter, we look at the operation of antiracist activism (e.g., alt-left, Antifa, Anti-Racist Alliance) in the United States, especially in the wake of the election of Donald Trump. This chapter looks at the state of Trump-era manifestations of antiracist organizations and their organizational missions, activities, and mobilizations for racial justice against white supremacy in a context of rapidly increasing state-sponsored racism. Specifically, we are interested in the place of white fragility and white guilt in racial justice–inclined social movements, as well as more proactive proclamations of white activists manifesting as "race traitors" who seek to give up illegitimate, unearned privilege. In order to investigate the contemporary space of white antiracist organizing, we have conducted a website analysis of some twenty-five groups' online presence (from novice MySpace and Facebook pages to professional, costly websites), looking at the missions, activities, discursive strategies, and goals designed for their white constituencies. Many of these groups are traditional nonprofits or 501(c)(3)-style organizations; we did not focus on college or university activism. Through this brief digital ethnography we consider how antiracist activism has encountered, managed, and shaped the experiences and attitudes of white activists in the work of white resistance in the twenty-first century. Ours is a pursuit of understanding the potential impact of the current political climate on antiracist activism for those organizations that appear to appeal online to whites.

In a now classic analysis, *Sincerity and Authenticity*, literary critic Lionel Trilling (1972) lays out his theory of the collective moral (read: white) transition from the central role of sincerity as a crucial interactional cement for social order to a twentieth-century role of authenticity and a "staying true to oneself." For Trilling, sincerity, conceptualized as the distance "between feeling and avowal," was a "salient, perhaps a definitive, characteristic of western culture for some four hundred years" (1972:6) and it "stood high in the cultural firmament and had dominion over men's [sic] imagination of how they ought to be" (12). But, alas, race has been referred to by critical sociologists as a "sincere fiction" wherein "white actions are still often legitimized by an overt or barely disguised racial mythology" (Feagin, Vera, and Batur 2000:190). Seligman et al. provide some additional thoughts about the place of sincerity within the acceptance of social convention ("ritual"—here, read: racism), saying that sincerity often grows out of a reaction against ritual by calling out ritual as "performance without belief.... The sincere mode of behavior seeks to replace 'mere convention' of ritual with a genuine and thoughtful state of internal conviction. Rather than becoming what we do in action through ritual, we do according to what we have become through self-examination" (2008:103). Sincerity is a utopian, romanticized, and, indeed, white utopian search for its etymological cognates "free," "pure," "whole," "unmingled," and "uncorrupt" (Seligman et al. 2008:112). What, then, is white sincerity? By extension, white sincerity is located in the distance between racial *affect* (white feelings within their racial mythology) and *actuality* (real acknowledgment of the veracity of those feelings).

STUDYING ANTIRACIST ORGANIZATIONS ONLINE

We began our investigation into the contemporary contours of white antiracist organizations almost one year to the day into the presidency of Donald Trump, in January 2018. Initially we searched the web using keywords *antiracism, antiracist, racial justice, activism, organizing, racial equality*, and so on, as well as various combinations of such key terms. It was quickly apparent that the terrain of antiracist organizations, organizations that include elements of antiracism in their missions, organized collectives of whites who engage in racial justice work, and other such iterations was vast, amorphous, and conceptually slippery. It is not within the scope of this chapter to map this complex virtual antiracist landscape, though future research should endeavor to do so. Rather, we focus on those organizations that consistently came up in our various searches while trying to stay very close to those that seemed primarily oriented toward the recruitment of whites (although not necessarily *by* whites) as well as those that had larger-than-parochial campus or local community operations (though, again, research should map these too).

Our sample (hereafter called "antiracist organizations") ultimately consisted of some twenty-five such organizations—distributed, in their founding, quite evenly across three decades. The 1980s saw the development of several early antiracist organizations, such as Race Forward, Crossroads, Skinheads Against Racial Prejudice, Friends Stand United, and, most notably, the People's Institute for Survival and Beyond. The next decade saw the rise of the internet as well as organizations such as By Any Means Necessary, The Heads Up Collective, and White People Challenging Racism. Our sample includes some eight organizations that were formed in the early years of the twenty-first century, including the formidable Anti-Racist Alliance (ARA), the Catalyst Project, Alliance of White Anti-Racists Everywhere, and the increasingly evident (especially on college campuses) Showing Up for Racial Justice. Numerous local organizations claim to be founded by the ARA. A couple of organizations were founded in the 2010s—Promoting Racial Equity and Awareness and the Anti-Racism Collaborative. Notably, we could find *no* such organizations founded *after* Trump announced his candidacy in late 2015.

ORGANIZATIONAL STRUCTURE AND GOALS

One important aspect of understanding contemporary white antiracist organizing and activism is understanding how these groups communicate and what they are trying to accomplish. In general, the functioning of these organizations is characterized by an outdated/inactive website or a calendar of events that is not updated. Almost all of the organizations focus on education/awareness and workshop planning around the often undefined idea of "racial justice." Occasionally there are updates on legislative activity, but many organizations simply publish reading lists or focus on research, while still others seem primarily interested in broadly conceived community building and leadership training. They seem to implicitly target other whites with materials that largely feature images of whites (particularly white women) who seek to engage with and mobilize other whites for discussions of multiracial coalitions or intersectional dialogue, fundraising, pledges, and networking. Many of the groups appear young and parochially based. They tend to report on extremist and right-wing movements and politics in the US and invoke John Brown, Anne Braden, and the Grimké sisters as models.

Given this general description, it can be broadly understood that these groups seek social and political change, but the scale of reform targeted and the tactics used differ from group to group. One of the largest and best-known antiracist organizations, operating until 2013, was the ARA. The ARA focused on front-line activism and overt forms of racism. In their words:

1. We go where they go. Whenever racists/fascists are organizing or active in public, we confront them and do our best to stop them.
2. We don't rely on the cops or courts to do our work or to protect us.
3. We defend and support each other in spite of our differences.
4. We are active with the goal of building a movement against racism, sexism, anti-Semitism, homophobia and discrimination against the disabled, the oldest, the youngest and the weakest of our society. (qtd. in O'Brien 2001:12–13)

Now disbanded, the ARA gave rise to Antifa, an autonomous group of antifascist activists who engage in direct action, fighting far-right and white supremacist ideology directly through militant protest tactics rather than through political measures. In late 2019, Trump announced that he intends to pursue the labeling of Antifa as a domestic terror organization.

Some groups work on particular issues, like immigration or policing. Occasionally, these groups even align over national campaigns, such as the

"Drop the 'i' word" (illegal) campaign regarding immigration or those seeking welfare reform for racial equity in foster care (spearheaded by ARA). These groups target legislative reforms and write letters to influence systemic stakeholders, but they also tend to focus more on public education and lobbying of all Congress and Senate writ large, not just the president and his cabinet. Related to this interest in influencing the political sphere, some organizations act as a resource center by compiling affiliated works, popular culture resources, and research. Given the longevity of the Internet, some web pages remain accessible even after the group has disbanded, such as the ARA's curriculum page. Some better-funded organizations, or ones that use alliances more fully to achieve their goals, conduct their own research and publish reports to influence change; one example is the Catalyst Project, which is aligned with the Tides Foundation.

Others groups, like the Coalition to Defend Affirmative Action, Integration, and Immigrant Rights and Fight for Equality By Any Means Necessary (commonly referred to as BAMN), seek the resignation or removal of President Trump, suggesting that the political figureheads are shaping the social atmosphere and hinting that swapping out the regime may help achieve a more just society.

Some organizations also spend a substantial portion of their time and money organizing institutes, events, and trainings, like the Unmasking Whiteness Institute of the Alliance of White Anti-Racists Everywhere (AWARE) or the YWCA's Unlearning Racism workshop. PISAB also conducts Undoing Racism workshops that look at covert and unintentional forms of racism as well as institutionalized racism. PISAB's principles include the following: (1) Racism has historically been the most critical barrier to unity in this country. (2) Culture is the life support system of the community. (3) Militarism is applied racism. (4) History is a guide to the future.

Catalyst began as a project of the Challenging White Supremacy (CWS) workshops in 2000. CWS was founded by Sharon Martinas and Mickey Ellinger in 1993. Both are long-time white antiracist organizers who were politicized by the black freedom struggle in the civil rights, Black Power, and antiwar movements of the 1960s and 1970s. In the late 1960s the Student Non-Violent Coordinating Committee (SNCC), which played a leading role in defining the political developments of the period, put forward an analysis and strategy that white people needed to organize other white people to challenge racism as a central barrier to building a multiracial movement for justice. In this organization, we see the antiracist work in the era of Trump not as a new and distinct kind of organizing but as a continuation of decades of racial justice struggles.

While the end goal of Catalyst workshops may have some similarities to the YWCA's Unlearning Racism or PISAB's Undoing Racism workshops, this effort seems to signal a different understanding of success as a moment in which people shed their ignorance about white privilege and also come together and make friends instead of living in isolation or segregation. While many of the attendees are asked to be Facebook page fans or to sign up for a newsletter, there is sometimes little concerted effort to engage people in policy reform or political advocacy. Success for some might be building a sense of community, even if that community only fundraises at a 5K instead of calling a US senator.

Of course, some organizations do both social networking and political organizing. Organizational advocacy may also mirror diverse individual strategies identified by O'Brien (2001), which include confrontations (in-the-moment, direct attention to the racist impact of others' speech or actions); challenges (more subtle ways of making opposition known); a "choosing your battles" continuum between direct/angry, direct/calm, delayed/calm, direct challenge, delayed challenge, and delayed; and privileged resistance, since whites, who face lesser and different consequences for the same actions, have the luxury of being more vocally confrontational than people of color can be. Kivel also outlines a famous list of basic organizing tactics (1996:103–4). In short, the multitude of approaches outlined by O'Brien and Kivel argue that, contrary to the "knee-jerk liberal" and other stereotypes, white antiracists are hardly reacting without thinking but are actually using carefully crafted strategies (Kivel 1996:82).

Communications platforms in the age of Trump are more sophisticated than ever. As Eileen O'Brien (2001) notes, college students in the late 1990s received most of their information about "race relations" from television. Today, televised and streamed comedy from Samantha Bee, Stephen Colbert, Bill Maher, John Oliver, and others provides political updates, while social media technology like Twitter and Facebook—and for some of the smaller groups, even MySpace still—provide the primary means of communication with antiracist advocates. The internet is an important contextual shift in antiracist organizing, but it is not the only one. Groups like Antifa also have used technology like Signal, an encrypted texting service, to build their peer organizing networks (Mallett 2017). Additionally, it is clear that some groups are swapping old in-person recruitment models for cheaper and more efficient technological introductions, including automated cell phone messages, predrafted chat group welcomes, and algorithm-suggested activities after a person RSVPs for an event. All of this suggests that technology might be changing the ethnographic playing field, allowing researchers to learn more about groups' motivations online than we ever could in the past. Such platforms likely are not sufficient by themselves to replace the value of ethnographic research, but the dependency of antiracist groups to organize via these modes should also foster more research into their content moving forward.

Since most antiracist groups operate on a decentralized basis, there is a striking lack of shared leadership on national problems. There are few strong and central leaders nationally; instead, there are numerous satellite chapters. There seems to be little concerted effort to unify around a national platform with specific legislative goals. Thousands of people have indeed signed on to the antiracist charge, in the last decade especially, but they seem to be doing very little by way of structural reform and profound racial change. Are these volunteers just in it to socialize and make friends? Do they wish to make more substantive changes but feel that their efficacy is somehow restricted? Is the government curtailing activism, or do they face hierarchical oppression prohibiting more meaningful reforms? These are all serious questions about the nature of white antiracist activism in the Trump era. In this way, the role that sincerity, sincere fictions, and other related strivings have played in generating genuine racial consciousness are important in understanding if there is to be any transformative antiracist activism in twenty-first-century advocacy. The platforms examined in this chapter provide one way to think about how the language used on these sites helps convey what these groups think about racial justice. The racial grammar employed is one aspect of the white habitus in action. By itself, it is not sufficient to cultivate robust antiracist practices, but it is nonetheless an important avenue to examine in present-day advocacy.

These questions reinforce the ongoing struggle to develop a vocabulary for antiracism, something that O'Brien (2001) suggests we have for different kinds of feminisms but not for antiracisms. Such open-endedness is at the heart of understanding precisely what antiracist activists identify as, and thus how they see their activism helping shape that identity. For O'Brien, in the late 1990s, antiracists were, "quite simply . . . people who have committed themselves, in thought, action and practice, to dismantling racism" (2001:4). Another potential definition is offered by bell hooks, who states that antiracism is to "daily vigilantly resist becoming reinvested in white supremacy" (qtd. in O'Brien 2001:5). O'Brien says that hooks's understanding mirrors how her respondents viewed their antiracism. A finding like this might be understandable if we compare the two demands: one suggests tackling systemic reforms to end racism whereas the other keeps the identity of an antiracist as a personal choice in which an individual rejects an ideology.

While we do not mean to suggest that interpersonal antiracism is easy, it is important to critique the narrowness of these reforms. Interpersonal activism limits the scope of dismantling racism to personal change, omitting vital societal or institutional changes for racial progress. The system has always been racist in the US, but some whites just want to get rid of a person who is seen as unjust or bad. In this way, whites who do not see the systemic injustice seek to remove a troubling symptom while nonwhites rebel against the government and other societal systems because those systems have never privileged or rewarded them. This fundamentally different outlook toward antiracist activism begs important questions about motivations and ideology, to be examined in the next section.

In a fairly representative statement, if one takes a cumulative birds-eye view of these organizations' approaches to communicating with whites and encouraging them to engage in antiracist action, comes from the ARA and was written by Phyllis Labanowski. For Labanowski and the ARA, an active white antiracist ally

> Names issue as racism
> Recognizes and makes unearned privilege visible
> Dismantles internalized dominance and the belief in the racial superiority of self as a white person
> Challenges other whites
> Interrupts collusion with other whites who seek to maintain their power and privilege
> Breaks silence and speaks up
> Seeks and validates critical feedback from People of Color
> Facilitates the empowerment of People of Color
> Consistently challenges prevailing patterns
> Takes personal responsibility
> Acts intentionally and overtly
> Behaves as a change agent
> Promotes and models change for other whites. (Labanowski n.d.)

MOTIVATION AND IDEOLOGICAL CHALLENGES

Numerous ideological and conceptual issues frame antiracist organizing. White people express a number of orientations regarding the historical, social, economic, and political privilege their race has delivered them. Antiracist organizing often seeks to unmask whiteness and overcome white fragility; no robust reform is possible if white fragility stands in the way. In addition to white fragility, some experience white guilt. This begs the important question at the heart of antiracist organizing: Can the white habitus be changed? Trepagnier (2010), using Pierre Bourdieu's concept of the habitus, looks at whether if race awareness is raised, the white habitus can be changed and result in "antiracist practice." Because racist practice (via the habitus, which Bourdieu says is based on routine rather than intention) has to become antiracist practice (routine), a change is ... very difficult. Trepagnier writes, "When I speak of antiracism, I am referring to individuals' personal behavior, not to the collective action of members in antiracist organizations" (2010:105).

Some whites engaged in antiracist activism also demonstrate a white savior complex. Perhaps this is understandable, given that O'Brien refers to the "historical amnesia" of there being too few whites as role models of white antiracist action. The white savior complex does appear to be a continuation of white supremacy, however well intentioned. Likewise, advocates of color blindness ignore the compounded white privilege their race has afforded them. This is not simply a historical oversight or some form of political forgiveness for many scholars. For example, both O'Brien (2001) and Feagin (2010) mention the lack of empathy many whites have for people of color. Feagin describes a process of sympathy, empathy, and autopathy and proposes a concerted effort at teaching whites the history of racial oppression.

Feagin is not alone in examining the conjunction of education and racial preferences. Interactional reforms, especially through housing and education, are often seen as valuable sources of antiracist progress. Bonilla-Silva, in his final chapter, encourages whites to read as much as they can on antiracism and to search for an antiracist organization in their area. This mindset has pitfalls, namely that it could make a person seem arrogant when they believe they are better than those they deem racist. Emirbayer and Desmond discuss how efforts to be antiracist come down to making racial interactions more democratic and educational, yet those efforts also need to be more confrontational. They suggest that it is necessary to disrupt "the ordinary workings of a racist order whenever and wherever they occur," even if such actions come "at the cost of considerable acrimony and personal discomfort" (2015:318). This raises important concerns about whether these strategies are too narrow to overturn racial domination or to effectively help white people manage their shame and guilt about unjust racial pasts carried out by the white race with which they identify.

Since the history of how racism is valued and lived in the US is deeply political, we also consider the impact of neoliberalism on the social justice activism. Does the interweaving of capitalism with democracy spur the creation of a market to buy and sell racial sincerity and front a desire for symbolic capital in the effort to gain (fetishize and desire) racial justice? Also, because American racism has always been intertwined with economics and restricting access to resources, it is a product to be sold and exchanged. Social movement activism may reveal responses to exclusion when white people are told they can't be part of the game. This is not necessarily anything new (consider Malcolm X's iconic response to what he calls a "well-meaning" white woman asking what she can do: "Nothing"), but the rise in globalization and overwhelming permeation of capitalism across all aspects of the US could arguably be compounding these effects. As a result, the interplay between racial threat and racial opportunism is informed, shaped, and given meaning through a neoliberal lens, much as the concept of racial capitalism has long predicted. Neoliberalism is one of the reasons that barriers to white antiracist action have materialized so profoundly in the era of Trump. As Melanie Bush describes, neoliberalism creates a "racialization of resistance" (2011:214), presenting a barrier for antiracist reforms. The "contact" hypothesis marks the importance of interracial relationships (especially between white women and nonwhite partners), but hypersegregation, further entrenched by neoliberalism, makes such relationships rare.

Such ideological concerns invite us to think about what larger forces give rise to or inhibit antiracist activism. Perhaps, in the era of Trump, we must reexamine what Bush describes as "cracks in the wall of whiteness." For Bush, the potential openings were idealism; ambiguities and contradictions; ambivalence (financial insecurities); knowledge/awareness; systemic downturns; confusion; exposure to diverse experiences; creativity and hybridity; courage/openness/understanding the stakes; and the increased visibility and higher levels of representation of nonwhites.

Miller and Davis (2020) published an article on white outgroup intolerance and levels of support for American democracy. They found that intolerant white people in the United States abandon democracy when they fear that democracy may benefit people they perceive as marginalized. They use surveys to show, for example, that white people who do not want to live near immigrants or people of other races and ethnicities are, unsurprisingly, more likely to support authoritarianism. In this way, such whites follow the logic of alt-right neofascist leader Richard Spencer. Today, the logic of fascism suggests that white rule essentially requires totalitarianism. Aggrieved white people still espouse patriotism and the country's cherished values of liberty and equality for all, but centuries of baked-in racism create a different lived reality.

White antiracist day-to-day activities are likely shaped by these ideological frames, which are important to understanding activists' motivations. Classic studies like Doug McAdam's *Freedom Summer* (1988) and Alphonso Pinkney's *The Committed* (1968) traced the motivations of 1960s white civil rights activists. These works found that religious or secular humanist values were important in compelling whites to become civil rights activists because they underscored the belief that it was the right thing to do.

When you consider the findings of McAdam (1988) and O'Brien (2001), three primary factors explain how and why whites become antiracist: (1) through activist networks, including organizational ties, prior participation in activism, and personal relations with others in movement; (2) by developing empathy for people of color by way of "approximating experiences," either by analogy to some oppression they have suffered themselves or through borrowed approximations (e.g., reading *Savage Inequalities* or listening to a story from a black friend); and (3) via a "planting seeds" or "turning point" moment, an early memory that is a combination of environment, status (especially gender), and life experiences. O'Brien (2001:106) shares psychologist Beverly Daniel Tatum's conclusion that pseudo-independence, immersion, and autonomy—the final three stages of racial identity, according to Janet Helms—may tip some toward antiracism.

Nativism and racial tribalism evoke the kind of whitelash discussed in Matthew Hughey's *White Bound* (2012). Hughey researched and attended the meetings of two white organizations, one white nationalist group and one antiracist group. From this research, Hughey concludes that while there are unsurprising political differences, there is also a perhaps surprising similarity. Both groups use racist worldviews and reactionary stories to bind them to their racial vantage point.

CONCLUSIONS

When one contemplates the role of white activism for racial justice in the twenty-first century, paying special attention to the prevalence of limited racial conscientiousness among whites for decades and particularly since the rise of fascism and bigotry incited by Trump's regime, it becomes necessary to question whether the old dichotomy of racial justice activism—namely a binary choice between allyship and self-emancipation—holds any longer. Some organizations, like the ARA, were founded by and made up largely of whites, while others, like PISAB, were founded and made up largely of African Americans. Allyship demands that white people recognize their privilege, identify ways in which they are complicit in practices that maintain and reproduce racial hierarchies, and work to withdraw from or interrupt such practices. White allies also must take direction from people of color on how they, as allies, are contributing to or perpetuating racial hierarchies, how they might act differently, and specific ways in which they should oppose racial hierarchies. Self-emancipation, on the other hand, treats the struggle against racism as an activity that ought to be wholly led and largely carried out by people of color themselves.

The binary activist choice asks whether whites should oppose racism as white people or as participants in allied movements. But perhaps the Trump regime demands a fresh look toward sincerity and liberation, in line with the old adage: "If you have come here to help me, you are wasting your time. But if you have come because your liberation is bound up with mine, then let us work together." However, despite the best intentions of white antiracist activism to date, this has not yet happened. In fact, some fear that as right-wing groups become more emboldened and more right-wing candidates are elected, we might see a decline in antiracist action, especially among whites. Indeed, we find ourselves at a unique turning point. Many scholars and activists, including Ibram Kendi, American University's director of the Antiracist Research and Policy Center, have observed the lack of a deep, societal challenge against racist ideas in our country. Yet, there is still time for massive and deliberate antiracism activism. The future of a racially just United States demands a movement against racist policies. Only when white supremacy is evicted from occupying its moral space in US democracy can a new century of liberatory promise emerge, breaking down old binaries and authorizing authentic activism to create a new, society-wide resistance to racist ideas in the US.

REFERENCES

Aptheker, Herbert. 1992. *Antiracism in U.S. History: The First Two Hundred Years*. New York: Greenwood.

Berlatsky, Noah. 2018. "The Trump Effect: New Study Connects White American Intolerance and Support for Authoritarianism." NBC News, May 27. Retrieved May 27, 2018 (nbcnews.com/think/opinion/trump-effect-new-study-connects-white-american-intolerance-support-authoritarianism-ncna877786).

Bonilla-Silva, Eduardo. 2012. "The Invisible Weight of Whiteness: The Racial Grammar of Everyday Life in Contemporary America." *Ethnic and Racial Studies* 35(2): 173–94

——. 2018. *Racism without Racists: Color-Blind Racism and the Persistence of Racial Inequality in America*. 5th edition. Lanham, MD: Rowman & Littlefield.

Bonnett, Alastair. 1999. *Anti-Racism.* New York: Routledge.

Bush, Melanie E. L. 2011. *Everyday Forms of Whiteness: Understanding Race in a "Post Racial" World.* 2nd edition. Lanham, MD: Rowman & Littlefield.

Doane, Ashley. 2006. "What Is Racism? Racial Discourse and Racial Politics." *Critical Sociology* 32(2–3): 255–74.

Emirbayer, Mustafa, and Matthew Desmond. 2015. *The Racial Order.* Chicago: University of Chicago Press.

Essed, Philomena. 1991. *Understanding Everyday Racism.* Thousand Oaks, CA: Sage.

Feagin, Joe R. 2010. *Racist America: Roots, Current Realities, and Future Reparations.* 2nd edition. New York: Routledge.

———. 2013. *The White Racial Frame: Centuries of Racial Framing and Counter-Framing.* New York: Routledge.

Feagin, Joe R., Hernán Vera, and Pinar Batu. 2000. *White Racism.* 2nd edition. New York: Routledge.

Frankenberg, Ruth. 1993. *White Women, Race Matters: The Social Construction of Whiteness.* Minneapolis: University of Minnesota Press.

Goldberg, Susan B., and Cameron Levin. 2018. "Towards a Radical White Identity." AWARE-LA. Retrieved May 3, 2018 (https://static1.squarespace.com/static/581e9e06ff7c509a5ca2fe32/t/588d4ff3414fb55621d5d0f1/1485656053135/Toward+a+Radical+White+Identity.pdf).

Hughey, Matthew. 2012. *White Bound: Nationalists, Antiracists, and the Shared Meanings of Race.* Stanford, CA: Stanford University Press.

Ignatiev, Noel, and John Garvey, eds. 1996. *Race Traitor.* New York: Routledge.

Kailin, Julie. 2002. *Antiracist Education: From Theory to Practice.* Lanham, MD: Rowman & Littlefield.

Kendi, Ibram X. 2017. *Stamped from the Beginning: The Definitive History of Racist Ideas in America.* New York: Nation Books.

Kivel, Paul. 1996. *Uprooting Racism: How White People Can Work for Racial Justice.* Gabriola Island, BC: New Society Publishers.

Labanowski, Phyllis. N.d. "Checklist of Characteristics of Active Anti-Racist Ally Behavior." Retrieved March 15, 2018 (http://www.antiracistalliance.com/allychar.html).

Lartey, Jamiles. 2018. "Oppression in America: 'To Root This Out, We Need a Movement against Racist Policies.'" *The Guardian*, June 6. Retrieved June 6, 2018 (theguardian.com/us-news/2018/jun/06/everyday-racism-in-america-how-to-fix-it).

Mallett, Whitney. 2017. "California Anti-Fascists Want Racists and the Trump Administration to Be Afraid." *Vice*, May 10.

McAdam, Doug. 1988. *Freedom Summer.* New York: Oxford University Press.

McIntosh, Peggy. 1988. "White Privilege: Unpacking the Invisible Knapsack." Excerpted from "White Privilege and Male Privilege: A Personal Account of Coming to See Correspondences through Work in Women's Studies." Working Paper 189, Wellesley College Center for Research on Women.

Miller, Steven V., and Nicholas T. Davis. 2020. "The Effect of White Social Prejudice on Support for American Democracy." *Journal of Race, Ethnicity, and Politics*. Published online, February 3. Retrieved May 12, 2020 (doi: 10.1017/rep.2019.55).

Mills, Charles. 1997. *The Racial Contract*. Ithaca, NY: Cornell University Press.

O'Brien, Eileen. 2001. *Whites Confront Racism: Antiracists and Their Paths to Action*. Lanham, MD: Rowman & Littlefield.

Olson, Joel. 2004. *The Abolition of White Democracy*. Minneapolis: University of Minnesota Press.

Omi, Michael, and Howard Winant. 2015. *Racial Formations in the United States*. 3rd edition. New York: Routledge.

Pinkney, Alphonso. 1968. *The Committed: White Activists in the Civil Rights Movement*. New Haven, CT: College and University Press.

Seligman, Adam B., Robert P. Weller, Michael J. Puett, and Bennett Simon. 2008. *Ritual and Its Consequences: An Essay on the Limits of Sincerity*. Cary, NC: Oxford University Press.

Thomas, James M. 2014. "Affect and the Sociology of Race: A Program for Critical Inquiry." *Ethnicities* 14(1):72–90.

Thompson, Becky W. 2001. *A Promise and a Way of Life: White Antiracist Action*. Minneapolis: University of Minnesota Press.

Trepagnier, Barbara. 2010. *Silent Racism: How Well-Meaning White People Perpetuate the Racial Divide*. Boulder, CO: Paradigm.

Trilling, Lionel. 1972. *Sincerity and Authenticity*. Cambridge, MA: Harvard University Press.

Wise, Tim. 2011. *White Like Me: Reflections on Race from a Privileged Son*. New York: Soft Skull Press.

CONCLUSIONS

*Where Do We Go from Here?: Structural and
Social Implications of Whitelash*

J. SCOTT CARTER, DAVID G. EMBRICK,
AND CAMERON D. LIPPARD

AND JUST LIKE that, the rise of Donald Trump to the presidency of the United States has seemingly ushered in a new era, one in which the dominant color-blind racial discourse has been altered. Overt racism, characterized by references to racial inferiority and once thought to be moved to the margins of society never to be seen again, has found its voice in prominent political debates and throughout the public sphere. From immigration to terrorism to inner-city violence, President Trump and other prominent right-wing pundits and organizations have become more emboldened to promote appeals to racial essentialism and overt racism over the past few years.

Trump has focused much of his inflammatory rhetoric toward people of color. Undocumented immigrants were described as animals, rapists, and just outright dangerous to American citizens (Korte and Gomez 2018). In striking discourse leading up to the election, then candidate Trump used such language to call for a ban on Muslims entering the US (Diamond 2015). He openly questioned their motives and referred to them as a threat. This rhetoric should not be surprising. Starting in 2011, before his remarkable and stunning presidential run in 2016, Trump became a spokesperson for the Birther movement, which denied the citizenship and thus eligibility for office of Barack Obama, the first African American president of the United States. It should be noted that this racist discourse was supported by many prominent individuals and groups (such as the Tea Party) as well as a large percentage of the US population. Thus, this support is not confined to marginalized individuals and groups who lurk in the shadows. It is found in the mainstream.

As highlighted throughout the various chapters of this book, Trump's denial of President Obama as a citizen and incendiary proclamations about immigration, Muslim terrorism, women's roles, and views of transgender military service did not occur in a vacuum. Rather, this era is marked by growing racial diversity in all facets of life, the election of the first African American president of the United States, prominent protests of police abuse (e.g., Black Lives Matter), a general push to disassemble systems oppression toward various groups (e.g., women and LGBTQIA individuals), and a push to remove Confederate memorials and other historical symbols. Thus, we see the rise of Trump and the seeming success of his openly racist rhetoric among supporters as an example of whitelash in the US, coming in reaction to marginalized groups fighting for equal rights and treatment.

However, we stress that the Trump phenomenon is simply one example of backlash reaction among whites. Indeed, Lee Cokorinos (2003:16) stated that "for as long as there has been civil rights law, conservatives have been developing the arguments and instruments to reverse it." During this era, before and during Trump's administration, the Tea Party gained social and political prominence for this very reason. In the *Washington Post*, Gervais and Morris (2018) wrote that what differentiated Tea Party conservatives from mainstream conservatives was not their fiscal positions but their hostile reactions to social and racial issues (e.g., DACA). Other instances of whitelash can be seen in the continued fight against affirmative action (see *Fisher v. The University of Texas at Austin*) and the dismantling of the Voting Rights Act. We also witnessed the rebirth of white supremacy in the form of the alt-right as well as the founding of the far-right website Breitbart News. Appropriately, as suggested by Gervais and Morris, growing diversity and movements such as Black Lives Matter set the stage for white backlash (or what we call whitelash) and Trump's election to the presidency of the United States.

While many have been shocked by the rise of Trump and hostile or provocative narratives surrounding race and racial issues, many critical race scholars are not. Research prominent in the social science literature and in this book have highlighted that while Jim Crow views of racial inferiority may have declined, a more insidious and buoyant ideology, color blindness, has taken its place—one that on its face seems even nice. This ideology seeks to minimize the notion that racism and discrimination persist while promoting views that act to prop up white dominance and maintain the racist system found in the US (Bonilla-Silva 2018). Accordingly, African Americans and other marginalized groups are blamed for the abject poverty and inequality many of them continue to experience today. This ideological position ignores persistent racism and discrimination while also outlining the mechanism used to reproduce such outcomes (Carter and Lippard 2020; Carter, Lippard, and Baird 2019). Scholars have consistently posited that while the caustic and mean-spirited ideology characteristic of the Jim Crow is "in your face," the new color-blind ideology is dangerous because, as Eduardo Bonilla-Silva stated, it is often produced and reproduced by racists and nonracists alike. However, as noted above, a new era may be dawning that ushers out this "nice," subtle racism in favor of returning to past aggressive and more hostile positions on race and racial issues. This observation may provide ample opportunity for future research looking at shifts in ideology that lean toward more overt racist narratives that blame marginalized groups, particularly African Americans, for their plight as well as for other problems in the US.

The Trump era does seem to be ushering in this new ideology in many ways. President Trump has eschewed traditional political etiquette consistent with past Republican presidents in favor of more caustic discourse, particularly when it comes to race-based issues. Past presidents' seemingly "cordial" repudiation of policies meant to improve the experiences of minorities is seemingly now replaced by a much more honest and scathing repudiation. However, as described in chapter 3, Trump attempts to straddle that line as well as he commonly claims to be the "least racist" person while using veiled racist language to deny any racial animosity. The Trump administration has also attempted to quiet and even dismiss prominent opponents. Trump constantly attempts to silence prominent media outlets by describing them as "fake news." He has also directly attacked celebrities and other prominent individuals who have opposed his presidency. His administration has also openly supported white nationalism; in response to alt-right violence in Charlottesville, Virginia, that resulted in one death, Trump openly stated that both sides had some bad people and some "very fine" ones (Stolberg and Rosenthal 2017). Furthermore, Trump labeled himself a nationalist and questioned how this is a bad thing, despite the history of the term. Such tactics provide ample opportunity to "other" marginalized groups and create a victimhood status among whites, a prominent frame used to describe whites as the true victims of race-based policies meant to alleviate racial inequality and promote diversity in the country.

An ideology that minimizes the role of race is problematic for many reasons; however, it is especially worrisome given the state of race relations and inequality in the US today. A few issues in particular raise concerns. First, the seeming liberalization of whites' attitudes toward principles of racial equality has not significantly resulted in a reduction in the disadvantages experienced by African Americans (Sears and Henry 2003). Research in the social sciences has clearly demonstrated that racial disparities continue to exist on several economic and social indicators, including income and education (Jones, Schmitt, and Wilson 2018). Second, while whites' attitudes appear to be growing more liberal with regard to race over time, their views toward ameliorative racial policies simply have not (Bobo and Smith 1994; Carter, Steelman et al. 2005; Schuman et al. 1997). For example, Carter and Lippard (2020) found very little support among whites toward affirmative action, a view that has remained quite stable since the 1970s. As such, this research poses that the lack of support reflects a backlash to any government attempt to minimize the impact of past racial harms.

This book addresses the broader notion of whitelash and how it relates to the rise of Trump. However, whitelash is not about Trump. We make no claim that Trump started the whitelash; rather, he is just one symptom of a broader pushback against changes in the status quo. In the face of the issues described above (e.g., growing diversity and the inclusion of minorities in positions of power such as President Obama), many whites and institutions have pushed back. As such, we define whitelash as individual, institutional, and structural countermeasures against the dismantling of white supremacy (the racial status quo) or against actions, real or imagined, that seek to remedy existing racial inequities. It is a reaction to growing diversity; it is reaction to those who would call out racism or white privilege; it is a reaction to the inclusion of members of marginalized groups in powerful positions. While they are not mutually exclusive, whitelash can take the form of white ideologies or institutional patterns and rules that block the success of marginalized groups.

DOES ANY OF THIS MATTER? EXPECTATIONS, IMPLICATIONS, AND CONCLUSIONS

The research by various critical racism scholars in the discipline makes it clear that we are living in turbulent times, particularly when it comes to the relevancy of race and racism. While there are several prevailing ideologies that demean, suppress, and cloak the continuing issues of racism, the Trump era has ushered in a not-so-nice period reminiscent of the Jim Crow era, Reconstruction, and even slavery. Rhetoric and narratives implying biological and temperament inferiority are taking root and being promoted by prominent individuals, including the president of the United States. Nonetheless, while the foundations of the color-blind ideology have been shaken, it is also clear that it is still a powerful component of US culture individually and institutionally. This book supports this conclusion.

However, the collective assessment of the chapters in this volume suggest that it is time to do more than just expose particular ideologies that prop up a racist system. Doane (2017:60) stated that "studying the racial attitudes of individuals can certainly be useful for exploring the prevalence of elements of racial ideologies, but at some point, the analysis needs to return to the macro-level or we risk equating ideology with individual beliefs and prejudice." This book succeeds in accomplishing this task. With whitelash as a theoretical guidepost, we demonstrate that whitelash takes on different forms and manifests itself in practices and rules of organizations and institutions. Indeed, even while discussing the contours of racial ideology in the US, these authors never veer too far from institutional-level issues and how they act to reproduce the racist system that benefits whites at the expense of marginalized groups. The authors describe these institutional practices as dangerous because they work to reproduce inequality and the racist system in seemingly nonracial and innocuous ways.

Where do we go from here? What ideas and arguments can we take from the collective chapters in this book? Further, what are the major implications of these readings? We offer five specific points that we contend need to be addressed moving forward: whitelash and the persistence of white supremacy; racial ideologies; institutional and organizational racism; a new civil rights movement; and demystifying white victimization. We address each of our points below.

Whitelash and the Persistence of White Supremacy

As we previously contended, whitelash is not new or unique to the Trump era. In fact, the history of the US is fraught with racial contestations that challenge changes to the status quo—one that is premised on the ideas of white normativity and white superiority. Whenever issues of race and racism, today and in the past, have come to the forefront, whites have mobilized to stymie change. We can see this during the Abolitionist movement that took place in the late 1820s leading up to (and beyond) the US Civil War and Emancipation. We saw the whitelash against indigenous peoples during McCarthyism in the 1950s, as conservative politicians argued for the dismantling and termination (read: genocide) of indigenous reservations that were argued to be dangerous communist safe havens within the US. We also witnessed whitelash against affirmative action policies throughout US history, beginning in the 1960s but really taking off during the Reagan era in the 1980s.

What these facts point to is that whitelash is not a new phenomenon but a collective and potentially dangerous set of mobilization efforts by whites (and some nonwhites) to maintain a racialized social system that exclusively benefits whites. Certainly, the founding of the United States was centered on keeping white, elite males in power (Feagin 2006). This means that the starting point for any conversation on the eradication of racism needs to be premised on the idea that the road to a more just and racially equitable society means uprooting the strong foundation that is centered on maintaining white supremacy. Arguably, it means dismantling racialized organizations that are the pillars holding up the racialized US social system. Such moves are sure to evoke whitelash, as we have seen in the Trumptopian era, where calls for revisiting the "good ol'" days are nostalgic walks down memory lane to a time when nonwhites knew their place as second-class citizens or perpetual foreigners.

Evolving Racial Ideologies

Meaningful change also means disrupting the existing racial ideology that demonizes African Americans and blames them for their current socioeconomic position. In so doing, the myth of white victims and the neoliberal idea that we live in meritocratic society need to be put to rest. The looming power of whiteness in the reproduction of white supremacy is still quite relevant. It is clear that future research needs to continue to shine a light on evolving racial ideologies in the US today. As we and others have argued, while color-blind and other racial ideologies clearly persist, the contours seem to be changing—ushering in new racial ideologies that borrow from traditional racist views of the past while propping up the color-blind ideology so prevalent today.

Accordingly, future research might do well to focus on the changing narrative and stories around race and how old, not-so-nice propositions are finding footing in today's discourse. While Eduardo Bonilla-Silva has described color-blind ideology's insidious role in reproducing inequality, he never stated that other ideologies did not exist or that no other ideologies were effective in maintaining white supremacy. We suggest that future research look at how prominent individuals and organizations act to reproduce these ideologies. Indeed, Herbert Blumer (1958) argued that racism, to a great degree, exists outside of the individual and is created by elite entities who have the ability to reach the ears of the masses with their message.

Research has shown that conservative think tanks and other organizations with resources play key roles in maintaining racist narratives in debates surrounding key cases reaching the US Supreme Court (Carter and Lippard 2020; Carter, Lippard, and Baird 2019). Bonilla-Silva (2018) similarly stated that those entities, who have greater access to resources, have the loudest voices and thus greater impact.

Institutional and Organizational Racism

While racist ideologies play a significant role in whitelash and the reproduction of white supremacy, institutional practices also stand as debilitating factors in the process. Put simply, some mechanisms (whether they be formal rules or informal norms) when implemented by whites (and some nonwhites) in institutions further support the persistence of the color line described by Du Bois over a century ago. Du Bois (1898) posed that unlike whites and other immigrant groups, African Americans experience a "peculiar environment" that complicates their lives and that actively reproduces inequality. Thus, future research should examine how institutional and organizational practices contribute to the racist system that benefits one group at the expense of others. The sociologist Wendy Leo Moore described how organizations, in this case elite law schools, maintain rules and practices that reproduce racism and racial inequality. Similarly, the sociologist Victor Ray (2019) posited that organizations maintain exclusionary mechanisms that promote white supremacy, including place, space, policies, programs, practices, methods, logic, and language.

With respect to the above, we argue that whitelash can be found above and beyond racial ideology; however, you would not know this from the extant research. Most researchers have not heeded the words of Du Bois and studied the peculiar conditions of African Americans. Rather, they have focused on intraindividual attitudes that reflect broader ideological tidbits. In addition, like Du Bois, who was excluded from mainstream sociology for decades because he was black, those who have challenged white supremacy and noted moments of whitelash have also faced reprisal for exposing these truths. Even with the creation of this volume of scholarly research, the editors and the press were concerned about white backlash. Specifically, one chapter was removed because of concerns around litigation risks. This provides another real-world example that underscores how whitelash can shape the actions of institutions and organizations, even for an academic press that publishes current theory and research. Because of the chapters that *were* included in this volume, we also better understand that the potential of whitelash is enough to play an instrumental role in the reproduction of white supremacy because it stifles discourse on the very subject. Thus, everyday institutional decisions that attempt to avoid the possibility of facing negative repercussions still benefit whites at the expense of African Americans and other marginalized groups. This conclusion is particularly true because even academics cannot fully tell the truth about whitelash if their research and writing cannot be published due to fear of reprisal. Furthermore, to keep these patterns and practices alive due to fear is to keep the system unchecked and unchanged to combat systemic racial oppression.

Rethinking a New Civil Rights Movement

As Bonilla-Silva (2003) and other scholars have argued, there needs to be a rebirth or rethinking of a new civil rights movement. Given the reentrenchment of white supremacy and accompanying whitelash, the support for the dominant color-blind ideology and the denial of persistent racism and discrimination, the emergence of narratives that evoke Jim Crow, and the role of institutions in maintaining the status quo, a need exists for broader societal and structural changes. As seen in this volume, this movement will most likely be led by women of color, who have for years led the charge against systemic oppression of all marginalized groups. Indeed, the 2018 midterm election may provide insight that such a movement is occurring right before our very eyes. In total, 117 women were elected or appointed to Congress, bringing the total number of women serving in the 116th Congress to 127 (102 in the House and 25 in the Senate). This is a record, as no more than 84 women have ever held seats in the US House of Representatives. As such, the inclusion of more women in general and women of color in politics and activism may be the key ingredient in the fight against whitelash. This movement would also need to reconsider and strengthen class coalitions, an issue that came up during the 2016 presidential election (see Basu 2018; Stonecash 2018).

Such movements could lead to the several outcomes. First, the movement could lead to structural changes that connect issues marginalized groups are having with persistent and historical racism and discrimination. As Thomas posed in chapter 4, rather than benignly celebrating diversity of all kinds, institutions must do real work to eliminate problems of racism and discrimination and must include persons of color in the process. As it stands now, whites hold dominant positions in most institutions, which means that they continue to create the narrative and they ultimately handle most decisions. Accordingly, research should continue to focus on uncovering persistent institutional practices that maintain the racial status quo.

Such a movement can further address the issue of "whiteness." Whites need to also come to terms with the notion of color-blind racism and how their whiteness contributes to the pernicious inequality that pervades the US. However, in chapter 2 Williams stated, "The historical and contemporary record counsels that self-identified whites' addiction to white license and materialism will probably never lend itself to ending their domination and exploitation of racialized Others" (p. 00). Therefore, it will take broader activism to bring about such change. When this occurs, changes to rules and practices in organizations can finally be considered. Furthermore, certain practices by elite organizations (e.g., interest groups) can be brought into the light and challenged. Such groups have prominently produced color-blind and "threat" narratives that reproduce the racial status quo (Carter, Lippard, and Baird 2019; Carter and Lippard 2015).

Such a movement may make institutions and organizations more likely to address other issues associated with whiteness that often deflect attempts to improve the well-being of marginalized groups: white fragility and white victimization. Feelings held by whites that they are under attack and that they ultimately are the victims of any diversification attempt are hampering the movement toward racial justice and inequality. It is clear that the problem of the color line is inherent not within marginalized groups but within whites who struggle to accept changing norms and diversification. Accordingly, the broader movement will need to deconstruct whiteness and provide evidence that such a viewpoint is deleterious to the utopian society of racial blindness and equality. As such, as Carter and Roos noted in chapter 3, victimization is the new rallying cry to protect white superiority and thus to exclude marginalized groups from coalition politics and movements that aim to achieve true racial equality.

Interestingly, white America has attempted to participate in moments of true reconciliation and cooperation to bring about civil rights and equal treatment. However, in this era, growing fears of the Other taking jobs and educational opportunities and threatening a way of life sustained for over four centuries muddles the possibilities of future coalition (see Painter 2010; Roediger 2007). However, DiAngelo (2018) noted that White America must come to understand their power in privilege as whites in society. They also have to toughen up a little because these privileges have saved them from hundreds of years of racial persecution and violence. Moreover, all Americans collectively must refute the notion that whites suffer just as much as other racial and ethnic groups, a notion based on some storied past that has been craftily rewritten to suggest that they are victims too. For example, should Americans believe that Confederate memorials honor fallen soldiers who had no real opinion about slavery and thus were innocent bystanders? Or should Americans, particularly white southern Americans, accept that these individuals lived in a racist society that encouraged them to fight as racists to hold on to a racist society that would benefit free white men?

White America must make four important ideological shifts in how they see racial equality. First, they must realize that race and racism in the past and within present-day America benefits only them and violates American views of equality. It is a serious double standard. Second, whites must embrace that they are to blame because whether they as individuals actively participate as neo-Nazis, Klansmen, or social justice warriors, American institutions and ideological structures still give them the benefit of the doubt based on the color of their skin. This is true even when controlling for other social characteristics such as social class, gender, and sexual orientation. As comedian Chris Rock once stated, "You all right because you all white!" Third, while whites have the power right now and can commit to change, people of color and other oppressed groups must go to the streets to fight for their dignity and livelihood. The only true and lasting successes in any social movements are those in which the majority at least tolerate, or better yet agree to, changes. Finally, whites must embrace the psychological, economic, and political pain that these changes will cause if we are to have a truly democratic and fair society where race does not matter. If we really want our society to be color blind and merit-based, then whites must bear the pain and realize that this kind of holistic annihilation of racism will be worth it. Even so, it will take generations, and still it will not cause as much pain for whites as what has happened to millions of people of color, crushed under the foot of racist oppression for centuries.

CONCLUSION

Whitelash is a historical process where whites have reacted against any challenges to the racial status quo or calls made for the rights of nonwhites and an end to racial and ethnic oppression, whether those challenges and calls be economical, political, social, psychological, or even philosophical. From slavery to the Reconstruction era to the rise of Donald Trump, the fight to maintain power and control is ongoing. We and the contributors in this volume view whitelash as collective effort to maintain hegemony in an ever changing society that is growing more diverse by the day. We feel that the theoretical framework of whitelash will provide future scholars with a conceptually and analytically agile tool to explain future actions and reactions among whites (and some nonwhites) to maintain power in the face of growing protest over unequal treatment and fairness.

REFERENCES

Basu, Amrita. 2018. *The Challenge of Local Feminisms: Women's Movements in Global Perspective*. New York: Routledge.

Blumer, Herbert. 1958. "Race Prejudice as a Sense of Group Position." *Pacific Sociological Review* 1: 3–7.

Bonilla-Silva, Eduardo. 2003. *Racism without Racists: Color-Blind Racism and the Persistence of Racial Inequality in America*. Lanham, MD: Rowman & Littlefield.

———. 2018. *Racism without Racists: Color-Blind Racism and the Persistence of Racial Inequality in America*. 5th edition. Lanham, MD: Rowman & Littlefield.

Bobo, Lawrence., and R. A. Smith. 1994. Antipoverty Policy, Affirmative Action, and Racial Attitudes. Pp. 365–95 in *Confronting Poverty: Prescriptions for Change*, edited by Sheldon H. Danziger, Gary D. Sandefur, and Daniel H. Weinberg. Cambridge, MA: Harvard University Press.

Carter, J. Scott, and Cameron D. Lippard. 2015. "Group Position, Threat, and Immigration: The Role of Interest Groups and Elite Actors in Setting the 'Lines of Discussion.'" *Sociology of Race and Ethnicity* 1(3): 394–408.

———. 2020. *The Death of Affirmative Action? Racialized Framing and the Fight against Racial Preference in College Admissions*. Bristol, UK: Bristol University Press.

Carter, J. Scott, Cameron Lippard, and Andrew F. Baird. 2019. "Veiled Threats: Color-Blind Frames and Group Threat in Affirmative Action Discourse." *Social Problems* 66(4): 503–18. Retrieved May 12, 2020 (https://doi.org/10.1093/socpro/spy020).

Carter, J. Scott, Lala Carr Steelman, Lynn M. Mulkey, and Casey Borch. 2005. "When the Rubber Meets the Road: The Differential Effects of Urban and Regional Residence on Principle and Implementation Measures of Racial Tolerance." *Social Science Research* 34(2): 408–25.

Cokorinos, Lee. 2003. *The Assault on Diversity: An Organized Challenge to Racial and Gender Justice*. Lanham, MD: Rowman & Littlefield.

Diamond, Jeremy. 2015. "Donald Trump: Ban All Muslim Travel in U.S." *CNN Politics*, December 8. Retrieved March 1, 2019 (https://www.cnn.com/2015/12/07/politics/donald-trump-muslim-ban-immigration/index.html).

DiAngelo, Robin. 2018. *White Fragility: Why It's So Hard for White People to Talk about Racism*. Boston: Beacon Press.

Doane, Ashley W. 2017. "Beyond Color-Blindness: (Re)Theorizing Racial Ideology." *Sociological Perspectives* 60(5): 975–91.

Du Bois, W. E. B. 1898. "The Study of the Negro Problems." *Annals of the American Academy of Political and Social Science* 1: 1–23.

Feagin, Joe R. 2006. *Systemic Racism: A Theory of Oppression.* New York: Routledge.

Gervais, Bryan T., and Irwin L. Morris. 2018. "How the Tea Party Paved the Way for Donald Trump." *Washington Post*, September 7.

Jones, Janelle, John Schmitt, and Valerie Wilson. 2018. "50 Years after the Kerner Commission: African Americans Are Better Off in Many Ways but Are Still Disadvantaged by Racial Inequality." Economic Policy Institute, February 26. Retrieved May 12, 2020 (https://www.epi.org/publication/50-years-after-the-kerner-commission/).

Korte, Gregory, and Alan Gomez. 2018. "Trump Ramps Up Rhetoric on Undocumented Immigrants: 'These aren't people. These are animals.'" *USA Today*, May 16.

Painter, Nell Irvin. 2010. *The History of White People.* New York: W. W. Norton.

Ray, Victor. 2019. "A Theory of Racialized Organizations." *American Sociological Review* 84: 26–53.

Roediger, David. 2007. *The Wages of Whiteness: Race and the Making of the American Working Class.* New York: Verso.

Schuman, Howard, Charlotte Steeh, Lawrence D. Bobo, and Maria Krysan. 1997. *Racial Attitudes in America: Trends and Interpretations.* Cambridge, MA: Harvard University Press.

Sears, David O., and P. J. Henry. 2003. "The Origins of Symbolic Racism." *Journal of Personality and Social Psychology* 85(2): 259–75.

Stolberg, Sheryl Gay, and Brian M. Rosenthal. 2017. "Man Charged after White Nationalist Rally in Charlottesville Ends in Deadly Violence." *New York Times*, August 12.

Stonecash, Jeffery. 2018. *Class and Party in American Politics.* New York: Routledge.

CONTRIBUTORS

FELICIA ARRIAGA is assistant professor of sociology at Appalachian State University. Her research interests are in the areas of race and ethnicity, immigration, and crimmigration (criminalization of immigration policy and procedure). She specifically examines how local policies and procedures relate to issues of criminal justice accountability, transparency, and reform.

EDUARDO BONILLA-SILVA is the James B. Duke Distinguished Professor of Sociology at Duke University. He is a recipient of the American Sociological Association's Cox-Johnson-Frazier Award and the ASA's Lewis A. Coser Memorial Award for Theoretical Agenda Setting. He is author or coeditor of several books, including *White Logic, White Methods*. He is a past president (2017–18) of the American Sociological Association and the Southern Sociological Society.

DAVID L. BRUNSMA is professor of sociology at Virginia Tech. He is cofounding editor of *Sociology of Race and Ethnicity* and has recently published *The Matrix of Race: Social Construction, Intersectionality, and Inequality* (with Coates and Ferber). He lives and loves with his family in Blacksburg, Virginia.

J. SCOTT CARTER is associate professor of sociology at the University of Central Florida. His research interests encompass several areas, including race and politics, racial attitudes, racial inequality in education, and southern and urban place.

C. DOUG CHARLES is a PhD student at the University of Central Florida with a focus on inequality. His research and interests focus on race and gender, conspiracy theorists, and online groups and movements.

DAVID DIETRICH is associate professor at Texas State University. He received his PhD from Duke University in 2011. His areas of interest are racial and ethnic relations, social movements, immigration, social stratification, and sociological theory.

ASHLEY ("WOODY") DOANE is professor of sociology, chair of the Department of Social Sciences, and Associate Dean for Academic Administration at the University of Hartford. His published work includes numerous articles and book chapters on color-blind racial ideology, racial discourse, and whiteness.

SILVIA DOMÍNGUEZ is associate professor of sociology at Northeastern University. She is an interdisciplinary scholar with degrees in sociology, psychology, forensic social work, and social welfare policy. She specializes in areas addressing the welfare of women, children, and minorities both in the United States and abroad, with additional emphasis on sexual violence, race, social networks, mental health, and immigration.

MARLESE DURR is a professor in the Department of Sociology/Anthropology at Wright State University. Her areas of specialization include work and occupations, race and labor markets, African Americans and social networks, entrepreneurship and inner-city neighborhoods, and stressful life events and African American women. She has served as president of the Society for the Study of Social Problems (2014–15) and Sociologists for Women in Society (2004–5) and Chair of Publications for *Gender & Society*. She is currently serving as an Advisory Board member for *Social Problems* and was a founding Editorial Board member for *Sociology of Race and Ethnicity*.

DAVID G. EMBRICK is associate professor in the Sociology Department and African Studies Institute at the University of Connecticut. He is a former American Sociological Association Minority Fellow, past president of the Southwestern Sociological Association, current vice president of the Society for the Study of Social Problems, and president-elect of the Association for Humanist Sociology.

CHARLES A. GALLAGHER is professor and chair of the Sociology and Criminal Justice Department at La Salle University. His research focuses on social inequality, race relations, and immigration, and he has published over fifty articles, reviews, and books on these topics.

KASEY HENRICKS is assistant professor of sociology at the University of Tennessee. His research interests lie in understanding how racial inequalities are reproduced over time through arrangements of public finance.

CAMERON D. LIPPARD is professor and chair of sociology at Appalachian State University. His research and teaching interests focus on race and ethnic relations, immigration, and research methods.

MARETTA MCDONALD is a Louisiana BOR/SREB doctoral fellow at Louisiana State University. Her primary research interests are race and ethnicity, crime, intersectionality, and public policy. She earned her master's degree from Southeastern Louisiana University in applied sociology.

BETHANY NELSON is a PhD candidate at the University of Tennessee with a concentration in criminology and critical race studies. Her research interests lie at the intersections of social suffering, exclusion, dark tourism, and cultural criminology.

J. MICAH ROOS is assistant professor of sociology at Virginia Tech. His interests focus on quantitative methods, sociology of knowledge and culture, stratification, and science and religion.

MARY K. RYAN is a doctoral candidate in social, political, ethical, and cultural thought at Virginia Tech, where she teaches in the Departments of Philosophy and Political Science. Her dissertation concerns structural racism in the United States federal government.

REBECCA R. SCOTT is associate professor of sociology at the University of Missouri. She is author of *Removing Mountains: Extracting Identity in the Appalachian Coalfields.* Her current work centers on environmental justice, racism, and settler culture in late fossil fuel society.

BHOOMI K. THAKORE is assistant professor and director of the Sociology Program at Elmhurst College. Her research interests include racial and ethnic inequality, underrepresentation in popular media, and issues of diversity in higher education.

JAMES M. THOMAS is assistant professor of sociology at the University of Mississippi. His research centers on historical and contemporary formations of race and racism in comparative perspective.

SIMÓN E. WEFFER is associate professor of sociology and Latino and Latin American studies at Northern Illinois University. His research includes understanding immigration protest, Latino social movement organizations, Latino adolescent obesity, urban inequality, race and space, and the link between protest and voting.

JOHNNY E. WILLIAMS is professor of sociology at Trinity College in Hartford, Connecticut. He specializes in social movements, political sociology, cultural sociology, racism, and science and religion.

INDEX

abolitionist movement, 259
acquisitive individualism, 120
affirmative action, 225, 258–59; *Fisher v. The University of Texas at Austin*, 256
All Lives Matter movement, 213
Allsup, 197
alt-left, 241
alt-right, 197, 225
AltRight.com, 157
American Civil Liberties Union (ACLU), 105–8, 110
American National Election Study, 62
American Renaissance, 154, 158
American-nationalist, 198
Anderson, Elijah, 94
anti-mountaintop removal movement (MTR), 121, 123, 124
anti-PC, 59
Anti-Racist Alliance, 241, 244–45, 248, 251
anti-Semitism, 157
Antifa, 241, 244
antiracism, 74
anti-racist activism, 241–42, 250
anti-racist organizations, 240, 244
apocalypticism, 205
Art Institute of Chicago, 180–82, 184–87, 189–90
Atomwaffen Division, 154

audience perception, 168–69
authoritarianism, xi
authoritarian populism, xi

Bacon's Rebellion, 30
Baldwin, James, 135
Baudelaire, Charles, 77
Bell, Sean, 95, 224–26
Berbrier, Mitch, 153, 155–56, 160
Bermuda Triangle of Whiteness, 190
Bernstein, Richard, 57
Beyond Coal Campaign, 124
Biko, Steve, 54
Birther movement, 37, 255
Black Codes, 30
Black Lives Matter movement, 17, 95, 120, 210–11, 213–19, 235, 256
bleaching syndrome, 166
Blue Lives Matter movement, 17, 210–11, 213–20
Blumer, Herbert, 12, 260
Bonilla-Silva, Eduardo, 9, 12, 27–28, 31, 33–34, 61–62, 73, 98, 213, 235, 260
Bourdieu, Pierre, 249
Breitbart News, 256
Brown, Michael, 95, 122, 215
Brown v. Board of Education, 89, 97
Buchanan, Patrick, 36
Bundy, Cliven, 121–22, 126, 128
Bundy Ranch standoff, 120

Carr, Edward, 45
Carter, J. Scott, 263
Challenging White Supremacy (CWS), 245
Chopra, Priyanka, 172, 174–75
civility, 51–52
Civil Rights Act, 227
Civil War, 259
Clarke, David, 216–17
Clarno, Andy, 136
classical racism, 31
Clinton, William J., 224
Clinton administrations, 225
Cohen, Stanley, 108
collective amnesia, 132, 134
color blindness, 14–16, 33, 89–90, 94–97, 99, 190, 256; rational color blindness, 90, 117. *See also* color-blind racism
color-blind racism, 91–92, 213, 263
commodification of crime, 112
consumer-created content, 165
consumer-oriented content, 165
Cooper, Brittney, 233
Copeland, Misty, 190
countermovements, 212
covert racism, 255
covert systemic racism, 213. *See also* systemic racism
cultural Marxists, 159
culture of poverty, 109

decentralization, 80–81
DiAngelo, Robin, 263
diversity, 47, 50, 71, 179–80
diversity initiatives, 15, 71, 73
diversity regimes, 71–72, 74, 81
Du Bois, W. E. B., 34, 261
Duke, David, 200
Durham, 169
Durham People's Alliance, 145

elite museums, 180
elitism, 180

Ellsworth, Elizabeth, 48
Emancipation, 259
ethnic cleansing, 29

Faludi, Susan, 6
Farm Labor Organizing Committee (FLOC), 141
Faye, Guillaume, 157
Feagin, Joe R., 9–10
Ferguson, Missouri, 122
Fisher v. The University of Texas at Austin, 256
flâneur, 77
Ford, Gerald, 225
frames, 199
Freedom of Employment Act, 225

Gallagher, B. J., 58
Gamergate, 7
Garner, Eric, 95
Goldwater, Barry, 97
good-white, 43, 50
grounded theory, 137–38, 215

Habitus, 249
Hagelin, Rebecca, 106
Hamer, Fannie Lou, 234
Hamilton, Charles, 183
Han, Sora, 98
Hannah, Darryl, 123
Harlan, John Marshall, 97
Harris-Perry, Melissa, 232
hate speech, 37
Hechinger Report, 47
Heyer, Heather, 93
Hochschild, Arlie, 3
Hopwood v. Texas, 97
hyperindividualism, 117

identarianism, 198, 204
Identity Evropa, 153–54, 157
ideology, 33; antiracist ideology, 33; blue lives matter ideology, 211;

color-blind ideology, 61, 109, 257, 259–60; diversity ideology, 72, 180; dominant ideology, 28; ideology of race, 29; oppositional ideology, 28; racial ideology, 27–30, 259; white ideology, 258
Illegal Immigration Reform and Immigrant Responsibility Act, 133
immigration, 20, 36
Immigration and Customs Enforcement, 132–33, 140
implicit bias, 50
inclusion, 180
individualism, 46, 135, 117–18; acquisitive individualism, 120; hyperindividualism, 117; liberal individualism, 118, 135
Indivisible movement, 138
institutional racism, 90–91, 95, 183

Jim Crow, 30, 257
Jones, Van, 4, 8, 113

Kaepernick, Colin, 7
Kaling, Mindy, 168, 170–71, 175
King, Steve, 180

Labanowski, Phyllis, 248
Lakshmi, Padma, 169–70
law and order, 36, 103, 135, 217
Lefebvre, Henri, 182
"less obtrusive" racism, 61
liberal individualism, 118, 135
Lipsitz, George, 183
"living while black," 93–94
Locke, John, 122
López, Ian Haney, 97

Make America Great Again (MAGA), 226, 228
Malcolm X, 250
Manifest Destiny, 30
Manuel-Miranda, Lin, 190

May, Reuben, 185
McCarthyism, 259
McDonald, Laquan, 95
Metzger, Tom, 198
Millennial Woes, 204
Mitra, Sreya, 174
Moore, Wendy Leo, 98, 183, 261
Morrison, Toni, 35, 49
mountaintop removal (MTR), 121, 123, 124
Mueller, Jennifer, 34
Muir, John, 123
multiculturalism, 72–73, 82

Nasty Women, 228
National Association for the Advancement of White People, 200
nationalism, 35, 204; new white nationalism, 33–34, 38; white nationalism, 35–37; white nationalists, 152
neoconservative racial project, 214
neoliberalism, 117, 120, 250; neoliberal feminism, 230, 234
new civil rights movement, 262
new racism, 7
new white nationalism, 33–34, 38
New World Order, 153, 156, 204
nice racism, 15, 43, 45–46, 50–51, 53
nonwhite groups, 179
North Carolina: Farm Act of 2017, 141; State Criminal Alien Assistance Program (SCAAP), 143, 143*fig*.
North Carolina Farm Act of 2017, 141

Obama, Barack, 103, 113, 121, 162, 226, 255–56, 258
Obama administration, 227
O'Brien, Eileen, 73, 246–47, 249
O'Keeffe Gallery, 187*fig*
Omi, Michael, 7, 9–11, 14, 104, 227, 229, 235

Patillo-McCoy, Mary, 185
Peinovich, Michael "Enoch," 154
perceptions of attractiveness, 166
Plessy v. Ferguson, 97
policing of space, 187
political correctness, 4, 13, 15, 57, 58–59, 66, 92
populism, 226, 228, 234
post-racism, 95
principled objection, 59, 61
prison reform, 104, 109
psychological wages of whiteness, 181

race, 43, 54, 242
race consciousness, 71–72, 74–75; hollow race consciousness, 81–82; white race consciousness, 71–72, 74
racecraft, 11
race realists, 198
race traitors, 242
racial conservatism, 227
racial discrimination, 182
racial formation, 9, 14, 229; racial formation theory, 213
racialism, 204
racialized immigration, 29
racialized social spaces, 181, 183
racialized social system, 27–28, 180
racial mechanisms, 186, 189
racial project, 104
racial resentment, 65*fig.*
Reconstruction, 264
Red Ice TV, 201
Regents of the University of California v. Bakke, 97
Republican National Convention, 216
respectable Negroes, 51–52
reverse discrimination, 31, 34
reverse racism, 90, 118
Right on Crime (RoC) movement, 105–7
Roe v. Wade, 212

Roos, J. Micah, 263
Rottenberg, Catherine, 230

Safran, Josh, 173
Sandberg, Sheryl, 230–31
second-wave feminism, 230
Sensenbrenner Bill (2005), 133
settler colonialism, 118, 126; settler colonial complex, 121, 124; settler complex, 119, 121, 124; white settler, 127
Seurat, George, 188
Sierra Club, 121–25, 128
skin lightening, 166
skin tone, 166
social movements, 211–12
Southern, Lauren, 199
spatiality, 186, 187*fig.*
Spencer, Richard, 32, 197
State Criminal Alien Assistance Program (SCAAP), 143, 143*fig.*
Stormfront.org, 198–99
structural racism, 11
Student Non-Violent Coordinating Committee (SNCC), 245
systemic white racism, 43–45, 46, 48; covert systemic racism, 213

Tea Party, 225
Texas State Vigilantes, 157, 160
Thomas, Clarence, 90
Thornhill, Ted, 50
Trump, Donald: anti-immigrant rhetoric of, 53, 226, 255; campaign and election of, 3, 27, 32, 37, 160, 226; and Colin Kaepernick, 7; and political correctness, 58–59, 67; racism of, 3, 27, 32, 160, 228; Trump effect, 34; women and, 228; and whitelash, 7, 30, 255, 258–59, 264; and white nationalism, 27, 37, 126; and white resistance, 29, 30, 92; and white supremacy, 160–61, 228, 240.

See also Birther movement; Make America Great Again (MAGA); Trump administration
Trump administration, 117, 257
trumpismo, xiii
trumpistas, xiii
Ture, Kwame, 183
Turner, Jennifer, 106
287(g) program, 133, 135–36, 140–42, 146, 137*table*
2007 Illegal Immigration Project/Sheriffs Immigration Enforcement Agreement, 142
2017 Farm Bill, 141

unblackening, 47, 51, 53–54
unconscious racism, 50
Unite the Right, 93, 151, 197
US Bureau of Land Management, 121
US Civil War, 259
Useem, Burt, 212

Vanguard America, 153–54, 156–57, 158
von Hassel-Davies, Cathy, 145
Voting Rights Act, 98, 227

Waters, Maxine, 226, 228
white activism, 251
white antiracist organizations, 243
white anxiety, 213–14
white art, 186
White Aryan Resistance, 198
white domination, 180
white environmentalism, 124
white features, 166
white fragility, 242, 248, 263
white identity, 153, 158, 161
white ignorance, 134
white ignore-ance, 45, 47–49
white innocence, 134;
whitelash, 5–8, 11–12, 13*fig.*, 18, 190, 258–62, 264

white license, 43–44, 263
white nationalism, 35–37
white nationalists, 152
whiteness: as an activity, 73; as background, 151–52; idea of, 30, 124; ideology of, 44, 48–49; and immigration, 30; problem of, 5, 263; and property, 118–19, 122; value of, 16–17, 124, 180, 183, 260. *See also* white privilege; white supremacy
white normativity, 183
white privilege, 43, 183, 258
white property, 118
white racial frame, 91–92
white resistance, 117
whites, 43, 44, 54, 180
white sanctuary, 182, 187
white savior, 133–34, 138; savior, 134–35; white savior complex, 121
white sincerity, 242
white spaces, 95–96, 180–82, 184–85, 190. *See also* white sanctuary
white spatial imaginary, 183
white structural dominance, 13*fig.*; racial domination, 29
white superiority, 263
white supremacy, 5, 16, 45–46, 74–75, 77, 180–83, 258
white victimization, 121, 152, 155, 156, 160
Wikstrom, Peter, 58
Williams, Christine, 230–31
Williamson, Abigail Fisher, 136
Winant, Howard, 7, 9–11, 14, 104, 227, 229, 234

YouTube, 197–98, 200–201
YWCA, 245–46

Zald, Mayer, 212